Working with Linux – Quick Hacks for the Command Line

Shell scripting hacks for Linux developers

Petru Işfan

Bogdan Vaida

BIRMINGHAM - MUMBAI

Working with Linux – Quick Hacks for the Command Line

First published: May 2017

Production reference: 1260517

Published by Packt Publishing Ltd.
Livery Place
35 Livery Street
Birmingham B3 2PB, UK.

ISBN 978-1-78712-918-4

www.packtpub.com

Credits

Authors
Petru Işfan
Bogdan Vaida

Commissioning Editor
Kartikey Pandey

Acquisition Editor
Prachi Bisht

Content Development Editor
Prachi Bisht
Trusha Shriyan

Technical Editor
Naveenkumar Jain

Copy Editor
Safis Editing

Project Coordinator
Kinjal Bari

Proofreader
Safis Editing

Indexer
Aishwarya Gangawane

Graphics
Kirk D'Penha

Production Coordinator
Melwyn Dsa

Cover Work
Melwyn Dsa

About the Authors

Petru Işfan is a full-stack developer, Linux evangelist, open source lover, and cloud pioneer. Petru has worked all his engineering life in Linux, and has tried all the major distributions out there. He specializes not only in software development, but in the whole software engineering stack, focusing on tools and workflows that enhance developer productivity and enjoyment.

An early adopter of technology, he uses passion and best practices to deliver software products, mainly for the Web and the mobile world, working with clients big and small. He is really enthusiastic about finding the most efficient and elegant solutions for all problems.

Bogdan Vaida burst onto the training scene in 2009 using extremely old Powerpoint presentations. Luckily, two years later, he switched to experiential training and learning by using methodologies that he practiced devotedly in all of his training. Known for his no-nonsense approach to getting results, Bogdan has been told that he helps participants get their own "insanely practical insights."

What does he do? He travels around the world doing experiential training in fields ranging from video editing to personality typologies and trainer training. While doing this, he also manages his online courses, which have over 10,000 students from all over the world.

In 2015, he beat the record for total time spent in airports.

www.PacktPub.com

eBooks, discount offers, and more

Did you know that Packt offers eBook versions of every book published, with PDF and ePub files available? You can upgrade to the eBook version at www.PacktPub.com and as a print book customer, you are entitled to a discount on the eBook copy. Get in touch with us at customercare@packtpub.com for more details.

At www.PacktPub.com, you can also read a collection of free technical articles, sign up for a range of free newsletters and receive exclusive discounts and offers on Packt books and eBooks.

https://www.packtpub.com/mapt

Get the most in-demand software skills with Mapt. Mapt gives you full access to all Packt books and video courses, as well as industry-leading tools to help you plan your personal development and advance your career.

Why subscribe?

- Fully searchable across every book published by Packt
- Copy and paste, print, and bookmark content
- On demand and accessible via a web browser

Customer Feedback

Thanks for purchasing this Packt book. At Packt, quality is at the heart of our editorial process. To help us improve, please leave us an honest review on this book's Amazon page at https://www.amazon.com/dp/1787129187.

If you'd like to join our team of regular reviewers, you can e-mail us at customerreviews@packtpub.com. We award our regular reviewers with free eBooks and videos in exchange for their valuable feedback. Help us be relentless in improving our products!

Table of Contents

Preface

Our mission is to save Linux users from their unproductive habits.

In this book, you will learn:

- What's one of the best terminals to use (just a hint: you need that split screen functionality).

- How clipboard managers memorize the things you copy, so you don't have to.

- How to use the greatest/biggest/most intelligent :)) console editor since humankind appeared. Yes, it's Vim. And we'll dive deep into its usefulness.

- Zsh and its awesome `oh-my-zsh` framework featuring over 200 plugins for developers and productivity seekers.

- Extensive lessons on terminal commands: how to find and replace text, parts of text, tiny bits of text or even non-text.

- How to use pipes and subshells to create customized commands that automate day-to-day tasks.

- And much more. This book is for all the programmers that are new to the Linux environment.

But who are we?

Petru: the infamous coder with many years of Linux experience. He types like crazy, loves doughnuts and has Linux wired in his brain! After discovering Linux and switching through a different distribution every week, annoying his girlfriend with tons of geeky stuff, now he annoys everybody with geek talks and the latest news in the tech world.

He spends his time coding frontends, backends, databases, Linux servers, and clouds.

Bogdan: the deserter! He went through more than 20 Linux and Unix distributions including Plan 9, HP-UX and all of the BSDs. But after his girlfriend left him because he spent way too much time in front of the computer he... switched to Mac.

Now he spends his time teaching over ten thousand students in his 8 online courses.

And we are here to help you double your terminal productivity!

If you don't know how to use `sed`, if you're not that used to `pipeing` commands, if you use the default terminal and if you are still using BASH then this book is for you.

Read it now and double your terminal productivity!

What this book covers

Chapter 1, *Introduction*, introduces the most basic tools needed to transform your user experience.

Chapter 2, *Productive Shells – Reinvent the Way You Work*, reinvents the way you work. Colors, editors, and custom configurations all tailored to your custom needs.

Chapter 3, *Vim kung fu*, explains the way of the terminal warrior. This includes configuration and advanced usage to cover the majority of needs.

Chapter 4, *CLI – The Hidden Recipe*, shows different ways of going from good to great and boosting the command-line capabilities to new frontiers.

Chapter 5, *Developers' Treasure*, explains how to maximize productivity with these simple hacks. It's the small things that produce the big difference.

Chapter 6, *Terminal Art*, prepares you to become amazed at what creativity can do with limited resources. This is where the fun begins.

What you need for this book

Ideally, you can equip yourself with a fresh Ubuntu operating system and go through the samples while reading. Remember there is a git repository available at `https://github.com/petruisfan/linux-for-developers`.

Go ahead and clone this locally so that you can use the project's sample files.

Who this book is for

This book is for Linux users who already have some form of basic knowledge and are looking to improve their skills and become more productive in the command-line environment. It is for users who want to learn tips and tricks that master's use, without going through all the trials and errors in the vast open source ocean of tools and technologies. It's for the users who want to feel at home at the terminal prompt and are eager to do the vast majority of tasks from there.

Conventions

In this book, you will find a number of text styles that distinguish between different kinds of information. Here are some examples of these styles and an explanation of their meaning.

Code words in text, database table names, folder names, filenames, file extensions, pathnames, dummy URLs, user input, and Twitter handles are shown as follows: "Open the terminator and type `sudo apt install zsh` to install `zsh`, as shown in."

A block of code is set as follows:

```
case ${CMD} in
    publicip)
        print_public_ip
        ;;
    ip)
        IFACE=$(getarg iface $@)
        print_ip $IFACE
        ;;
    *)
        echo "invalid command"
esac
```

Any command-line input or output is written as follows:

```
sh -c "$(curl -fsSL https://raw.githubusercontent.com/robbyrussell/oh-my-zsh/master/tools/install.sh)"
```

New terms and **important words** are shown in bold. Words that you see on the screen, for example, in menus or dialog boxes, appear in the text like this: "Go to shell and enable **Open new tab in current directory**."

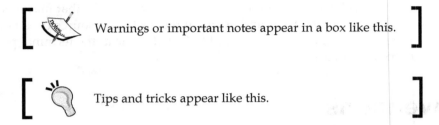

> Warnings or important notes appear in a box like this.

> Tips and tricks appear like this.

Reader feedback

Feedback from our readers is always welcome. Let us know what you think about this book—what you liked or disliked. Reader feedback is important for us as it helps us develop titles that you will really get the most out of.

To send us general feedback, simply e-mail feedback@packtpub.com, and mention the book's title in the subject of your message.

If there is a topic that you have expertise in and you are interested in either writing or contributing to a book, see our author guide at www.packtpub.com/authors.

Customer support

Now that you are the proud owner of a Packt book, we have a number of things to help you to get the most from your purchase.

Errata

Although we have taken every care to ensure the accuracy of our content, mistakes do happen. If you find a mistake in one of our books—maybe a mistake in the text or the code—we would be grateful if you could report this to us. By doing so, you can save other readers from frustration and help us improve subsequent versions of this book. If you find any errata, please report them by visiting http://www.packtpub.com/submit-errata, selecting your book, clicking on the **Errata Submission Form** link, and entering the details of your errata. Once your errata are verified, your submission will be accepted and the errata will be uploaded to our website or added to any list of existing errata under the Errata section of that title.

To view the previously submitted errata, go to https://www.packtpub.com/books/content/support and enter the name of the book in the search field. The required information will appear under the **Errata** section.

Piracy

Piracy of copyrighted material on the Internet is an ongoing problem across all media. At Packt, we take the protection of our copyright and licenses very seriously. If you come across any illegal copies of our works in any form on the Internet, please provide us with the location address or website name immediately so that we can pursue a remedy.

Please contact us at copyright@packtpub.com with a link to the suspected pirated material.

We appreciate your help in protecting our authors and our ability to bring you valuable content.

Questions

If you have a problem with any aspect of this book, you can contact us at questions@packtpub.com, and we will do our best to address the problem.

1
Introduction

This book is split into multiple parts. In part 1, we'll explore a new terminal and show you how to install and configure it. In part 2, we will concentrate on configuring your shell, adding plugins, understanding regular expressions, and working with pipes and subshells. Everything will then be coagulated into a shell scripting lesson. In part 3, we'll work with Vim, our recommended editor. We will cover everything from configuring it, to learning keyboard shortcuts, installing plugins, and even using it as a password manager. So let's get started.

In the following chapter, we will learn the following topics:

- Understanding the working of Terminator
- Using Guake for your quick commands or long running tasks
- Using ClipIt to copy-paste text

So, we will start with a terminal after which everything will be wild! When it comes to working long hours in a terminal, our choice is to use Terminator for its fast and easy split screen functionality. Then, we will focus on Guake, a terminal that opens really fast and wherever you are. Towards the end, you will understand the working of Clipit and use its copy and paste feature effectively.

Are you ready?

We will dive deep into the Linux environment, giving you tips and tricks to increase your productivity, make you more comfortable with the command line, and automate your tasks.

The book is based on Ubuntu Linux version 16.04, which is the latest long-term support version. We chose Ubuntu because it's the most common Linux distribution out there, it's really simple to use, has a lot of graphical tools, and you can find a huge online community ready to answer all your questions. Ubuntu is also the most supported Linux distribution. This means that companies that create software, especially graphics software, and offer them for Linux, usually start with Ubuntu.

This makes it easier for us to use tools such as Skype, Slack, or Visual Studio Code. Although the book is based on Ubuntu, most of the commands are not related to Ubuntu, so you can easily use another distribution and apply the same lessons. A large part of the book can even be applied applicable to Mac, as we can have the same tools installed on Mac — bash, zsh, vim all work the same way across Linux and Mac--and with the release of Windows 10, bash support is built in, so tools such as zsh and vim can easily be installed and used. Before Windows 10, there were tools such as cygwin that let you use the Linux command line in a Windows environment.

We recommend you to read and practice in an open terminal so that you can execute the commands and check their results. Before we start, you want to download all the source files from our GitHub repository (located here: `https://github.com/petruisfan/linux-for-developers`).

https://github.com/petruisfan/linux-for-developers

Terminator – the ultimate terminal

The first thing you need to do in order to become productive is to have a good terminal. Throughout the book, we will be working mostly with the command line, which means that the primary piece of software we will be using is our terminal. A great terminal that we recommend is **Terminator**, which can be installed from the software center.

Let's go to our launcher and click on the software center icon. After it opens, click on the search input and write `terminator`, as shown in the following screenshot. It will probably be first in the list of results. Click on **Install**.

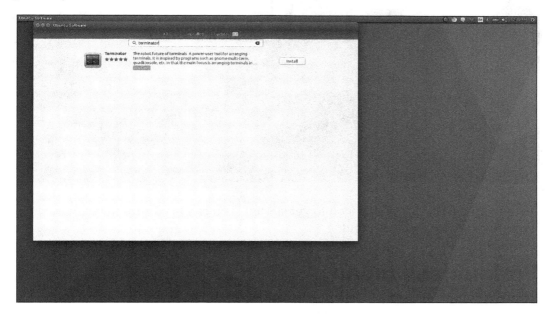

After installing Terminator, it's a good idea to drag its icon to the Launcher. For this, you just open the dash by hitting the Windows key, write `terminator` and drag and drop its icon into the Launcher:

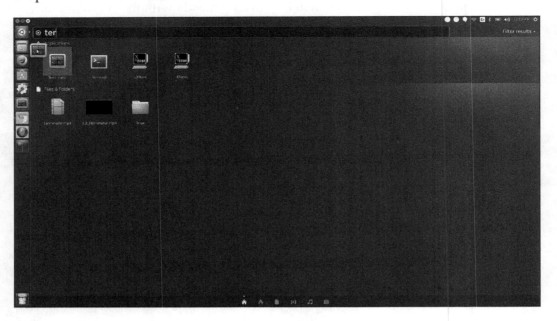

Alright, now let's click on the icon to get started. You can maximize the window to have more space to play around.

Preferences menu

It's an customizing terminal, where good surprises can be found in form of fonts styles and other tools. What you see right now are the default settings. Let's go into the preferences menu and see what we can update. First of all, let's hide the title bar because it doesn't give us that much information and it's always a good idea to have as much free screen space as possible (and as few distractions as possible).

Now let's look at some other preferences:

1. Let's change the font. We will make it a bit larger than usual so that it is easy to read. Let's go with Monospace 16, as shown in the following screenshot:

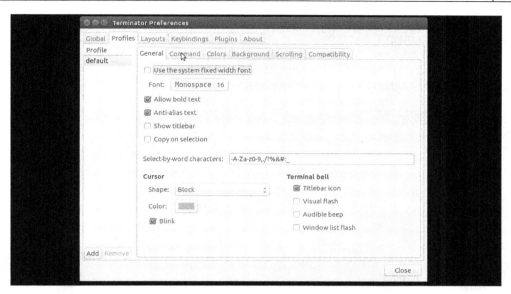

2. We also want to have good contrast so that it's easy to distinguish the letters. And for this, we will choose a black on white color theme.

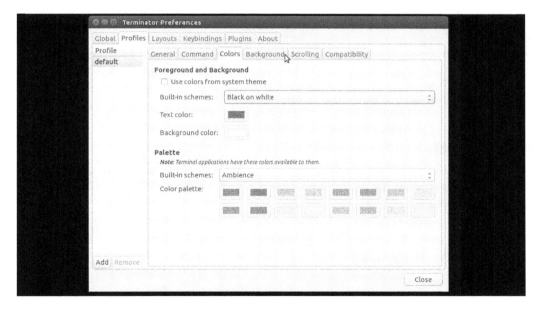

3. It's also a good idea to enable infinite scroll, because you don't want your terminal output to be trimmed after 500 lines. A lot of the time, you just want to scroll and see the previous output. Also, while scrolling, if there is a lot of text, you probably don't want to be brought back to the bottom of the page, so uncheck the **Scroll on output** option.

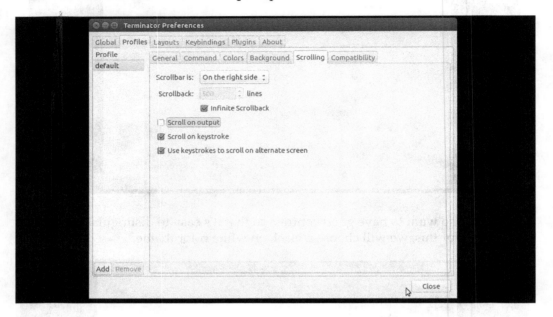

And voila! This is our newly configured terminal. And now it's time to check what we can do with this **new** terminal. Here comes the *Features* section!

Features

Now it's time to look at some of Terminator's useful features and their keyboard shortcuts. This is what the normal Terminator interface looks like:

Let's play around with it now:

- Split screen: *Ctrl* + *Shift* + *O* for a horizontal split:

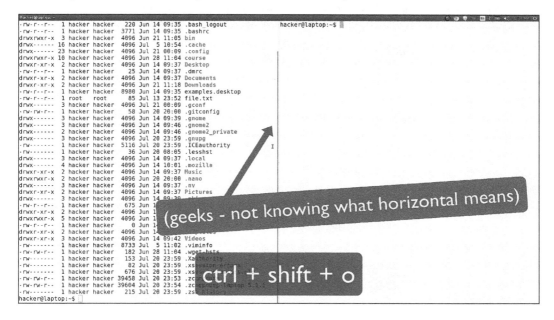

- *Ctrl + Shift + E* for a vertical split:

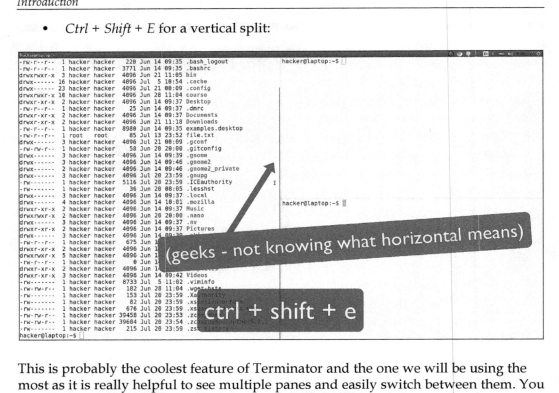

This is probably the coolest feature of Terminator and the one we will be using the most as it is really helpful to see multiple panes and easily switch between them. You can split the screen any number of times, in any combination you want.

Resize screen: *Ctrl + Shift + Arrow* or just drag and drop:

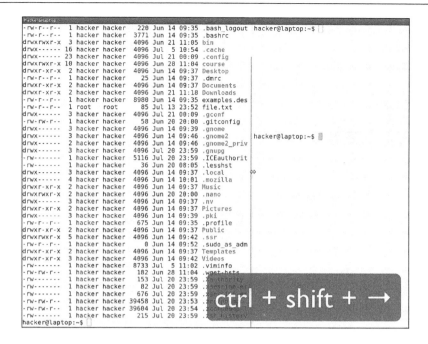

- Easily move between Windows with *Ctrl + Shift + Arrow*.

- Close screen using *Ctrl + Shift + W* or *Ctrl + D*.

- Create tabs with *Ctrl + Shift + T*. This is for when you don't have any more space to split the screen:

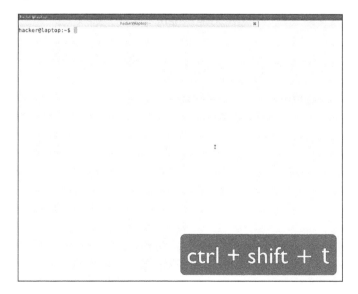

- Text zoom: *Ctrl + +* and *Ctrl + -* — useful for when you need to present or when you have a person with a bad eyesight:

```
hacker@laptop:~
-rw-r--r--   1 hacker hacker    25 Jun 14 09:37 .dmrc
drwxr-xr-x   2 hacker hacker  4096 Jun 14 09:37 Documents
drwxr-xr-x   2 hacker hacker  4096 Jun 21 11:18 Downloads
-rw-r--r--   1 hacker hacker  8980 Jun 14 09:35 examples.desktop
-rw-r--r--   1 root   root      85 Jul 13 23:52 file.txt
drwx------   3 hacker hacker  4096 Jul 21 00:09 .gconf
-rw-rw-r--   1 hacker hacker    58 Jun 20 20:00 .gitconfig
drwx------   3 hacker hacker  4096 Jun 14 09:39 .gnome
drwx------   3 hacker hacker  4096 Jun 14 09:46 .gnome2
drwx------   2 hacker hacker  4096 Jun 14 09:46 .gnome2_private
drwx------   3 hacker hacker  4096 Jul 20 23:59 .gnupg
-rw-------   1 hacker hacker  5116 Jul 20 23:59 .ICEauthority
-rw-------   1 hacker hacker    36 Jun 20 08:05 .lesshst
drwx------   3 hacker hacker  4096 Jun 14 09:37 .local
drwx------   4 hacker hacker  4096 Jun 14 10:01 .mozilla
drwxr-xr-x   2 hacker hacker  4096 Jun 14 09:37 Music
drwxrwxr-x   2 hacker hacker  4096 Jun 20 20:00 .nano
drwx------   3 hacker hacker  4096 Jun 14 09:37 .nv  I
drwxr-xr-x   2 hacker hacker  4096 Jun 14 09:37 Pictures
drwx------   3 hacker hacker  4096 Jun 14 09:39 .pki
-rw-r--r--   1 hacker hacker   675 Jun 14 09:35 .profile
drwxr-xr-x   2 hacker hacker  4096 Jun 14 09:37 Public
drwxrwxr-x   5 hacker hacker  4096 Jun 14 09:42 .ssr
-rw-r--r--   1 hacker hacker     0 Jun 14 09:52 .sudo_as_admin_successful
drwxr-xr-x   2 hacker hacker  4096 Jun 14 09:37 Templates
drwxr-xr-x   3 hacker hacker  4096 Jun 14 09:42 Videos
-rw-------   1 hacker hacker  8733 Jul  5 11:02 .viminfo
-rw-rw-r--   1 hacker hacker   182 Jun 28 11:04 .wget-hsts
-rw-------   1 hacker hacker   153 Jul 20 23:59 .Xauthority
-rw-------   1 hacker hacker    82 Jul 20 23:59 .xsession-errors
-rw-------   1 hacker hacker   676 Jul 20 23:53 .xsession-errors.old
-rw-------   1 hacker hacker 39458 Jul 20           .npdump
-rw-rw-r--   1 hacker hacker 39604 Jul 20           
-rw-------   1 hacker hacker   215 Jul 20           history
hacker@laptop:~$ 
```

`ctrl + + / ctrl + -`

Being able to divide the screen in order to arrange the terminal in a grid, and being able to split, switch, and resize panes with keyboard shortcuts are the biggest advantages of Terminator. One big productivity killer that a lot of people don't realize is switching between using the mouse and using the keyboard. And although most people prefer using the mouse, we suggest using the keyboard as much as possible and learning the keyboard shortcuts of your most commonly used computer programs.

Being productive ultimately means having more time to focus on the things that are really important, instead of wasting time struggling to use the computer.

Hasta la vista terminal! Welcome Terminator!

Guake – not Quake!

Terminator works well for all sorts of tasks, especially when working long sessions on multiple items. However, sometimes there are scenarios where you need to quickly access a terminal in order to run a command, check a status, or run a task in the foreground for a long time--all of these without opening too many tabs. Guake is excellent in such situations. It is a handy, easy-to-use terminal that you can open on any workspace on top of your existing windows, by pressing *F12*.

We will install it right now by using a simple command line. As shown below, open your terminal and type sudo apt install guake:

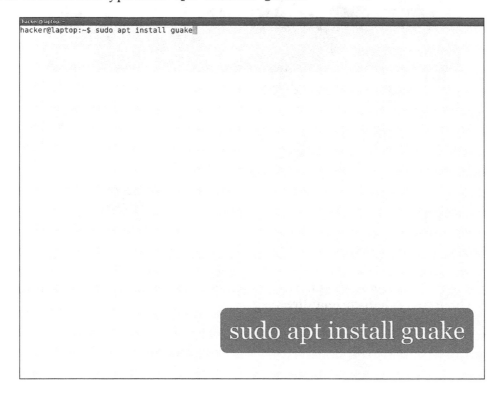

[

apt is the new package manager that Ubuntu launched in version 16.04 and is meant to be an easier-to-use version of the apt-get command, with some added eye candy.
]

Now that Guake is installed, we will go to dash and open it. To do this, we just press *F12*. Once it is running, you can see the notification on the top-right side of the screen. This is what it should look like:

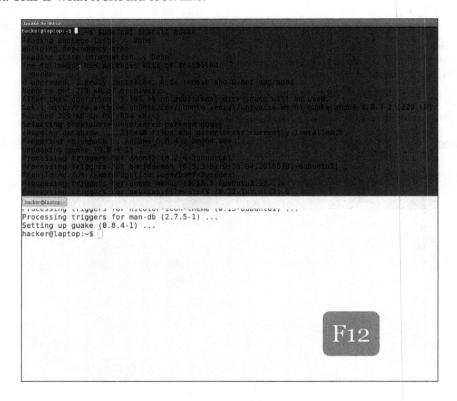

Just like with Terminator, we will check its preferences. First of all, go to shell and enable **Open new tab in current directory**:

I believe you can guess what this does. Then, go scrolling and insert a really big number, like 99,999. Also, make sure **Scroll | On output** is unchecked:

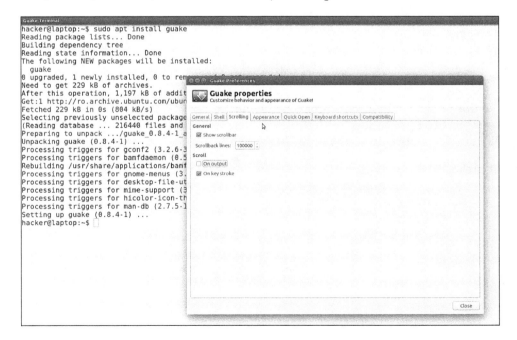

Again, we will change the default font to `Monospace 16`, set the **Cursor blink mode** to off, and hit **Close**:

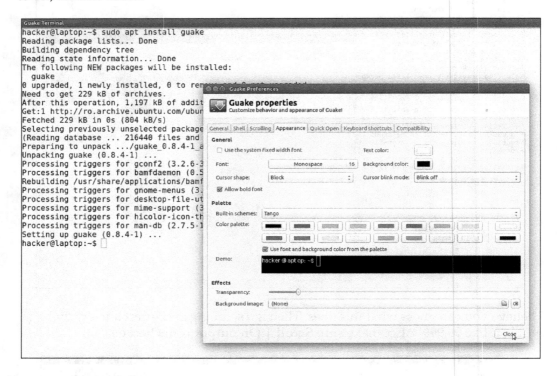

We can use Guake in full screen by hitting *F11* and we can also resize it by dragging the margin. If you want, you can play around with the default settings to see what suits you best.

Guake does not start automatically when Ubuntu reboots, so we will have to add it to our startup application for that. To do this, open dash again, type startup applications and click add. Just type Guake in all three fields, add, and close.

What makes it so handy is the fact that you can open it on top of your current windows at any time, quickly type a command, and reopen it again later to check the status of the command.

What we actually do is to also make it a little bit transparent so that when it opens on top of a web page where we have some commands written, we can still read the content on the page and type the commands as we read, without switching windows. Another awesome productivity tip!

ClipIt – copy-paste at its finest

We believe that one of the greatest inventions of mankind is copy-paste. The ability to take a piece of text from some random place and insert it to another not-so-random place is a huge time saver! Mankind would still be ages behind if computers didn't have this feature! Just imagine having to type every little command, every URL, every block of code you read! It would be a huge waste of time! And so, being such an important feature, copy-paste deserves a tool of its own for managing all the important text you copied. These types of tools are called clipboard managers. There are a lot of options for every operating system, and one good free one for Ubuntu is called clipIt. Open the terminal and type `sudo apt install clipit` to install it.

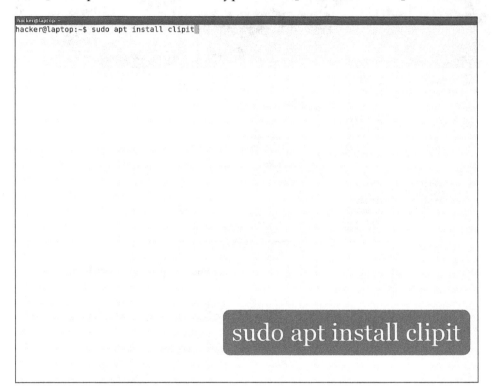

A good scenario for using Guake is to run `ClipIt` in it. By default, `ClipIt` occupies a terminal window but, with the help of Guake, we just hide it away!

```
Guake Terminal
hacker@laptop:~$ clipit
Reading package lists... Done
Building dependency tree
Reading state information... Done
The following additional packages will be installed:
  libxdo3 xdotool
The following NEW packages will be installed:
  clipit libxdo3 xdotool
0 upgraded, 3 newly installed, 0 to remove and 0 not upgraded.
Need to get 119 kB of archives.
After this operation, 592 kB of additional disk space will be used.
Do you want to continue? [Y/n]
Get:1 http://ro.archive.ubuntu.com/ubuntu xenial/universe amd64 libxdo3 amd64 1:3.20150503.1-2 [20.7 kB]
Get:2 http://ro.archive.ubuntu.com/ubuntu xenial/universe amd64 xdotool amd64 1:3.20150503.1-2 [39.3 kB]
Get:3 http://ro.archive.ubuntu.com/ubuntu xenial/universe amd64 clipit amd64 1.4.2-1ubuntu1 [59.4 kB]
Fetched 119 kB in 0s (415 kB/s)
Selecting previously unselected package libxdo3:amd64.
(Reading database ... 216516 files and directories currently installed.)
Preparing to unpack .../libxdo3_1%3a3.20150503.1-2_amd64.deb ...
Unpacking libxdo3:amd64 (1:3.20150503.1-2) ...
```

```
hacker@laptop:~
Preparing to unpack .../xdotool_1%3a3.20150503.1-2_amd64.deb ...
Unpacking xdotool (1:3.20150503.1-2) ...
Selecting previously unselected package clipit.
Preparing to unpack .../clipit_1.4.2-1ubuntu1_amd64.deb ...
Unpacking clipit (1.4.2-1ubuntu1) ...
Processing triggers for man-db (2.7.5-1) ...
Processing triggers for hicolor-icon-theme (0.15-0ubuntu1) ...
Processing triggers for bamfdaemon (0.5.3~bzr0+16.04.20160701-0ubuntu1) ...
Rebuilding /usr/share/applications/bamf-2.index...
Processing triggers for gnome-menus (3.13.3-6ubuntu3.1) ...
Processing triggers for desktop-file-utils (0.22-1ubuntu5) ...
Processing triggers for mime-support (3.59ubuntu1) ...
Setting up libxdo3:amd64 (1:3.20150503.1-2) ...
Setting up xdotool (1:3.20150503.1-2) ...
Setting up clipit (1.4.2-1ubuntu1) ...
Processing triggers for libc-bin (2.23-0ubuntu3) ...
hacker@laptop:~$
```

The tool is automatically added to the startup applications, so it will start the next time you reboot.

In order to invoke `ClipIt`, hit *Ctrl + Alt + H* or click the clipboard image in the menu bar.

```
4  1:3.20150503.1-2 [20.7 kB]
4  1:3.20150503.1-2 [39.1 kB]
 1.4.2-1ubuntu1 [59.4 kB]
```

The first times it starts, it warns you that it stores data in plain text, so it might not be safe to use if other users use your account. Currently, it contains only the latest clipboard element.

Let's do a quick example of its usage.

We cat the content of the .profile file. And let's say we want to copy some lines of text and run them in another terminal, which looks like this:

```
hacker@laptop:~$ cat .profile
# ~/.profile: executed by the command interpreter for login shells.
# This file is not read by bash(1), if ~/.bash_profile or ~/.bash_login
# exists.
# see /usr/share/doc/bash/examples/startup-files for examples.
# the files are located in the bash-doc package.

# the default umask is set in /etc/profile; for setting the umask
# for ssh logins, install and configure the libpam-umask package.
#umask 022

# if running bash
if [ -n "$BASH_VERSION" ]; then
    # include .bashrc if it exists
    if [ -f "$HOME/.bashrc" ]; then
        . "$HOME/.bashrc"
    fi
fi

# set PATH so it includes user's private bin if it exists
if [ -d "$HOME/bin" ] ; then
    PATH="$HOME/bin:$PATH"
fi
hacker@laptop:~$ 
```

For example, we might want to update the PATH variable, then source the `.bashrc` file and update the PATH variable again. Instead of copying the content again from our file, we just hit *Ctrl + Alt + H* and choose what we want to paste from our clipboard history:

```
hacker@laptop: ~
Unpacking libxdo3:amd64 (1:3.20150503.1-2) ...
Selecting previously unselected package xdotool.
Preparing to unpack .../xdotool_1%3a3.20150503.1-2_amd64.deb ...
Unpacking xdotool (1:3.20150503.1-2) ...
Selecting previously unselected package clipit.
Preparing to unpack .../clipit_1.4.2-1ubuntu1_amd64.deb ...
Unpacking clipit (1.4.2-1ubuntu1) ...
Processing triggers for man-db (2.7.5-1) ...
Processing triggers for hicolor-icon-theme (0.15-0ubuntu1) ...
Processing triggers for bamfdaemon (0.5.3~bzr0+16.04.20160701-0ubuntu1) .
Rebuilding /usr/share/applications/bamf-2.index...
Processing triggers for gnome-menus (3.13.3-6ubuntu3.1) ...
Processing triggers for desktop-file-utils (0.22-1ubuntu5) ...
Processing triggers for mime-support (3.59ubuntu1) ...
Setting up libxdo3:amd64 (1:3.20150503.1-2) ...
Setting up xdotool (1:3.20150503.1-2) ...
Setting up clipit (1.4.2-1ubuntu1) ...
Processing triggers for libc-bin (2.23-0ubuntu3) ...
hacker@laptop:~$ cat .profile
# ~/.profile: executed by the command interpreter for login shells.
# This file is not read by bash(1), if ~/.bash_profile or ~/.bash_login
# exists.
# see /usr/share/doc/bash/examples/startup-files for examples.
# the files are located in the bash-doc package.

# the default umask is set in /etc/profile; for setting the umask
# for ssh logins, install and configure the libpam-umask package.
#umask 022

# if running bash
if [ -n "$BASH_VERSION" ]; then
    # include .bashrc if it exists
    if [ -f "$HOME/.bashrc" ]; then
        . "$HOME/.bashrc"
    fi
fi

# set PATH so it includes user's private bin if it exists
if [ -d "$HOME/bin" ] ; then
    PATH="$HOME/bin:$PATH"
fi
hacker@laptop:~$ 
```

```
hacker@laptop:~$ PATH="$HOME/bin:$PATH"
hacker@laptop:~$ . "$HOME/.bashrc"
hacker@laptop:~$ 
```

> "$HOME/.bashrc"
> PATH="$HOME/bin:$PATH"
> 1.3_guake

ctrl + alt + h

This is a very basic example. ClipIt mostly comes in handy when you work long hours on your computer and need to paste something that you copied from a website hours earlier. It comes with a default history size of 50 items and it will show you the last 10 items in your floating window. You can increase these limits in the settings:

With ClipIt, you can copy and paste as many times as you want without losing any data. It's like a time machine for your clipboard!

2
Productive Shells – Reinvent the way you work

In this chapter, we will start off with a short introduction to Vim and look at the most basic commands to help you get started with basic CRUD (create, read, update, delete) operations. We will then upgrade the shell interpreter to zsh and also give it superpowers with the awesome `oh-my-zsh` framework. We will look at some basic regular expressions such as searching some text using grep. Then, we will unleash the power of Unix pipes and run embedded commands using subshells. The later part of the chapter will help us understand how we can boost productivity and automate a lot of our day-to-day work by showing some of the more advanced shell scripting techniques.

In this chapter, we will cover the following:

- Working with Vim
- Managing zsh using the `oh-my-zsh` framework
- Writing and running super powerful one line commands using pipes and subshells
- Exploring the shell scripting libraries

We will focus on editing files. For that we need to choose a file editor. There are a bunch of options but considering that the fastest way to edit files is, of course, without leaving the terminal. We recommend Vim. Vim is an awesome editor! It has a lot of configuration options with a huge community that has produced lots of plugins and beautiful themes. It also features advanced text editing, which makes it ultra-configurable and super-fast.

So, let's proceed. Open the terminator and type `sudo apt install vim` to install Vim:

```
hacker@laptop:~$ sudo apt install vim
```

sudo apt install vim

Vim is renowned for its exotic keyboard controls and a lot of people avoid using Vim because of it. But once you get the basics, it's super easy to use.

Let's start `vim` with no arguments:

```
                        VIM - Vi IMproved

                        version 7.4.1689
                     by Bram Moolenaar et al.
        Modified by pkg-vim-maintainers@lists.alioth.debian.org
             Vim is open source and freely distributable

                    Help poor children in Uganda!
           type  :help iccf<Enter>        for information

           type  :q<Enter>                to exit
           type  :help<Enter>  or  <F1>   for on-line help
           type  :help version7<Enter>    for version info

                                                       0,0-1          All
```

This is the default screen; you can see the version on the second line.

- To start editing text, press the *Insert* key; this will take us to the insert mode, where we can start typing. We can see we are in the insert mode at the bottom of the screen:

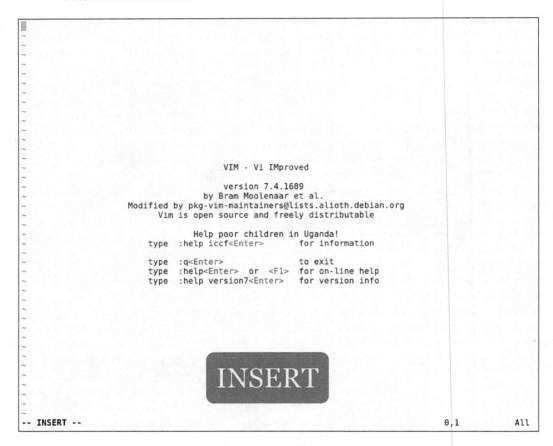

```
                      VIM - Vi IMproved

                      version 7.4.1689
                    by Bram Moolenaar et al.
       Modified by pkg-vim-maintainers@lists.alioth.debian.org
            Vim is open source and freely distributable

                  Help poor children in Uganda!
         type  :help iccf<Enter>        for information

         type  :q<Enter>                to exit
         type  :help<Enter>  or  <F1>   for on-line help
         type  :help version7<Enter>    for version info
```

INSERT

```
-- INSERT --                                        0,1           All
```

- Press the *Insert* key again to go to replace the mode and override text.
- Press the *Esc* key to exit insert or replace.
- Type *yy* to copy a line.
- Type *p* to paste the line.

- Type *dd* to cut the line.
- Type *:w* to save any changes. Optionally, specify a filename:

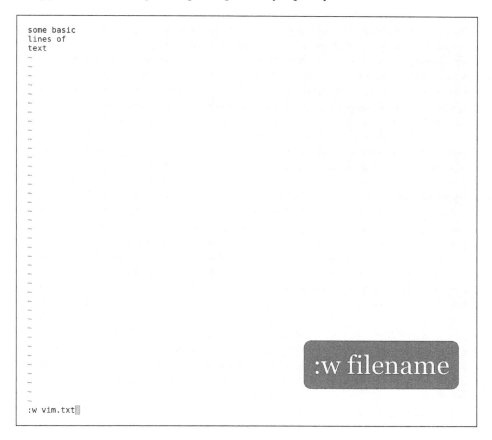

- To save the file in editing text, type `vim.txt`
- Type `:q` to exit Vim

Let's open the file again and do a small change:

- `:wq`: Write and exit at the same time
- `:q!`: Exit without saving

Now you are familiar with these commands, we can do basic file editing directly from the command line. This is the bare minimum that anybody needs to know when working with Vim, and we will use this knowledge in the chapters to come.

We will also have an entire section about Vim, where we will go into more detail about being productive in the coolest terminal editor today!

Oh-my-zsh – your terminal never felt this good before!

Bash is probably the most commonly used shell. It has lots of features and powerful scripting capabilities, but when it comes to user interaction, zsh is better. Most of its power comes from the awesome framework oh-my-zsh. In this section, we will be installing zsh.

Let's get started with the oh-my-zsh framework and we will be looking at some basic configuration options:

- Open the terminator and type sudo apt install zsh to install zsh, as shown in the following image:

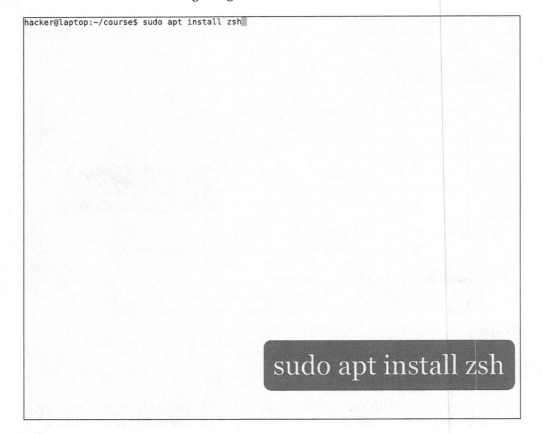

```
hacker@laptop:~/course$ sudo apt install zsh
```

sudo apt install zsh

After installing it, go to this link, `https://github.com/robbyrussell/oh-my-zsh`, and follow the instructions for installing the `oh-my-zsh` framework. The installation process is a one-line command with `curl` or `wget`. Let's install it using both the command one by one:

Via curl:

`sh -c "$(curl -fsSL https://raw.githubusercontent.com/robbyrussell/oh-my-zsh/master/tools/install.sh)"`

Via wget:

`sh -c "$(wget https://raw.githubusercontent.com/robbyrussell/oh-my-zsh/master/tools/install.sh -O -)"`

You will see that the command is giving an error saying that `git` is not installed, so we need to install that too. The following command-line is used to install git:

`sudo apt install git`

```
hacker@laptop:~/course$ sudo apt install git



                                    sudo apt install git

```

Notice how easy it is to install software in Ubuntu. This is also a big productivity booster; every common software package we might need is already prepackaged in the remote software repository and it takes us just one command to add new software to our computer.

Now that we have `git` installed, let's run the command again. We can see that this time it's working successfully and it's bringing us to our new shell. `Oh-my-zsh` also changes the default shell to `zsh`.

After installation, the first thing to do is go pick a theme. To see all available themes, run this:

```
ls ~/.oh-my-zsh/themes
```

You can also go to the `git` repo and check out the themes, together with their screenshots. We will be using the *candy* theme, because it has a lot of useful information in the prompt: *username, hostname, time, folder* and *git* branch/*git* status.

Time can be very useful, for example if you want to know how long a command took to execute and you didn't use the *time* utility to measure your command's total runtime. Then, you can check out the prompt and see the time when the command started and the prompt to know when it was finished, and thus you can calculate the total time.

To change the theme, `open ~/.zshrc` and modify the `ZSH_THEME` variable. Save the file and open a new terminal window. Let's initialize an empty `git` directory so we can see how the prompt looks. You can see we are on the master branch:

```
hacker@laptop:~/course$ zsh
                    [10:29:55 AM]
-> % mkdir git-demo
                    [10:30:16 AM]
-> % cd git-demo
                    [10:30:19 AM]
-> % git init
Initialized empty Git repository in /home/hacker/course/git-demo/.git/
                    [10:30:22 AM]          [master]
-> %
```

Let's create a file, say readme.md. The * in the prompt shows that the directory is not clean. We can verify this with the git status command:

```
hacker@laptop:~/course$ zsh
                    [10:29:55 AM]
-> % mkdir git-demo
                    [10:30:16 AM]
-> % cd git-demo
                    [10:30:19 AM]
-> % git init
Initialized empty Git repository in /home/hacker/course/git-demo/.git/
                    [10:30:22 AM]                [master]
-> % touch readme.md
                    [10:30:30 AM]                [master *]
-> % git status
```

git status

You can see how it gets verified. After we've cleaned up the directory, the * is gone. If we change branch, the prompt shows that we are on the new branch.

Let's quickly create a demo. Run the following commands on your terminal:

```
git branch test
git checkout test
```

```
-> % git init
Initialized empty Git repository in /home/hacker/course/git-demo/.git/
hacker@laptop [10:30:22 AM] [~/course/git-demo] [master]
-> % touch readme.md
hacker@laptop [10:30:30 AM] [~/course/git-demo] [master *]
-> % git status
On branch master

Initial commit

Untracked files:
  (use "git add <file>..." to include in what will be committed)

        readme.md

nothing added to commit but untracked files present (use "git add" to track)
hacker@laptop [10:30:35 AM] [~/course/git-demo] [master *]
-> % git add readme.md
hacker@laptop [10:30:39 AM] [~/course/git-demo] [master *]
-> % git commit -m "added readme"
[master (root-commit) c5d8885] added readme
 1 file changed, 0 insertions(+), 0 deletions(-)
 create mode 100644 readme.md
hacker@laptop [10:30:46 AM] [~/course/git-demo] [master]
-> % vim readme.md
hacker@laptop [10:30:58 AM] [~/course/git-demo] [master *]
-> % git commit -m "added readme"
On branch master
Changes not staged for commit:
        modified:   readme.md

no changes added to commit
hacker@laptop [10:31:04 AM] [~/course/git-demo] [master *]
-> % git commit -a -m "added readme"
[master b2d072a] added readme
 1 file changed, 1 insertion(+)
hacker@laptop [10:31:11 AM] [~/course/git-demo] [master]
-> % git branch test
hacker@laptop [10:31:17 AM] [~/course/git-demo] [master]
-> % git checkout test
Switched to branch 'test'
hacker@laptop [10:31:21 AM] [~/course/git-demo] [test]
-> %
```

You can now see the branch name in the prompt, and there are some other cool features that you might like to explore:

- **Command completion**: Start typing, for example, ip, and press *Tab*. We can see all the commands that start with IP and we can hit *Tab* again to start navigating through the different options. You can use the arrow keys to navigate and hit *Enter* for the desired command:

```
                    [10:31:39 AM]
-> % ip
ip                       ip6tables-save          ipmaddr                   iptables               iptables-xml
ip6tables                ipcmk                   ipod-read-sysinfo-extended iptables-apply        iptunnel
ip6tables-apply          ipcrm                   ipod-time-sync            iptables-restore       iputil
ip6tables-restore        ipcs                    ippusbxd                  iptables-save
```

- **Params completion**: For example type ls - and press *Tab*, and we can see here all the options and a short description for each. Press *Tab* again to start navigating through them and *Enter* to select.

```
-> % ls --almost-all
-1                         -- single column output
--all                  -a  -- list entries starting with .
--almost-all           -A  -- list all except . and ..
--author                   -- print the author of each file
--block-size               -- specify block size
-c                         -- status change time
-C                         -- list entries in columns sorted vertically
--classify             -F  -- append file type indicators
--dereference          -L  -- list referenced file for sym link
--directory            -d  -- list directory entries instead of contents
--dired                -D  -- generate output designed for Emacs' dired mode
--escape               -b  -- print octal escapes for control characters
-f                         -- unsorted, all, short list
--file-type            -p  -- append file type indicators except *
--full-time                -- list both full date and full time
-g                         -- long listing but without owner information
--help                     -- display help information
--hide-control-chars   -q  -- hide control chars
--human-readable       -h  -- print sizes in human readable form
--ignore               -I  -- don't list entire matching pattern
--ignore-backups       -B  -- don't list entries ending with ~
--inode                -i  -- print file inode numbers
--kilobytes            -k  -- use block size of 1k
-l                         -- long listing
--literal              -N  -- print raw characters
-m                         -- comma separated
--no-group             -G  -- inhibit display of group information
--numeric-uid-gid      -n  -- numeric uid, gid
-o                         -- no group, long
--quote-name           -Q  -- quote names
--recursive            -R  -- list subdirectories recursively
--reverse              -r  -- reverse sort order
-S                         -- sort by size
--si                   -H  -- sizes in human readable form; powers of 1000
--size                 -s  -- display size of each file in blocks
-t                         -- sort by modification time
--tabsize              -T  -- specify tab size
--time                     -- specify time to show
--time-style               -- show times using specified style
-u                         -- access time
-U                         -- unsorted
-v                         -- sort by version (filename treated numerically)
```

- **History navigation**: Click on arrow up key to search in history, filtering by the string that is written before the cursor. For example, if I type `vim` and press the arrow up key, I can see all the files opened with Vim in my history.

- **History search**: Press *Ctrl + R* and start typing, and press *Ctrl + R* again to search the same occurrence in history. For example ~, and *Ctrl + R* to see all commands that have ~ in the string.

- **Navigating**: Here press *Ctrl +* arrow left/right to jump one word, *Ctrl + W* to delete one word, or *Ctrl + U* to delete the whole line.

- **cd completion case insensitive**: For example, `cd doc` will expand into `cd` `Documents`.

- **cd directory completion**: If you are lazy and want to specify only a few key letters in a path, we can do that too. For example, `cd /us/sh/zs` + *Tab* will expand into `cd /usr/share/zsh`.

- **Kill completion:** Just type `kill` and *Tab* and you will see a list of `pids` to kill. From there you can choose which process to kill.

- **chown completion**: Type `chown` and tab to see a list of users to change owner to. The same applies to groups.

- **Argument expansion**: Type `ls *` and hit *Tab*. You see * expanded to all files and folders in the current directory. For a subset, type `ls Do*` and press *Tab*. It will only expand to documents and downloads.

- **Adds lots of aliases:** Just type alias to see a full list. Some very useful ones are:

```
.. - go up one folder
... - go up two folders
- - cd o the last directory
ll - ls with -lh
```

```
 5395 hacker    unity-music-dae
 5442 hacker    notify-osd
 8128 hacker    gvfsd-metadata
 9225 hacker    python2
 9230 hacker    gnome-pty-helpe
 9231 hacker    bash
 9268 hacker    bash
10322 hacker    bash
11006 hacker    clipit
11185 hacker    /usr/bin/termin
11197 hacker    gnome-pty-helpe
11891 hacker    chrome
12933 hacker    firefox
13080 hacker    chrome
17156 hacker    bash
17179 hacker    zsh
17350 hacker    zsh
17351 hacker    ps
0
              [10:33:16 AM]
-> % alias
 ='cd -'
..=../..
...=../../..
....=../../../..
.....=../../../../..
......=../../../../../..
1='cd -'
2='cd -2'
3='cd -3'
4='cd -4'
5='cd -5'
6='cd -6'
7='cd -7'
8='cd -8'
9='cd -9'
_=sudo
afind='ack -il'
d='dirs -v | head -10'
g=git
ga='git add'
gaa='git add --all'
gapa='git add --patch'
gb='git branch'
```

alias

To see a list of shortcuts, run the `bindkey` command. The terminal is one of the places where you will spend a lot time, so it's really important to master our shell and use it as efficiently as possible. Knowing good shortcuts and viewing relevant and condensed information, such as our prompt, can make our job much easier.

Basic regular expressions

You have a problem and you want to solve it with regular expressions? Now you have two problems! This is just one of the many regular expression jokes on the Internet.

In this section, you will learn how regular expressions work, as we will be using them in the upcoming chapters. We have prepared a file for our playground and if you want to try the grep commands on your own, you can take it from the GitHub repository.

Let's start by opening our text file so we can see its contents, and then splitting the screen so we can see both the file and the command side by side.

First of all, the simplest and probably the most common regular expression is to find a single word.

For this we will use the `grep "joe" file.txt` command:

```
hacker@laptop: ~/course
wordoftheday                        hacker@laptop [10:41:59 AM] [~/course]
[one and two]                       -> % grep "Joe" file.txt

2445343
a:-b:-b

a2s3c4
ALL CAPS LOCK
Joe, Bill - Alice!
~
~
~
~
~
~
~
~
~
~
~
~
~
~
~
~
~
~
         1,1            All
```

`joe` is the string we are searching for and `file.txt` is the file where we perform the search. You can see that grep printed the line that contained our string and the word is highlighted with another color. This will only match the exact case of the word (so, if we use lowercase `j`, this regex will not work anymore). To do a case insensitive search, `grep` has an `-i` option. What this means is that grep will print the line that contains our word even if the word is in a different case, like JoE, JOE, joE, and so on:

```
grep -i "joe" file.txt
```

```
hacker@laptop: ~/course
wordoftheday                    hacker@laptop [10:41:59 AM] [~/course]
[one and two]                   -> % grep "Joe" file.txt
                                Joe, Bill - Alice!
2445343                         hacker@laptop [10:42:08 AM] [~/course]
a:-b:-b                         -> % grep "joe" file.txt
                                hacker@laptop [10:42:13 AM] [~/course]
a2s3c4                          -> % grep -i "joe" file.txt
ALL CAPS LOCK                   Joe, Bill - Alice!
Joe, Bill - Alice!              hacker@laptop [10:42:16 AM] [~/course]
~                               -> % ▓
~
~
~
~
~
~
~
~
~
~
~
~
~
~
~
~
~
~
~
        1,1             All
```

If we don't know exactly what characters are there in our string, we can use `.*` to match any number of characters. For example, to find a sentence beginning with "word" and ending with "day", we'd use the `grep "word.*day" file.txt` command:

- `.` - matches any character
- `*` - matches previous character multiple times

Here you can see that it matched the first line in the file.

A very common scenario is to find empty lines in a file. For this we use the `grep "^\s$" file.txt` command:

- Where `\s` : This stands for space,
- `^` : It's for the beginning of the line.
- `$` : It's for its ending.

We have two empty lines with no space. If we add a space between the lines, it will match the lines containing one space. These are called **anchors**.

grep can do a neat little trick to count the number of matches. For this, we use the -c parameter:

```
hacker@laptop: ~/course
wordoftheday                          hacker@laptop [10:41:59 AM] [~/course]
[one and two]                         -> % grep "Joe" file.txt
                                      Joe, Bill - Alice!
2445343                               hacker@laptop [10:42:08 AM] [~/course]
a:-b:-b                               -> % grep "joe" file.txt
                                      hacker@laptop [10:42:13 AM] [~/course]
a2s3c4                                -> % grep -i "joe" file.txt
ALL CAPS LOCK                         Joe, Bill - Alice!
Joe, Bill - Alice!                    hacker@laptop [10:42:16 AM] [~/course]
~                                     -> % grep "word.*day" file.txt
~                                     wordoftheday
~                                     hacker@laptop [10:42:26 AM] [~/course]
~                                     -> % grep "^\s$" file.txt
~                                     hacker@laptop [10:42:41 AM] [~/course]
~                                     -> % grep "^\s$" file.txt
~
~
~                                     hacker@laptop [10:44:13 AM] [~/course]
~                                     -> % grep -c "^\s$" file.txt
~                                     2
~                                     hacker@laptop [10:44:20 AM] [~/course]
~                                     -> %

                                      grep -c "^\s$" file.txt


<9L, 87C written  6,1        All
```

To find all the lines that have only letters and space, use:

- grep
- "": Open quotes
- ^$: From the beginning of the line to the end
- [] *: Match these characters any number of times
- A-Za-z: Any upper and lower case letter

If we run the command up to here, we get only the first line. If we add:

- - 0-9 any number we match another two lines,
- And if we add: - \s any space, we also match the empty lines and the all caps line
- If we run the command until here, we get only the first line from the output, the rest is not displayed

- Then, if we add 0-9 we match any number (so the first two lines get matched)
- And if we add \s we match any type of space (so the empty lines are matched as well)

```
grep "^[A-Za-z0-9\s]*$" file.txt
```

```
hacker@laptop: ~/course
wordoftheday                          hacker@laptop [10:41:59 AM] [~/course]
[one and two]                         -> % grep "Joe" file.txt
                                      Joe, Bill - Alice!
2445343                               hacker@laptop [10:42:08 AM] [~/course]
a:-b:-b                               -> % grep "joe" file.txt
                                      hacker@laptop [10:42:13 AM] [~/course]
a2s3c4                                -> % grep -i "joe" file.txt
ALL CAPS LOCK                         Joe, Bill - Alice!
Joe, Bill - Alice!                    hacker@laptop [10:42:16 AM] [~/course]
~                                     -> % grep "word.*day" file.txt
~                                     wordoftheday
~                                     hacker@laptop [10:42:26 AM] [~/course]
~                                     -> % grep "^\s$" file.txt
~                                     hacker@laptop [10:42:41 AM] [~/course]
~                                     -> % grep "^\s$" file.txt
~
~
~                                     hacker@laptop [10:44:13 AM] [~/course]
~                                     -> % grep -c "^\s$" file.txt
~                                     2
~                                     hacker@laptop [10:44:20 AM] [~/course]
~                                     -> % grep "^[A-Za-z0-9\s]*$" file.txt
~                                     wordoftheday
~                                     2445343
~                                     a2s3c4
~                                     hacker@laptop [10:44:54 AM] [~/course]
~                                     -> %
~
~
~
~
~
~
~                           grep "^[A-Za-z0-9\s]*$" file.txt
~
<9L, 87C written  6,1        All
```

Sometimes we need to search for something that's not in the string:

```
grep "^[^0-9]*$" file.txt
```

This command will find all the lines that do not have only numeric characters. [^] means match all characters that are not inside, in our case, any non-number.

The square brackets are markers in our regular expression. If we want to use them in our search string, we have to escape them. So, in order to find lines that have content between square brackets, do this:

```
grep "\[.*\]" file.txt
```

This is for any line that has characters in square brackets. To find all lines that have these character !, type this:

```
grep "\!" file.txt
```

Now let's have a look at a basic `sed`, lets find `Joe` word and replace with `All` word:

```
sed "s/Joe/All/g" file.txt
```

```
hacker@laptop: ~/course
wordoftheday                    hacker@laptop [10:46:01 AM] [~/course]
[one and two]                   -> % grep "[\!]" file.txt
                                Joe, Bill - Alice!
2445343                         hacker@laptop [10:47:47 AM] [~/course]
a:-b:-b                         -> % grep "\!" file.txt
                                Joe, Bill - Alice!
a2s3c4                          hacker@laptop [10:47:52 AM] [~/course]
ALL CAPS LOCK                   -> % sed "s/Joe/All/g" file.txt
Joe, Bill - Alice!              wordoftheday
                                [one and two]

                                2445343
                                a:-b:-b

                                a2s3c4
                                ALL CAPS LOCK
                                All, Bill - Alice!
                                hacker@laptop [10:48:29 AM] [~/course]
                                -> %

<9L, 87C written  6,1           All
```

This will replace every occurrence of the string `Joe` with the string `All`. We will deep dive into this in the upcoming chapters.

Regular expressions, such as Vim, are one of the things many people are afraid of because they seem complicated to learn in the beginning. Although they might seem cryptic, regular expressions are handy companions once mastered: they are not limited to our shell because the syntax is very similar in most programming languages, databases, editors, and any other place that includes searching for strings. We will go into more detail about regular expressions in the upcoming chapters.

Pipes and subshells – your shell's salt and pepper

In this section, we will be looking at ways to improve your productivity using your shell. The Linux command line is great because it has a variety of tools we can use. What makes it even greater is the fact that we can chain these tools together to form greater, more powerful tools that will make us even more productive. We will not go into basic shell commands; instead we will be looking at some cool pipe and subshell combinations that can make our lives easier.

Let's start with a basic pipe; in this example, we are counting the length of the current path using the following command:

```
pwd | wc -c
```

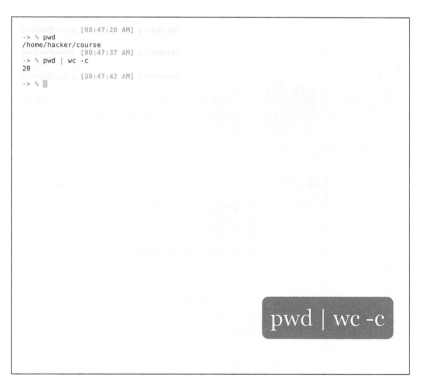

pwd, as you probably know, stands for print working directory. The | is the pipe symbol, and what it does is send the output of the command on the left to the command on the right. In our case, pwd is sending its output to wc -c, which counts the number of characters. The coolest thing about pipes is that you can create a chain of any number of pipes.

Let's see another example where we will see how to find used space on the drive:

```
df -h | grep /home | tr -s " " | cut -f 2 -d " "
```

```
hacker@laptop [08:47:20 AM] [~/course]
-> % pwd
/home/hacker/course
hacker@laptop [08:47:37 AM] [~/course]
-> % pwd | wc -c
20
hacker@laptop [08:47:42 AM] [~/course]
-> % df -h
Filesystem      Size  Used Avail Use% Mounted on
udev            3.9G     0  3.9G   0% /dev
tmpfs           784M  9.6M  775M   2% /run
/dev/sda5        46G   15G   29G  35% /
tmpfs           3.9G   12M  3.9G   1% /dev/shm
tmpfs           5.0M  4.0K  5.0M   1% /run/lock
tmpfs           3.9G     0  3.9G   0% /sys/fs/cgroup
/dev/sda1       952M  3.6M  948M   1% /boot/efi
/dev/sda3       173G   67G   98G  41% /home
tmpfs           784M  4.0K  784M   1% /run/user/108
tmpfs           784M   60K  784M   1% /run/user/1001
hacker@laptop [08:47:49 AM] [~/course]
-> % df -h | grep /home
/dev/sda3       173G   67G   98G  41% /home
hacker@laptop [08:47:56 AM] [~/course]
-> % df -h | grep /home | tr -s " "
/dev/sda3 173G 67G 98G 41% /home
hacker@laptop [08:48:07 AM] [~/course]
-> % df -h | grep /home | tr -s " " | cut -f 2 -d " "
173G
hacker@laptop [08:48:19 AM] [~/course]
-> % 
```

df -h | grep /home | tr -s " " | **cut -f 2 -d " "**

- `"df -h"`: This shows the disk usage in a human-readable format
- `"| grep /home"`: This shows only the home directory
- `'| tr -s " "'`: This substitutes multiple spaces for just one space
- `'| cut -f 2 -d " "'`: This selects the second column using a space as the delimiter

As you can see, the command printed out 173G, the size of the /home partition. This is a common use case when chaining multiple commands, each command reducing the output until we get the desired information and nothing else. In our case, this is the used disk space.

To count all the directories in a folder, use the following command:

```
ls -p | grep / | wc -l
```

```
                    [08:47:20 AM]  [~/course]
-> % pwd
/home/hacker/course
                    [08:47:37 AM]  [~/course]
-> % pwd | wc -c
20
                    [08:47:42 AM]  [~/course]
-> % df -h
Filesystem      Size  Used Avail Use% Mounted on
udev            3.9G     0  3.9G   0% /dev
tmpfs           784M  9.6M  775M   2% /run
/dev/sda5        46G   15G   29G  35% /
tmpfs           3.9G   12M  3.9G   1% /dev/shm
tmpfs           5.0M  4.0K  5.0M   1% /run/lock
tmpfs           3.9G     0  3.9G   0% /sys/fs/cgroup
/dev/sda1       952M  3.6M  948M   1% /boot/efi
/dev/sda3       173G   67G   98G  41% /home
tmpfs           784M  4.0K  784M   1% /run/user/108
tmpfs           784M   60K  784M   1% /run/user/1001
                    [08:47:49 AM]  [~/course]
-> % df -h | grep /home
/dev/sda3       173G   67G   98G  41% /home
                    [08:47:56 AM]  [~/course]
-> % df -h | grep /home | tr -s " "
/dev/sda3 173G 67G 98G 41% /home
                    [08:48:07 AM]  [~/course]
-> % df -h | grep /home | tr -s " " | cut -f 2 -d " "
173G
                    [08:48:19 AM]  [~/course]
-> % ls -p
file.txt  git-demo/  lorem.txt
                    [08:48:32 AM]  [~/course]
-> % ls -p | grep /
git-demo/
                    [08:48:43 AM]  [~/course]
-> % ls -p | grep / | wc -l
1
                    [08:48:47 AM]  [~/course]
-> %
```

```
ls -p | grep / | wc -l
```

The basic idea is to count all the lines that end with /. Here we can see we have only one directory.

Pipes are a great option to find and kill processes. Say we want to find the process ID of `nautilus`, and `kill all` running instances. For this we use:

```
ps aux | grep nautilus | grep -v grep | awk '{print $2}' | xargs kill
```

```
hacker    5906  0.0  0.9 769016 74312 ?        Sl   08:21   0:00 /opt/google/chrome/chrome --type=renderer --enable-features=UsePasswordSeparatedSi
hacker    5942  0.4  2.0 1476368 168808 ?      Sl   08:21   0:07 /opt/google/chrome/chrome --type=renderer --enable-features=UsePasswordSeparatedSi
hacker    5963  0.8  2.8 1415500 230916 ?      Sl   08:21   0:14 /opt/google/chrome/chrome --type=renderer --enable-features=UsePasswordSeparatedSi
hacker    6169  0.6  2.2 2066108 177148 ?      Sl   08:21   0:11 /opt/google/chrome/chrome --type=renderer --enable-features=UsePasswordSeparatedSi
hacker    6182  5.6  3.2 1123068 263284 ?      Sl   08:21   1:33 /opt/google/chrome/chrome --type=renderer --enable-features=UsePasswordSeparatedSi
hacker    6215  0.0  0.8 741716 70264 ?        Sl   08:21   0:00 /opt/google/chrome/chrome --type=renderer --enable-features=UsePasswordSeparatedSi
hacker    6768  0.0  0.0 435296  6824 ?        Sl   08:21   0:00 /usr/lib/gvfs/gvfsd-network --spawner :1.8 /org/gtk/gvfs/exec_spaw/4
hacker    6791  0.0  0.0 444064  7072 ?        Sl   08:21   0:00 /usr/lib/x86_64-linux-gnu/deja-dup/deja-dup-monitor
hacker    6889  0.0  0.0 194540  4460 ?        Sl   08:21   0:00 /usr/lib/gvfs/gvfsd-metadata
hacker    6816  0.0  0.0 370320  6704 ?        Sl   08:21   0:00 /usr/lib/gvfs/gvfsd-dnssd --spawner :1.8 /org/gtk/gvfs/exec_spaw/6
hacker    6873 21.2  5.1 1551112 409560 ?      Sl   08:22   5:39 simplescreenrecorder --logfile
hacker    6896  0.2  0.7 784740 56856 ?        Rl   08:22   0:03 /usr/bin/python /usr/bin/terminator
hacker    6989  0.0  0.0  14872  1844 ?        S    08:22   0:00 gnome-pty-helper
hacker    6918  0.0  0.0  55348  5860 pts/2    Ss   08:22   0:00 /usr/bin/zsh
root      6968  0.0  0.0      0     0 ?        S    08:23   0:00 [kworker/u16:0]
root      6981  0.0  0.0      0     0 ?        S    08:25   0:00 [kworker/2:2]
root      7041  0.0  0.0      0     0 ?        S    08:31   0:00 [kworker/5:1]
root      7057  0.0  0.0      0     0 ?        S    08:34   0:00 [kworker/6:0]
root      7072  0.0  0.0      0     0 ?        S    08:36   0:00 [kworker/u16:2]
```

```
ps aux | grep nautilus | grep -v grep | awk '{print $2}' | xargs kill
```

```
root      7442  0.0  0.0      0     0 ?        S    08:46   0:00 [kworker/0:0]
hacker    7446  0.8  0.9 1127124 79012 ?       Sl   08:46   0:01 /usr/bin/nautilus --gapplication-service
root      7470  0.0  0.0      0     0 ?        S    08:46   0:00 [kworker/u16:1]
root      7474  0.1  0.0      0     0 ?        S    08:47   0:00 [kworker/6:2]
root      7504  0.0  0.0      0     0 ?        S    08:47   0:00 [kworker/5:0]
hacker    7578  0.0  0.0  45960  3276 pts/2    R+   08:48   0:00 ps aux
hacker@laptop [08:48:55 AM] [~/course]
-> % ps aux | grep nautilus
hacker    7446  0.7  0.9 1127124 79012 ?       Sl   08:46   0:01 /usr/bin/nautilus --gapplication-service
hacker    7584  0.0  0.0  22820   984 pts/2    S+   08:49   0:00 grep --color=auto --exclude-dir=.bzr --exclude-dir=CVS --exclude-dir=.git --exclud
e-dir=.hg --exclude-dir=.svn nautilus
hacker@laptop [08:49:02 AM] [~/course]
-> % ps aux | grep nautilus | grep -v grep
hacker    7446  0.7  0.9 1127124 79012 ?       Sl   08:46   0:01 /usr/bin/nautilus --gapplication-service
hacker@laptop [08:49:09 AM] [~/course]
-> % ps aux | grep nautilus | grep -v grep | awk '{print $2}'
7446
hacker@laptop [08:49:27 AM] [~/course]
-> % ps aux | grep nautilus | grep -v grep | awk '{print $2}' | xargs kill
```

- `ps aux`: This prints all processes with PID
- `| grep nautilus`: Find the ones matching nautilus
- `| grep -v grep`: Inverts `grep` to exclude the `grep` process
- `| awk '{print $2}'`: Selects the second word in the line, which is the PID
- `| xargs kill`: Here `xargs` is used to distribute each PID to a kill command. It is especially used for commands that do not read arguments from standard input.

Now we've killed `nautilus`. This was purely a demonstrative example. There are other ways of doing this.

Let's open `nautilus` again and send it to the background by hitting *Ctrl + Z* followed by the `bg` command.

Now let's run the following command:

```
pgrep nautilus
```

To see all the `pids` of `nautilus` and to send the kill signal to all those processes, use the following command line:

```
pkill nautilus
```

Now it's time for some networking! You probably know the `ifconfig` command, which is used to print information about the network interfaces. To get the IP address of a specific interface (in our case the wireless interface `wlp3s0`), run this:

```
ifconfig wlp3s0 | grep "inet addr:" | awk '{print $2}' | cut -f 2 -d ":"
```

```
                collisions:0 txqueuelen:1000
                RX bytes:0 (0.0 B)  TX bytes:0 (0.0 B)

lo              Link encap:Local Loopback
                inet addr:127.0.0.1  Mask:255.0.0.0
                inet6 addr: ::1/128 Scope:Host
                UP LOOPBACK RUNNING  MTU:65536  Metric:1
                RX packets:883 errors:0 dropped:0 overruns:0 frame:0
                TX packets:883 errors:0 dropped:0 overruns:0 carrier:0
                collisions:0 txqueuelen:1
                RX bytes:91069 (91.0 KB)  TX bytes:91069 (91.0 KB)

wlp3s0          Link encap:Ethernet  HWaddr 68:17:29:bf:e2:67
                inet addr:192.168.0.159  Bcast:192.168.0.255  Mask:255.255.255.0
                inet6 addr: fe80::18e9:533a:d12f:82de/64 Scope:Link
                UP BROADCAST RUNNING MULTICAST  MTU:1500  Metric:1
                RX packets:37453 errors:0 dropped:0 overruns:0 frame:0
                TX packets:23870 errors:0 dropped:0 overruns:0 carrier:0
                collisions:0 txqueuelen:1000
                RX bytes:42402459 (42.4 MB)  TX bytes:3735603 (3.7 MB)

ifconfig wlp3s0 | grep "inet addr:" | awk '{print $2}' | cut -f 2 -d ":"

wlp3s0          Link encap:Ethernet  HWaddr 68:17:29:bf:e2:67
                inet addr:192.168.0.159  Bcast:192.168.0.255  Mask:255.255.255.0
                inet6 addr: fe80::18e9:533a:d12f:82de/64 Scope:Link
                UP BROADCAST RUNNING MULTICAST  MTU:1500  Metric:1
                RX packets:37466 errors:0 dropped:0 overruns:0 frame:0
                TX packets:23874 errors:0 dropped:0 overruns:0 carrier:0
                collisions:0 txqueuelen:1000
                RX bytes:42406711 (42.4 MB)  TX bytes:3736306 (3.7 MB)

         [08:50:30 AM]
-> % ifconfig wlp3s0 | grep 'inet addr:'
                inet addr:192.168.0.159  Bcast:192.168.0.255  Mask:255.255.255.0
         [08:50:43 AM]
-> % ifconfig wlp3s0 | grep 'inet addr:' | awk '{print $2}'
addr:192.168.0.159
         [08:50:56 AM]
-> % ifconfig wlp3s0 | grep 'inet addr:' | awk '{print $2}' | cut -f 2 -d ":"
192.168.0.159
         [08:51:10 AM]
-> %
```

- `ifconfig wlp3s0`: Prints networking information for the `wlp3s0` interface
- `| grep "inet addr:"`: Gets the line with the IP address
- `| awk '{print $2}'`: Selects the second word in the line (we could have used cut as well)
- `| cut -f 2 -d ":"`: This is split by `":"`, and only prints the second word

And now, we see your `private ip` address on the screen.

A common use case that might also arise is counting the word frequency in a file.

Here we have a standard lorem ipsum text contained in `lorem.txt`. In order to get the word frequency, use this:

```
cat lorem.txt | tr " " "\n" | grep -v "^\s*$" | sed "s/[,.]//g" | sort | uniq -c | sort -n
```

```
      1 est
      1 et
      1 eu
      1 ex
      1 Excepteur
      1 exercitation
      1 fugiat
      1 id
      3 in
      1 incididunt
      1 ipsum
      1 irure
      1 labore
      1 laboris
      1 laborum
      1 Lorem
      1 magna
      1 minim
      1 mollit
      1 nisi
      1 non
      1 nostrud
      1 nulla
      1 occaecat
      1 officia
      1 pariatur
      1 proident
      1 qui
      1 quis
      1 reprehenderit
      1 sed
      1 sint
      1 sit
      1 sunt
      1 tempor
      1 ullamco
      2 ut
      1 Ut
      1 velit
      1 veniam
      1 voluptate
mackze@isa.com [08:53:15 AM] [~/course]
-> % cat lorem.txt | tr " " "\n" | grep -v "^\s*$" | sed "s/[,.]//g" | sort | uniq -c | sort -n
```

    cat lorem.txt | tr " " "\n" | grep -v "^\s*$" |
           sed "s/[,.]//g" | sort | uniq -c | sort -n

- `cat lorem.txt`
- `| tr " " "\n"`: Transforms each space into a new line character
- `| grep -v "^\s*$"`: Eliminates empty lines
- `| sed "s/[,.]//g"`: Eliminates commas (,) and periods (.) to select only the words
- `| sort`: Sort the results alphabetically
- `| uniq -c`: Show only unique lines
- `| sort -n`: Sorts by numerical value

Append `grep -w id` to find the frequency of the word ID, or `grep -w 4` to see all words that appear four times.

Now let's move on to our first subshell example. Subshells can be written by either enclosing them in `$()`, or using backticks (`` ` ``). Backticks are usually found under the *Esc* key on your keyboard. In all our examples, we will be using the first form because it's easier to read.

Our first example is to list all the folders in our current folder:

```
ls $(ls)
```

The `ls` subshell returns the files and folders in the current directory and the `ls` from outside the subshell will list those individually, showing additional details:

- Counting all files and directories in the current directory
- Given the fact that commas (,) and periods (.) are hard links that mark the current and parent directory, we need to count all entries minus these two
- This can be done using the `expr $(ls -a | wc -l ) - 2` command:

```
      1 mollit
      1 nisi
      1 non
      1 nostrud
      1 nulla
      1 occaecat
      1 officia
      1 pariatur
      1 proident
      1 qui
      1 quis
      1 reprehenderit
      1 sed
      1 sint
      1 sit
      1 sunt
      1 tempor
      1 ullamco
      1 Ut
      1 velit
      1 veniam
      1 voluptate
      2 dolor
      2 dolore
      2 ut
      3 in
               [08:53:24 AM]
-> % ls $(ls)
file.txt  lorem.txt

git-demo:
readme.md
               [08:54:29 AM]
-> % ls
file.txt  git-demo  lorem.txt
               [08:54:36 AM]
-> % ls -a | wc -l
5
               [08:54:51 AM]
-> % expr $(ls -a | wc -l) - 2
3
               [08:55:07 AM]
-> % 
```

$$expr \; \$(ls \; -a \; | \; wc \; -l \;) - 2$$

Here, the subshell will return the number of entries (five, in this case). The number we are looking for is the number of entries minus the special folders ("." and ".."). In order to do arithmetic operations, we use the `expr` command, as in our example.

Notice that the subshell contains a pipe. The good thing is that we can combine pipes and subshells in any way in order to obtain the desired result.

Imagine pipes and subshells as Lego pieces for your shell. They expand way beyond its capabilities and give you access to new possibilities with infinite combinations. In the end, it all depends on your imagination and how well you learn to use them.

Shell scripting for fun and profit

Pipes and subshells are one way of expanding the capabilities of our shell. The ultimate way is by writing shell scripts. These scenarios must be taken into consideration when dealing with complex tasks that can't be automated with a one-line command.

The good news is that almost all the tasks can be automated with the use of shell scripts. We won't go over an introduction to shell scripts. Instead, we will be looking at some more advanced use cases for writing them.

Let's start our journey into shell scripting! First thing, let's open a file called `script.sh` and split the screen so that we can test while writing. Every shell should start with `#!`, followed by the interpreter it uses. This line is called a **shebang**. We will be using bash as our default interpreter.

It's a good idea to use bash, because it's a common interpreter that comes with most Linux distributions and also OS X:

```
#!/bin/bash
```

Let's start with a simple use case: reading the arguments passed into the command line. We will assign the value of the first command line argument, `$1`, to a variable called ARG, and then print it back to the screen:

```
ARG=${1}
echo ${ARG}
```

Let's save our script, assign it execution permissions, and then run it with one argument:

```
./script.sh test
```

```
#!/bin/bash

ARG=${1}
echo $ARG
~
~
~
~
~
~
~
~
~
~
~
~
~
~
~
~
~
~
~
~
~
~
~
~
~
~
~
~
~
~
~
~
~
~
~
~
                    4,11        All
```

```
                 [09:42:49 AM]
-> % ll
total 16K
-rw-r--r-- 1 hacker hacker   87 Jul 21 10:44 file.txt
drwxrwxr-x 3 hacker hacker 4.0K Jul 21 10:30 git-demo
-rw-rw-r-- 1 hacker hacker  447 Jul 27 08:37 lorem.txt
-rw-rw-r-- 1 hacker hacker   34 Jul 27 09:42 script.sh
                 [09:42:50 AM]
-> % chmod +x script.sh
                 [09:42:55 AM]
-> % ll
total 16K
-rw-r--r-- 1 hacker hacker   87 Jul 21 10:44 file.txt
drwxrwxr-x 3 hacker hacker 4.0K Jul 21 10:30 git-demo
-rw-rw-r-- 1 hacker hacker  447 Jul 27 08:37 lorem.txt
-rwxrwxr-x 1 hacker hacker   34 Jul 27 09:42 script.sh
                 [09:43:01 AM]
-> % ./script.sh test
test
                 [09:43:06 AM]
-> %
```

As you can see, the value test is printed back to the screen. In some cases, we want to assign default values to variables. In order to do this, add ":-" to the variable assignment, followed by the default value:

```
ARG=${1:-"default value"}
```

Now if we re-run the script, we can see that passing no arguments will echo default value. And just like pipes, we can chain multiple default value assignments together. We can define another variable AUX, assign it the value 123, and use the same syntax to assign its value to the ARG variable, before using the "default value" script like so:

```
AUX="123"
ARG=${1:-${AUX:-"default value"}}
```

```
#!/bin/bash

AUX="123"
ARG=${1:-${AUX:-"default value"}}
echo ${ARG}
~
~
~
~
~
~
~
~
~
~
~
~
~
~
~
~
~
~
~
~
~
~
~
~
~
~
"script.sh" 5L, 69C written     4,33        All
```

```
hacker@laptop [09:42:49 AM] [~/course]
-> % ll
total 16K
-rw-r--r-- 1 hacker hacker   87 Jul 21 10:44 file.txt
drwxrwxr-x 3 hacker hacker 4.0K Jul 21 10:30 git-demo
-rw-rw-r-- 1 hacker hacker  447 Jul 27 08:37 lorem.txt
-rw-rw-r-- 1 hacker hacker   34 Jul 27 09:42 script.sh
hacker@laptop [09:42:50 AM] [~/course]
-> % chmod +x script.sh
hacker@laptop [09:42:55 AM] [~/course]
-> % ll
total 16K
-rw-r--r-- 1 hacker hacker   87 Jul 21 10:44 file.txt
drwxrwxr-x 3 hacker hacker 4.0K Jul 21 10:30 git-demo
-rw-rw-r-- 1 hacker hacker  447 Jul 27 08:37 lorem.txt
-rwxrwxr-x 1 hacker hacker   34 Jul 27 09:42 script.sh
hacker@laptop [09:43:01 AM] [~/course]
-> % ./script.sh test
test
hacker@laptop [09:43:06 AM] [~/course]
-> % ./script.sh
default value
hacker@laptop [09:43:20 AM] [~/course]
-> % ./script.sh
123
hacker@laptop [09:43:41 AM] [~/course]
-> % 
```

ARG=${1:-${AUX:-"default value"}}

In this case, ARG will always receive 123 as its default value.

Now let's look at string selectors. To select a substring, use ":", plus the starting position plus ":", plus the number of characters:

```
LINE="some long line of text"
echo "${LINE:5:4}"
```

```
#!/bin/bash                                  hacker@laptop [09:42:49 AM] [~/course]
                                             -> % ll
AUX="123"                                    total 16K
ARG=${1:-${AUX:-"default value"}}            -rw-r--r-- 1 hacker hacker   87 Jul 21 10:44 file.txt
#echo ${ARG}                                 drwxrwxr-x 3 hacker hacker 4.0K Jul 21 10:30 git-demo
                                             -rw-rw-r-- 1 hacker hacker  447 Jul 27 08:37 lorem.txt
LINE="some long line of text"                -rw-rw-r-- 1 hacker hacker   34 Jul 27 09:42 script.sh
echo "${LINE:5:4}"                           hacker@laptop [09:42:50 AM] [~/course]
~                                            -> % chmod +x script.sh
~                                            hacker@laptop [09:42:55 AM] [~/course]
~                                            -> % ll
~                                            total 16K
~                                            -rw-r--r-- 1 hacker hacker   87 Jul 21 10:44 file.txt
~                                            drwxrwxr-x 3 hacker hacker 4.0K Jul 21 10:30 git-demo
~                                            -rw-rw-r-- 1 hacker hacker  447 Jul 27 08:37 lorem.txt
~                                            -rwxrwxr-x 1 hacker hacker   34 Jul 27 09:42 script.sh
~                                            hacker@laptop [09:43:01 AM] [~/course]
~                                            -> % ./script.sh test
~                                            test
~                                            hacker@laptop [09:43:06 AM] [~/course]
~                                            -> % ./script.sh
~                                            default value
~                                            hacker@laptop [09:43:20 AM] [~/course]
~                                            -> % ./script.sh
~                                            123
~                                            hacker@laptop [09:43:41 AM] [~/course]
~                                            -> % ./script.sh
~                                            long
~                                            hacker@laptop [09:44:14 AM] [~/course]
~                                            -> %
~
~
~
~
~
~
~
~
~
"script.sh" 8L, 120C written    8,18         All
```

In our case, we will be selecting four characters, starting from the fifth character. After running the script, we can see the value long printed on the screen.

Most shell scripts are designed to run from the command line and receive a variable number of arguments. In order to read command line arguments without knowing the total number of arguments, we'll use a `while` statement that checks whether the first argument is not null using the -z (or not equal to 0) conditional expression. In the while loop, let's echo the variable's value and run shift, which shifts command line arguments one position to the left:

```
while [[ ! -z ${1} ]]; do
echo ${1}
shift  # shift cli arguments
done
```

```
#!/bin/bash                                    hacker@laptop [09:42:49 AM] [~/course]
                                               -> % ll
AUX="123"                                      total 16K
ARG=${1:-${AUX:-"default value"}}              -rw-r--r-- 1 hacker hacker  87 Jul 21 10:44 file.txt
#echo ${ARG}                                   drwxrwxr-x 3 hacker hacker 4.0K Jul 21 10:30 git-demo
                                               -rw-rw-r-- 1 hacker hacker 447 Jul 27 08:37 lorem.txt
LINE="some long line of text"                  -rw-rw-r-- 1 hacker hacker  34 Jul 27 09:42 script.sh
#echo "${LINE:5:4}"                            hacker@laptop [09:42:50 AM] [~/course]
                                               -> % chmod +x script.sh
while [[ ! -z ${1} ]]; do                      hacker@laptop [09:42:55 AM] [~/course]
        echo $1                                -> % ll
        shift                                  total 16K
done                                           -rw-r--r-- 1 hacker hacker  87 Jul 21 10:44 file.txt
~                                              drwxrwxr-x 3 hacker hacker 4.0K Jul 21 10:30 git-demo
~                                              -rw-rw-r-- 1 hacker hacker 447 Jul 27 08:37 lorem.txt
~                                              -rwxrwxr-x 1 hacker hacker  34 Jul 27 09:42 script.sh
~                                              hacker@laptop [09:43:01 AM] [~/course]
~                                              -> % ./script.sh test
~                                              test
~                                              hacker@laptop [09:43:06 AM] [~/course]
~                                              -> % ./script.sh
~                                              default value
~                                              hacker@laptop [09:43:20 AM] [~/course]
~                                              -> % ./script.sh
~                                              123
~                                              hacker@laptop [09:43:41 AM] [~/course]
~                                              -> % ./script.sh
~                                              long
~                                              hacker@laptop [09:44:14 AM] [~/course]
~                                              -> % ./script.sh a b c
~                                              a
~                                              b
~                                              c
~                                              hacker@laptop [09:45:07 AM] [~/course]
~                                              -> % ▊
~
~
~
~
~
~
~
"script.sh" 13L, 169C written  12,6-13    All
```

If we run our script with the arguments *a b c*, we can see that our while looped through the parameters and printed each one on a separate line. Now let's extend our CLI arguments parser and add a *case* statement for interpreting the arguments.

Let's assume that our script will have a help option. The Posix standard recommends doing a long argument version with --, and a short version with only one -. So both -h and --help will print the help message. Also, it is recommended to always have a default case and print a message when the user sends invalid options and then exits with a non-zero exit value:

```
while [[ ! -z ${1} ]]; do
    case "$1" in
        --help|-h)
            echo "This is a help message"
            shift
            ;;
        *)
            echo "invalid option"
            exit 1
            ;;
    esac
done
```

```
#!/bin/bash                                            hacker@laptop [09:42:49 AM] [~/course]
                                                       -> % ll
AUX="123"                                              total 16K
ARG=${1:-${AUX:-"default value"}}                      -rw-r--r-- 1 hacker hacker   87 Jul 21 10:44 file.txt
#echo ${ARG}                                           drwxrwxr-x 3 hacker hacker 4.0K Jul 21 10:30 git-demo
                                                       -rw-rw-r-- 1 hacker hacker  447 Jul 27 08:37 lorem.txt
LINE="some long line of text"                          -rw-rw-r-- 1 hacker hacker   34 Jul 27 09:42 script.sh
#echo "${LINE:5:4}"                                    hacker@laptop [09:42:50 AM] [~/course]
                                                       -> % chmod +x script.sh
while [[ ! -z ${1} ]]; do                              hacker@laptop [09:42:55 AM] [~/course]
  case "$1" in                                         -> % ll
    --help|-h)                                         total 16K
      echo "This is a help message"                    -rw-r--r-- 1 hacker hacker   87 Jul 21 10:44 file.txt
      shift                                            drwxrwxr-x 3 hacker hacker 4.0K Jul 21 10:30 git-demo
      ;;                                               -rw-rw-r-- 1 hacker hacker  447 Jul 27 08:37 lorem.txt
    *)                                                 -rwxrwxr-x 1 hacker hacker   34 Jul 27 09:42 script.sh
      echo "Invalid option"                            hacker@laptop [09:43:01 AM] [~/course]
      exit 1                                           -> % ./script.sh test
      ;;                                               test
  esac                                                 hacker@laptop [09:43:06 AM] [~/course]
done                                                   -> % ./script.sh
~                                                      default value
~                                                      hacker@laptop [09:43:20 AM] [~/course]
~                                                      -> % ./script.sh
~                                                      123
~                                                      hacker@laptop [09:43:41 AM] [~/course]
~                                                      -> % ./script.sh
~                                                      long
~                                                      hacker@laptop [09:44:14 AM] [~/course]
~                                                      -> % ./script.sh a b c
~                                                      a
~                                                      b
~                                                      c
~                                                      hacker@laptop [09:45:07 AM] [~/course]
~                                                      -> % ./script.sh -h
~                                                      This is a help message
~                                                      hacker@laptop [09:46:26 AM] [~/course]
~                                                      -> % ./script.sh --help
~                                                      This is a help message
~                                                      hacker@laptop [09:46:30 AM] [~/course]
~                                                      -> %
"script.sh" 21L, 304C written   21,1          All
```

If we run our script with -h, we can see the help message printed, the same as if we had used `--help`. If we run the script with any other option, the invalid option text is printed and the script exits with the exit code 1. To get the exit code of the last command, use `"$?"`.

Now let's look at basic functions in shell. The syntax is pretty similar to other programming languages. Let's write a function called `print_ip` that will print the IP of the interface specified as the first argument. We will use a subshell and assign the value to a variable called IP. We already have the full command inside our clipboard; it's the same one we saw in the lesson about pipes:

```
function print_ip() {
    IP=$(
        ifconfig ${1} | \
        grep "inet addr:" | \
        awk '{print $2}' | \
        cut -f 2 -d ":"
    )
    echo ${IP}
}
```

```
#!/bin/bash

AUX="123"
ARG=${1:-${AUX:-"default value"}}
#echo ${ARG}

LINE="some long line of text"
#echo "${LINE:5:4}"

function print_ip() {
  IP=$(ifconfig ${1} |\
  grep 'inet addr:' |\
  awk '{print $2}' | \
  cut -f 2 -d ":")
  echo ${IP}
}

while [[ ! -z ${1} ]]; do
  case "$1" in
    --ip|-i)
      print_ip ${2}
      shift
      shift
      ;;
    --help|-h)
      echo "This is a help message"
      shift
      ;;
    *)
      echo "Invalid option"
      exit 1
      ;;
  esac
done
~
~
~
~
~
~
~
"script.sh" 34L, 503C written   24,8          All
```

```
hacker@laptop [09:46:51 AM] [~/course]
-> % ifconfig
docker0   Link encap:Ethernet  HWaddr 02:42:3f:08:70:c0
          inet addr:172.17.0.1  Bcast:0.0.0.0  Mask:255.255.0.0
          UP BROADCAST MULTICAST  MTU:1500  Metric:1
          RX packets:0 errors:0 dropped:0 overruns:0 frame:0
          TX packets:0 errors:0 dropped:0 overruns:0 carrier:0
          collisions:0 txqueuelen:0
          RX bytes:0 (0.0 B)  TX bytes:0 (0.0 B)

enp2s0    Link encap:Ethernet  HWaddr 20:89:84:f4:50:97
          UP BROADCAST MULTICAST  MTU:1500  Metric:1
          RX packets:0 errors:0 dropped:0 overruns:0 frame:0
          TX packets:0 errors:0 dropped:0 overruns:0 carrier:0
          collisions:0 txqueuelen:1000
          RX bytes:0 (0.0 B)  TX bytes:0 (0.0 B)

lo        Link encap:Local Loopback
          inet addr:127.0.0.1  Mask:255.0.0.0
          inet6 addr: ::1/128 Scope:Host
          UP LOOPBACK RUNNING  MTU:65536  Metric:1
          RX packets:1315 errors:0 dropped:0 overruns:0 frame:0
          TX packets:1315 errors:0 dropped:0 overruns:0 carrier:0
          collisions:0 txqueuelen:1
          RX bytes:151317 (151.3 KB)  TX bytes:151317 (151.3 KB)

wlp3s0    Link encap:Ethernet  HWaddr 68:17:29:bf:e2:67
          inet addr:192.168.0.159  Bcast:192.168.0.255  Mask:255.255.255.0
          inet6 addr: fe80::18e9:533a:d12f:82de/64 Scope:Link
          UP BROADCAST RUNNING MULTICAST  MTU:1500  Metric:1
          RX packets:107221 errors:0 dropped:0 overruns:0 frame:0
          TX packets:70867 errors:0 dropped:0 overruns:0 carrier:0
          collisions:0 txqueuelen:1000
          RX bytes:133203550 (133.2 MB)  TX bytes:9574542 (9.5 MB)

hacker@laptop [09:49:06 AM] [~/course]
-> % ./script.sh --ip wlp3s0
192.168.0.159
hacker@laptop [09:49:16 AM] [~/course]
-> %
```

Now let's add another case to our switch statement, for the -i or --ip option. The option will be followed by the name of the interface, which we will then pass to the print_ip function. Having two arguments for one option means we need to call the shift command twice:

```
--ip|-i)
    print_ip ${2}
    shift
    shift
    ;;
```

Let's do an ifconfig to get the name of our wireless interface. We can see it's wlp3s0.

Now let's run:

```
./script.sh --ip wlp3s0
```

We can see the IP address. This is a very basic use case, where we can see how command line arguments can be passed. We can add unlimited options to our case statement, define functions for handling the arguments, and even chain multiple options together to form complex scripts that receive well-structured information as command line arguments.

Being effective means running tasks faster-- really fast! And when it comes to speed, bash is not the first choice in terms of script interpreters. Luckily, we still have some tricks up our sleeves! If a shell script needs to run multiple independent tasks, we can use the & symbol to send the process to the background and move forward to the next command.

Let's create two functions, long_running_task 1 and 2, and add a sleep command inside, to simulate a long_running task:

```
function long_running_task_1() {
    sleep 1
}

function long_running_task_2() {
    sleep 2
}
```

The first long running task function will sleep for one second, and the next will sleep for two seconds.

Then, for testing purposes, let's add another case to our switch statement, called `-p` / `--parallel`, and run the two long running tasks:

```
--parallel|-p)
    long_running_task_1
    long_running_task_2
```

Now, if we run this:

```
./script.sh -p
```

It will take a total of three seconds for the script to finish. We can measure this with the *time* utility:

```
#!/bin/bash

AUX="123"
ARG=${1:-${AUX:-"default value"}}
#echo ${ARG}

LINE="some long line of text"
#echo "${LINE:5:4}"

function print_ip() {
  IP=$(ifconfig ${1} |\
   grep 'inet addr:' |\
   awk '{print $2}' | \
   cut -f 2 -d ":")
  echo ${IP}
}

function long_running_task_1() {
  sleep 1
}

function long_running_task_2() {
  sleep 2
}

while [[ ! -z ${1} ]]; do
  case "$1" in
    --ip|-i)
      print_ip ${2}
      shift
      shift
      ;;

    --parallel|-p)
      long_running_task_1
      long_running_task_2
      shift
      ;;

    --help|-h)
      echo "This is a help message"
      shift
      ;;
   *)
"script.sh" 47L, 687C written  33,18        Top
```

```
-> % time ./script.sh -p
./script.sh -p  0.00s user 0.00s system 0% cpu 3.005 total
-> %
```

If we run both functions in the background, we can reduce the running time to the longest running time of both functions (because of the wait). When running long running tasks, we probably want the script to wait for the longest-running task to finish, in our case task 2. We can achieve this by grabbing the `pid` of the second task. Here `$!` is used to grab the `pid` of the last run command. Then we use the wait shell built in to wait for the execution to finish:

```
--parallel|-p)
    long_running_task_1 &
    long_running_task_2 &
    PID=$!
    wait ${PID}
```

After running the script again with the time utility, we can see it takes us a total of two seconds to complete the task.

Who would've thought we can do parallel processing in a shell?

If the executions take a longer time, we can add a notification when the script finishes:

```
notify-send script.sh "execution finished"
```

This way we can start the script, work on some other tasks, and receive a notification when the script finishes. You can let your imagination go wild on the things you can achieve with parallel processing and notifications.

In this chapter, we have seen some common predefined shell variables. They were:

- `$1`: First argument
- `$?`: Return code of the last command
- `$!`: The `pid` of the last command run

Other commonly used predefined shell variables include:

- `$#`: Number of parameters
- `$*`: List of parameters
- `$@`: All the parameters
- `$0`: Name of the shell/script
- `$$`: PID of current running shell

Bash has a lot of features and we recommend going through its man page to get more information about them.

Shell scripts are amazing when used the right way. They can fine-tune system commands, as we saw in our example when we got only the IP address, without the whole `ifconfig` output and much more. You, as a pragmatic terminal user, should identify what tasks you most commonly do in the command line and what can be automated using shell scripts. You should create your own collection of shell scripts and add them your path, so that they are easily accessible from any directory.

Shell scripting libraries

To really take advantage of automating tasks using shell scripts, it's important to organize all common tasks into reusable commands and have them available in the path. To do this, it's a good idea to create a `bin` folder inside the home directory for the scripts, and a `bin/lib` directory for storing common pieces of code. When working with lots of shell scripts, it's important to reuse large pieces of functionality. This can be achieved by writing library functions for your shell scripts, functions that you can call from multiple places.

Here we will create a library script called `util.sh`, which will be sourced in other scripts. By sourcing the script, we get access to functions and variables from inside the library script.

We will start by adding the `print_ip` function from a previous script.

Now we will add another function called `getarg`, which will be used by other scripts for reading command line arguments and values. We will simply paste it from our clipboard history, using ClipIt to select it.

You can learn more about ClipIt by checking out our ClipIt section!

```
Function to read cli argument:
function getarg() {
    NAME=${1}
    while [[ ! -z ${2} ]]; do
        if [[ "--${NAME}" == "${2}" ]]; then
            echo "${3}"
            break
        fi
        shift
    done
}
```

```
#!/bin/bash

function print_ip() {
 IP=$(ifconfig ${1} |\
   grep 'inet addr:' |\
   awk {print $2}' | \
   cut -f 2 -d ":")
 echo ${IP}
}

function getarg() {
   NAME=${1}
   while [[ ! -z ${2} ]]; do
     if [[ "--${NAME}" == "${2}" ]]; then
        echo "${3}"
        break
     fi
     shift
   done
}


-- INSERT --                                                          21,1        All
```

This is just a simple function that will receive a parameter name as the first argument, the list of CLI arguments as the second parameter, and it will search inside the list of CLI arguments to find the parameter name. We will see it in action later on.

The last function we're going to create is called `get_public_ip`. It is similar in terms of functionality to the `print_ip` function, except that it will be used to print the computer's public IP. That means that, if you are connected to a wireless router and you access the Internet, you will get the IP of the router, which is the IP that other sites see. The `print_ip` function just shows the IP address from the private subnet.

The command is already copied in the clipboard. It's called **dig** and we're using it to access `https://www.opendns.com/` in order to read the public `ip`. You can find more information about it in its man page or by Googling it:

```
function get_public_ip() {
    dig +short myip.opendns.com @resolver1.opendns.com
}
```

Now that we have our library functions in place, let's go and create our productivity booster scripts. Let's create a script called **iputils** where we will add some common tasks for reading IP addresses.

We'll start by adding the shebang, followed by a neat little trick for making sure we are always in the same folder as the executed script. We will be using the BASH_SOURCE variable to determine the value of the **current working directory** (or **CWD**) variable. You see here that we are using nested subshells in order to achieve this:

```
CWD=$( cd "$(dirname "${BASH_SOURCE[0]}" )/" && pwd )
cd ${CWD}
```

Next, we will source the `util` script, so that the library functions are exported into memory. Then, we can access them from the current script:

```
source ${CWD}/lib/util.sh
```

Let's add a simple call to our `getarg` function using a subshell, and search for the `cmd` argument. Also, let's echo what we've found, so that we can test our script:

```
CMD=$(getarg cmd $@)
echo ${CMD}
```

The next thing we need to do is to give the script execution rights using the chmod command. Also, in order to run the script from anywhere, the bin folder must be in the PATH variable. Echo the variable and check that the bin folder is there and, if not, update the variable in ~/.zshrc.

Let's test the script by reading a command line parameter with the getarg function and echoing it.

If you are searching for the iputils command in the terminal using tab for autocomplete and the command doesn't seem to exist, that is probably because you need to tell zsh to reload its path commands. To do this, issue the "rehash" command.

Now run:

```
iputil --cmd ip
```

This should work from within any folder, and it should print ip on the screen.

Now that we've verified everything is alright, let's write some code for our command line arguments. If we run the script with the --cmd ip flags, the script should print that on the screen. This can be done with the already-familiar case statement. Here we also want to pass in another argument, --iface, to get the interface that's needed for printing the IP. It's also a good practice to add a default case and echo a message saying invalid argument:

```
case ${CMD} in
    ip)
        IFACE=$(getarg iface $@)
        print_ip ${IFACE}
        ;;
    publicip)
        get_public_ip
        ;;
    *)
        echo "Invalid argument"
esac
```

Save the script, and let's test it.

First, let's get the interface name from the `ifconfig` command, and then let's go and test the script by running this command:

```
iputil --cmd ip --iface wlp3s0
```

```
#!/bin/bash                                              #!/bin/bash

function print_ip() {                                    CWD=$( cd "$( dirname "${BASH_SOURCE[0]}" )/" && pwd )
  IP=$(ifconfig ${1} |\                                  cd ${CWD}
    grep 'inet addr:' |\
    awk '{print $2}' | \                                 source ${CWD}/lib/util.sh
    cut -f 2 -d ":")
  echo ${IP}                                             CMD=$(getarg cmd $@)
}                                                        #echo ${CMD}

function getarg() {                                       case ${CMD} in
  NAME=${1}                                                 ip)
  while [[ ! -z ${2} ]]; do                                     IFACE=$(getarg iface $@)
    if [[ "--${NAME}" == "${2}" ]]; then                        print_ip ${IFACE}
      echo "${3}"                                               ;;
      break                                                *)
    fi                                                       echo "Invalid command"
    shift                                                  esac
  done
}                                                        "iputils" 18L, 277C written                    17,30      All

function get_public_ip() {                                   inet6 addr: ::1/128 Scope:Host
  dig +short myip.opendns.com @resolver1.opendns.com          UP LOOPBACK RUNNING  MTU:65536  Metric:1
}                                                            RX packets:17434 errors:0 dropped:0 overruns:0 frame:0
                                                            TX packets:17434 errors:0 dropped:0 overruns:0 carrier:0
                                                            collisions:0 txqueuelen:1
                                                            RX bytes:1072674 (1.0 MB)  TX bytes:1072674 (1.0 MB)

                                                wlp3s0   Link encap:Ethernet  HWaddr 68:17:29:bf:e2:67
                                                            inet addr:192.168.0.159  Bcast:192.168.0.255  Mask:255.255.255.0
                                                            inet6 addr: fe80::18e9:533a:d12f:82de/64 Scope:Link
                                                            UP BROADCAST RUNNING MULTICAST  MTU:1500  Metric:1
                                                            RX packets:626337 errors:0 dropped:0 overruns:0 frame:0
                                                            TX packets:309964 errors:0 dropped:0 overruns:0 carrier:0
                                                            collisions:0 txqueuelen:1000
                                                            RX bytes:875811764 (875.8 MB)  TX bytes:35967052 (35.9 MB)

                                                Hackergladcop [11:33:07 PM] |~/bin|
                                                -> % iputils --cmd ip --iface wlp3s0
                                                192.168.0.159
                                                Hackergladcop [11:33:31 PM] |~/bin|
                                                -> %
```

We can see it's printing our private `ip` on the screen.

Now let's add our last `cmd` to the script: `publicip`.

For this we just call the `get_public_ip` function from our `lib` utility. Save it and run this:

```
iputil --cmd publicip
```

We see that the command worked; our public `ip` is printed on the screen. Here is the complete script:

```
#!/bin/bash

CWD=$( cd "$( dirname "${BASH_SOURCE[0]}" )/" && pwd )
cd ${CWD}

source ${CWD}/lib.sh

CMD=$(getarg cmd $@)

case ${CMD} in
    publicip)
        print_public_ip
        ;;
    ip)
        IFACE=$(getarg iface $@)
        print_ip $IFACE
        ;;
    *)
        echo "invalid command"
esac
```

To give you an example, a while ago there were a bunch of articles on the Internet about a man who used to automate everything that took him more than 90 seconds to do. The scripts he wrote included instructing the coffee machine to start making a latte, so that by the time he got to the machine, the latte was finished and he didn't need to wait. He also wrote a script that sent a text message "late at work" to his wife and automatically picked a reason from a preset list whenever there was activity with his login on the company's servers after 9 p.m.

Of course, this example is a little bit complex, but in the end it's all about your imagination. Well-written automation scripts can take care of your routine work and leave you to explore your creative potential.

3
Vim kung fu

Vim's default configuration is usually pretty average. In order to better use Vim's powers, we will unleash its full potential through the help of its config files. Then, we will learn to explore some keyboard shortcuts that will help us speed up our workflow. We will also look at some commonly used plugins that make Vim even better. We will see how Vim can come in handy with its option of encrypting files for storing your passwords. The chapters will end by showing how we can automate Vim and configure a work environment easily.

In this chapter, we will be covering the following:

- Working with Vim
- Exploring Plugin steroids for Vim
- Using the Vim password manager to store passwords
- Automating Vim configuration

When it comes to being productive in the terminal, one important aspect is to never leave the terminal! And when getting stuff done, a lot of the time we find ourselves having to edit files and opening an external (GUI) editor.

Bad move!

To double our productivity, we need to leave those days behind and get the job done right there, in the terminal, without opening full-fledged IDEs just to edit one simple line of text. Now, there is a lot of debate going on about which is the best text editor for your terminal, and each one has its pros and cons. We recommend Vim, an editor which is ultra-configurable and, once mastered, can even outmatch an IDE.

The first thing we need to do in order to kickstart our Vim productivity is to have a well configured `vimrc` file.

Supercharging Vim

Let's start by opening a new hidden file called `.vimrc` in our `home` folder and pasting a few lines:

```
set nocompatible
filetype off

" Settings to replace tab. Use :retab for replacing tab in existing
files.
set tabstop=4
set shiftwidth=4
set expandtab

" Have Vim jump to the last position when reopening a file
if has("autocmd")
    au BufReadPost * if line("'\"") > 1 && line("'\"") <= line("$") |
exe "normal! g'\"" | endif

" Other general vim options:
syntax on
set showmatch       " Show matching brackets.
set ignorecase      " Do case insensitive matching
set incsearch       " show partial matches for a search phrase
set nopaste
set number
set undolevels=1000
```

```
 1 set nocompatible
 2 filetype off
 3
 4 " Settings to replace tab. Use :retab for replacing tab in existing files.
 5 set tabstop=4
 6 set shiftwidth=4
 7 set expandtab
 8
 9 " Have Vim jump to the last position when reopening a file
10 if has("autocmd")
11     au BufReadPost * if line("'\"") > 1 && line("'\"") <= line("$") | exe "normal! g'\"" | endif
12 endif
13
14 " Other general vim options:
15 syntax on
16 set showmatch        " Show matching brackets.
17 set ignorecase       " Do case insensitive matching                    I
18 set incsearch        " show partial matches for a search phrase
19 set nopaste
20 set number           " show line number
21 set undolevels=1000
22 
```

Now let's close and reopen the file, so that we can see the configuration take effect. Let's go into a little more detail regarding some of the options.

First of all, as you've probably guessed, the lines starting with " are comments, so they can be ignored. Lines 5, 6, and 7 tell vim to always use spaces instead of tabs and to set the tab size to 4 spaces. Lines 10 to 12 tell vim to always open a file and set the cursor in the same position as the last time the file was open:

- syntax on: This enables syntax highlighting, so it is easier to read code
- set nopaste: This sets nopaste mode, which means you can paste code without having Vim try to guess how to format it
- set number: This tells Vim to always show the line numbers
- set undolevels=1000: This tells Vim to remember the last 1000 changes we made to the file, so that we can easily undo and redo

Now, most of these features can be easily turned on or off. Say, for example, we want to copy, paste some lines from a file opened in Vim to another file. With this configuration, we are also going to paste the line number. What can be done is to quickly switch off the line number by typing :set nonumber, or, if the syntax is annoying, we can easily switch it off by running syntax off.

Another common feature is the status line, which can be configured by pasting these options:

```
" Always show the status line
set laststatus=2

" Format the status line
set statusline=\ %{HasPaste()}%F%m%r%h\ %w\ \ CWD:\ %r%{getcwd()}%h\ \
\ Line:\ %l\ \ Column:\ %c

" Returns true if paste mode is enabled
function! Has Paste()
    if &paste
        return 'PASTE MODE  '
    en
    return ''
end function
```

Close the file and open it again. Now we can see at the bottom of the page a status bar with extra information. This is also ultra-configurable, so we can put a lot of different stuff inside. This particular status bar contains the name of the file, the current directory, the line and column numbers and also the paste mode (on or off). To set it to on, we use :set paste and the changes will be showed in the status bar.

Vim also has the option of changing the color scheme. To do this, go to /usr/share/ vim/vim74/colors and choose a color scheme from there:

```
                  [07:13:03 AM]
-> % pwd
/home/hacker
                  [07:15:03 AM]
-> % vim .vimrc
                  [07:15:14 AM]
-> % vim .vimrc
                  [07:17:25 AM]
-> % vim .vimrc
                  [07:18:42 AM]
-> % ll /usr/share/vim/vim74/colors
total 76K
-rw-r--r-- 1 root root 2.5K Jun 17 09:47 blue.vim
-rw-r--r-- 1 root root 3.0K Jun 17 09:47 darkblue.vim
-rw-r--r-- 1 root root  548 Jun 17 09:47 default.vim
-rw-r--r-- 1 root root 2.5K Jun 17 09:47 delek.vim
-rw-r--r-- 1 root root 2.8K Jun 17 09:47 desert.vim
-rw-r--r-- 1 root root 1.7K Jun 17 09:47 elflord.vim
-rw-r--r-- 1 root root 2.5K Jun 17 09:47 evening.vim
-rw-r--r-- 1 root root 2.0K Jun 17 09:47 industry.vim
-rw-r--r-- 1 root root 3.4K Jun 17 09:47 koehler.vim
-rw-r--r-- 1 root root 2.5K Jun 17 09:47 morning.vim
-rw-r--r-- 1 root root 2.0K Jun 17 09:47 murphy.vim
-rw-r--r-- 1 root root 1.1K Jun 17 09:47 pablo.vim
-rw-r--r-- 1 root root 2.7K Jun 17 09:47 peachpuff.vim
-rw-r--r-- 1 root root 2.6K Jun 17 09:47 README.txt
-rw-r--r-- 1 root root 1.4K Jun 17 09:47 ron.vim
-rw-r--r-- 1 root root 2.7K Jun 17 09:47 shine.vim
-rw-r--r-- 1 root root 2.4K Jun 17 09:47 slate.vim
-rw-r--r-- 1 root root 1.6K Jun 17 09:47 torte.vim
-rw-r--r-- 1 root root 1.8K Jun 17 09:47 zellner.vim
                  [07:18:56 AM]
-> %
```

/usr/share/vim/vim74/colors

Let's choose desert!

Color scheme desert

Close and reopen the file; you will see it's not that different from the previous color theme. If we want a more radical one, we can set the color scheme to blue, which will drastically change the way Vim looks. But during the rest of this course, we will stick to **desert**.

Vim can also be supercharged with the help of external tools. In the world of programming, we often find ourselves editing JSON files and that can be a very difficult task if the JSON is not indented. There is a Python module that we can use to automatically indent JSON files and Vim can be configured to use it internally. All we need to do is to open the configuration file and paste the following line:

```
map j !python -m json.tool<CR>
```

Essentially this is telling Vim that, when in visual mode, if we press *J*, it should call Python with the selected text. Let's manually write a `json` string, go to visual mode by pressing *V*, select the text using our arrows, and hit *J*.

And, with no extra packages, we added a JSON formatting shortcut:

```
  3
  4 " Settings to replace tab. Use :retab for replacing tab in existing f    -> % cd course
    iles.                                                                    -> % vim file.json
  5 set tabstop=4                                                            -> % sudo apt install libxml2-utils
  6 set shiftwidth=4
  7 set expandtab
  8
  9 " Have Vim jump to the last position when reopening a file
 10 if has("autocmd")
 11     au BufReadPost * if line("'\"") > 1 && line("'\"") <= line("$") |
    exe "normal! g'\"" | endif
 12 endif
 13
 14 " Other general vim options:
 15 syntax on
 16 set showmatch          " Show matching brackets.
 17 set ignorecase         " Do case insensitive matching
 18 set incsearch          " show partial matches for a search phrase
 19 set nopaste
 20 set number             " show line number
 21 set undolevels=1000
 22
 23 " Always show the status line         sudo apt install libxml2-utils
 24 set laststatus=2
 25
 26 " Format the status line
 27 set statusline=\ %{HasPaste()}%F%m%r%h\ %w\ \ CWD:\ %r%{getcwd()}%h\
    \ \ Line:\ %l\ \ Column:\ %c
 28
 29 " Returns true if paste mode is enabled
 30 function! HasPaste()
 31     if &paste
 32         return 'PASTE MODE '
 33     en
 34     return ''
 35 endfunction
 36
 37 colorscheme desert
 38
 39 map j !python -m json.tool<CR>              " format JSON
 40 []
 ~/.vimrc    CWD: /home/hacker   Line: 40   Column: 0
```

We can do the same thing for `xml` files, but first we need to install a tool for working with them:

```
sudo apt install libxml2-utils
```

```
  3                                                            [07:20:14 AM]
  4 " Settings to replace tab. Use :retab for replacing tab in existing f  -> % cd course
    iles.                                                       [07:20:43 AM]
  5 set tabstop=4                                              -> % vim file.json
  6 set shiftwidth=4                                            [07:23:52 AM]
  7 set expandtab                                              -> % sudo apt install libxml2-utils
  8
  9 " Have Vim jump to the last position when reopening a file
 10 if has("autocmd")
 11     au BufReadPost * if line("'\"") > 1 && line("'\"") <= line("$") |
    exe "normal! g'\"" | endif
 12 endif
 13
 14 " Other general vim options:
 15 syntax on
 16 set showmatch       " Show matching brackets.
 17 set ignorecase      " Do case insensitive matching
 18 set incsearch       " show partial matches for a search phrase
 19 set nopaste
 20 set number          " show line number
 21 set undolevels=1000
 22
 23 " Always show the status line
 24 set laststatus=2
 25
 26 " Format the status line
 27 set statusline=\ %{HasPaste()}%F%m%r%h\ %w\ \ CWD:\ %r%{getcwd()}%h\
    \ \ Line:\ %l\ \ Column:\ %c
 28
 29 " Returns true if paste mode is enabled
 30 function! HasPaste()
 31     if &paste
 32         return 'PASTE MODE  '
 33     en
 34     return ''
 35 endfunction
 36
 37 colorscheme desert
 38
 39 map j !python -m json.tool<CR>                 " format JSON
 40
~/.vimrc   CWD: /home/hacker    Line: 40  Column: 0
```

sudo apt install libxml2-utils

To install the XML utility package, we must add the following line to our configuration file:

```
map l !xmllint --format --recover -<CR>
```

This maps the *L* key when in visual mode to `xmllint`. Let's write a HTML snippet, which is actually a valid `xml` file, hit *v* for visual mode, select the text, and press *L*.

This type of extension (and also spell checkers, linters, dictionaries, and much more) can be brought to Vim and be instantly available to use.

A well configured `vim` file can spare you a lot of time in the command line. Although it might take some time in the beginning to get things set up and to find the configuration that is right for you, this investment can pay off bigtime in the future, as time passes and we spend more and more time in Vim. A lot of times we don't even have the luxury of opening a GUI editor, like when working remotely through an `ssh` session. Believe it or not, command line editors are life savers and productivity is hard to achieve without them.

Keyboard kung fu

Now that we have Vim all set up, it's time to learn some more command line shortcuts. The first thing we will be looking at is indentation.

Indentation can be done in Vim by going into visual mode and typing V for selecting portions of text or V for selecting full lines, followed by > or < to indent right or left. Afterwards press . to repeat the last operation:

```
 1  #!/bin/bash
 2
 3  CWD=$( cd "$( dirname "${BASH_SOURCE[0]}" )/" && pwd )
 4  cd ${CWD}
 5
 6  AUX="123"
 7  ARG=${1:-${AUX:-"default value"}}
 8  echo ${ARG}
 9
10  LINE="some long line of text"
11  #echo "${LINE:5:4}"
12
13  function print_ip() {
14    IP=$(ifconfig ${1} |\
15      grep 'inet addr:' |\
16      awk '{print $2}' | \
17      cut -f 2 -d ":")
18    echo ${IP}
19  }
20
21  function longRunningTask1() {
22    sleep 1
23  }
24
25  function longRunningTask2() {
26    sleep 2
27  }
28
29  while [[ ! -z ${1} ]]; do
30    case "$1" in
31      --ip|-i)
32        print_ip ${2}
33        shift
34        shift
35        ;;
36      --parallel|-p)
37        longRunningTask1 &
38        longRunningTask2 &
39        PID=$!
40        wait ${PID}
41        notify-send script.sh "execution finished"
~/course/script.sh    CWD: /home/hacker/course    Line: 8   Column: 1
-- VISUAL LINE --
```

Any operation can be undone by hitting u and can then be redone by hitting *Ctrl + R* (as in undo and redo). This is the equivalent of *Ctrl + Z* and *Ctrl + Shift + Z* in most popular editors.

When in visual mode, we have the option of changing the case of letters by hitting *U* to make all text upper case, *u* for lower case and ~ to reverse current case:

```
 1 #!/bin/bash
 2
 3 CWD=$( cd "$( dirname "${BASH_SOURCE[0]}" )/" && pwd )
 4 cd ${CWD}
 5
 6                 AUX="123"
 7                 ARG=${1:-${AUX:-"default value"}}
 8                 #echo ${ARG}
 9
10 LINE="SOME LONG LINE OF TEXT"
11 #echo "${LINE:5:4}"
12
13 function print_ip() {
14   IP=$(ifconfig ${1} |\
15     grep 'inet addr:' |\
16     awk '{print $2}' | \
17     cut -f 2 -d ":")
18   echo ${IP}
19 }
20
21 function longRunningTask1() {
22   sleep 1
23 }
24
25 function longRunningTask2() {
26   sleep 2
27 }
28
29 while [[ ! -z ${1} ]]; do
30   case "$1" in
31     --ip|-i)
32       print_ip ${2}
33       shift
34       shift
35       ;;
36     --parallel|-p)
37       longRunningTask1 &
38       longRunningTask2 &
39       PID=$!
40       wait ${PID}
41       notify-send script.sh "execution finished"
~/course/script.sh[+]    CWD: /home/hacker/course    Line: 10  Column: 7
```

Other handy shortcuts are:

- G: Go to end of file
- gg: Go to start of file
- Select all: This is not really a shortcut, but a combination of commands: gg V G, as in go to start of file, select full line, and move to the end.

Vim also has a handy shortcut for opening man pages for the word under the cursor. Just hit K and a man page will show up for that specific word (if there is one, that is):

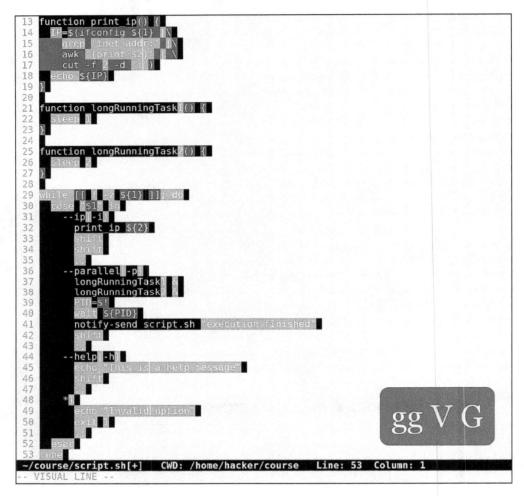

```
13 function print_ip() {
14     IP=$(ifconfig ${1} | \
15     grep 'inet addr:' | \
16     awk '{print $2}' | \
17     cut -f 2 -d ':')
18     echo ${IP}
19 }
20
21 function longRunningTask1() {
22     sleep 1
23 }
24
25 function longRunningTask2() {
26     sleep 2
27 }
28
29 while [[ ! -z ${1} ]]; do
30     case "$1" in
31     --ip|-i)
32         print_ip ${2}
33         shift
34         shift
35         ;;
36     --parallel|-p)
37         longRunningTask1 &
38         longRunningTask2 &
39         PID=$!
40         wait ${PID}
41         notify-send script.sh "execution finished"
42         shift
43         ;;
44     --help|-h)
45         echo "This is a help message"
46         shift
47         ;;
48     *)
49         echo "Invalid option"
50         exit
51         ;;
52     esac
53 one
```

`~/course/script.sh[+]    CWD: /home/hacker/course   Line: 53   Column: 1`
`-- VISUAL LINE --`

Finding text in Vim is as easy as hitting /. Just type / + the text to find, and hit *Enter* to start searching. Vim will go to the first occurrence of that text. Hit n for next occurrence, *N* for previous occurrence.

Our favorite editor has a powerful find and replace feature, similar to the sed command. Let's say we want to replace all occurrences of the string CWD with the string DIR. For this, just type:

```
:1,$s/CWD/DIR/g
```

```
:1,$ - start from line one, till the end of the file
```

```
s - substitute
```

```
/CWD/DIR/ - replace CWD with DIR
```

```
g - global, replace all occurrences.
```

```
 1 #!/bin/bash
 2
 3 DIR=$( cd "$( dirname "${BASH_SOURCE[0]}" )/" && pwd )
 4 cd ${DIR}
 5
 6                   AUX="123"
 7                   ARG=${1:-${AUX:-"default value"}}
 8                   #echo ${ARG}
 9
10 LINE="some long line of text"
11 #echo "${LINE:5:4}"
12
13 function print_ip() {
14   IP=$(ifconfig ${1} |\
15     grep 'inet addr:' |\
16     awk '{print $2}' | \
17     cut -f 2 -d ":")
18   echo ${IP}
19 }
20
21 function longRunningTask1() {
22   sleep 1
23 }
24
25 function longRunningTask2() {
26   sleep 2
27 }
28
29 while [[ ! -z ${1} ]]; do
30   case "$1" in
31     --ip|-i)
32       print_ip ${2}
33       shift
34       shift
35       ;;
36     --parallel|-p)
37       longRunningTask1 &
38       longRunningTask2 &
39       PID=$!
40       wait ${PID}
41       notify-send script.sh "execution finished"
~/course/script.sh[+]    CWD: /home/hacker/course    Line: 4  Column: 1
:1,$s/CWD/DIR/g
```

`:1,$s/CWD/DIR/g`

Let's do another common example that often comes up in programming: commenting lines of code. Let's say that we want to comment out lines 10 to 20 in a shell script. To do this, type:

`:10,20s/^/#\ /g`

```
 1 #!/bin/bash
 2
 3 DIR=$( cd "$( dirname "${BASH_SOURCE[0]}" )/" && pwd )
 4 cd ${DIR}
 5
 6                 AUX="123"
 7                 ARG=${1:-${AUX:-"default value"}}
 8                 #echo ${ARG}
 9
10 LINE="some long line of text"
11 #echo "${LINE:5:4}"
12
13 function print_ip() {
14   IP=$(ifconfig ${1} |\
15     grep 'inet addr:' |\
16     awk '{print $2}' | \
17     cut -f 2 -d ":")
18   echo ${IP}
19 }
20
21 function longRunningTask1() {
22   sleep 1
23 }
24
25 function longRunningTask2() {
26   sleep 2
27 }
28
29 while [[ ! -z ${1} ]]; do
30   case "$1" in
31     --ip|-i)
32       print_ip ${2}
33       shift
34       shift
35       ;;
36     --parallel|-p)
37       longRunningTask1 &
38       longRunningTask2 &
39       PID=$!
40       wait ${PID}
41       notify-send script.sh "execution finished"
~/course/script.sh[+]    CWD: /home/hacker/course    Line: 4  Column: 1
:10,20s/^/#\ /g
```

`:10,20s/^/#\ /g`

```
 1 #!/bin/bash
 2
 3 DIR=$( cd "$( dirname "${BASH_SOURCE[0]}" )/" && pwd )
 4 cd ${DIR}
 5
 6                  AUX="123"
 7                  ARG=${1:-${AUX:-"default value"}}
 8                  #echo ${ARG}
 9
10 # LINE="some long line of text"
11 # #echo "${LINE:5:4}"
12 #
13 # function print_ip() {
14 #    IP=$(ifconfig ${1} |\
15 #      grep 'inet addr:' |\
16 #      awk '{print $2}' | \
17 #      cut -f 2 -d ":")
18 #    echo ${IP}
19 # }
20 ▒
21 function longRunningTask1() {
22    sleep 1
23 }
24
25 function longRunningTask2() {
26    sleep 2
27 }
28
29 while [[ ! -z ${1} ]]; do
30    case "$1" in
31      --ip|-i)
32        print_ip ${2}
33        shift
34        shift
35        ;;
36      --parallel|-p)
37        longRunningTask1 &
38        longRunningTask2 &
39        PID=$!
40        wait ${PID}
41        notify-send script.sh "execution finished"
~/course/script.sh[+]   CWD: /home/hacker/course   Line: 20  Column: 1
11 substitutions on 11 lines
```

This means substitute the beginning of the line with # and space. For deleting lines of text, type:

`:30,$d`

This will delete everything from line 30 till the end.

More information about regular expressions can be found in the chapters. Also check out the parts on `sed` for more text manipulation examples. These commands are some of the longest in Vim and often we get them wrong. To edit the command we just wrote and run it again, we can open the command history by hitting *q:*, navigate to the line containing the command to edit, press Insert, update the line, and press *Esc* and *Enter* to run the command. It's as simple as that!

```
 3 DIR=$( cd "$( dirname "${BASH_SOURCE[0]}" )/" && pwd )
 4 cd ${DIR}
 5
 6                    AUX="123"
 7                    ARG=${1:-${AUX:-"default value"}}
 8                    #echo ${ARG}
 9
10 LINE="some long line of text"
11 #echo "${LINE:5:4}"
12
13 function print_ip() {
14   IP=$(ifconfig ${1} |\
15     grep 'inet addr:' |\
16     awk '{print $2}' | \
17     cut -f 2 -d ":")
18   echo ${IP}
19 }
20
21 function longRunningTask1() {
22   sleep 1
23 }
24
25 function longRunningTask2() {
26   sleep 2
27 }
28
29 while [[ ! -z ${1} ]]; do
30   case "$1" in
31     --ip|-i)
32       print_ip ${2}
33       shift
34       shift
35       ;;
~/course/script.sh[+]     CWD: /home/hacker/course    Line: 10   Column: 1
: 45 q!
: 46 w
: 47 q
: 48 1,$s/CWD/DIR/g
: 49 10,15s/^/#\ /g
: 50 30,$d
: 51
[Command Line]    CWD: /home/hacker/course    Line: 49   Column: 6
-- INSERT --
```

Another operation that is often useful is sorting. Let's create a file with unsorted lines of text from the classic lorem ipsum text:

```
cat lorem.txt | tr " " "\n" | grep -v "^\s*$" | sed "s/[,.]//g" > sort.txt
```

```
                    [07:36:39 AM]
-> % ls
file.html  file.json  file.txt  git-demo  lorem.txt
                    [07:36:46 AM]
-> % vim script.sh

[No write since last change]

Press ENTER or type command to continue
[No write since last change]

Press ENTER or type command to continue
                    [07:42:44 AM]
-> % ls
file.html  file.json  file.txt  git-demo  lorem.txt
                    [07:42:45 AM]
-> % cat lorem.txt
Lorem ipsum dolor sit amet, consectetur adipiscing elit, sed do eiusmod tempor incididunt ut labore et dolore magna aliqua. Ut enim ad minim veniam
, quis nostrud exercitation ullamco laboris nisi ut aliquip ex ea commodo consequat. Duis aute irure dolor in reprehenderit in voluptate velit esse
 cillum dolore eu fugiat nulla pariatur. Excepteur sint occaecat cupidatat non proident, sunt in culpa qui officia deserunt mollit anim id est labo
rum.

                    [07:42:49 AM]
-> % cat lorem.txt | tr " " "\n" | grep -v "^\s*$" | sed "s/[,.]//g" > sort.txt
```

Open `sort.txt` and run `:sort`. We see that the lines are all sorted alphabetically.

```
 1 Lorem
 2 ipsum
 3 dolor
 4 sit
 5 amet
 6 consectetur
 7 adipiscing
 8 elit
 9 sed
10 do
11 eiusmod
12 tempor
13 incididunt
14 ut
15 labore
16 et
17 dolore
18 magna
19 aliqua
20 Ut
21 enim
22 ad
23 minim
24 veniam
25 quis
26 nostrud
27 exercitation
28 ullamco
29 laboris
30 nisi
31 ut
32 aliquip
33 ex
34 ea
35 commodo
36 consequat
37 Duis
38 aute
39 irure
40 dolor
41 in
~/course/sort.txt   CWD: /home/hacker/course   Line: 1  Column: 1
"sort.txt" 69L, 438C
```

Now let's move forward to window management. Vim has the option to split the screen for editing files in parallel. Just write `:split` for horizontal split, and `:vsplit` for vertical split:

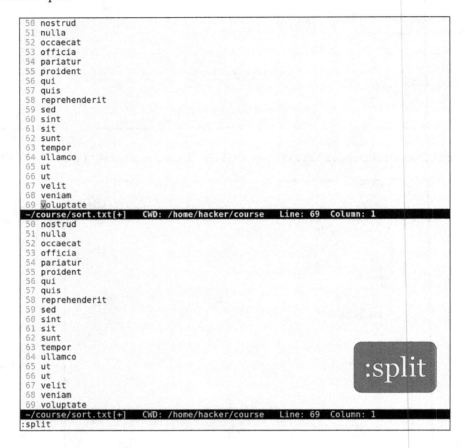

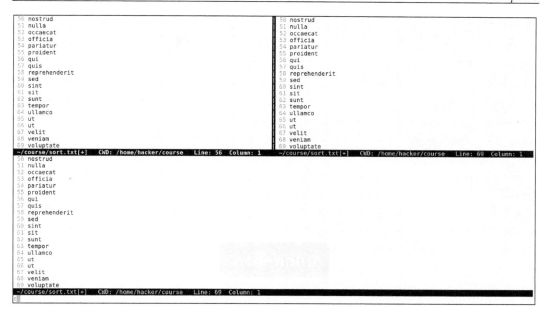

When Vim splits the screen, it opens the same file in the other pane; to open another file just hit :e. The good thing here is that we have autocomplete, so we can just hit *Tab* and Vim will start writing filenames for us. If we don't know what files we want to choose, we can just run any arbitrary shell command directly from Vim and come back once we've finished. For example, when we type :!ls, the shell opens, shows us the output of the command, and waits until we hit *Enter* to come back to the file.

When in split mode, press *Ctrl + W* to switch between windows. To close a window, press :q. If you want to save a file under a different name (think of the save as command from other editors), just hit :w followed by the new file name, say mycopy. txt.

Vim also has the option of opening multiple files at once; just specify a list of files after the vim command:

```
vim file1 file2 file3
```

After the files are open, use :bn to move to the next file. To close all the files, hit :qa.

Vim also has an built in explorer. Just open Vim and hit :Explore. After this, we can navigate through the directory layout and we can open new files:

```
" ======================================================================
" Netrw Directory Listing                        (netrw v155)
"    /home/hacker/course
"    Sorted by      name
"    Sort sequence: [\/]$,\<core\%(\.\d\+\)\)=\>,\.h$,\.c$,\.cpp$,\~\=\*$,*,\.o$,\.obj$,\.info$,\.swp$,\.bak$,\~$
"    Quick Help: <F1>:help  -:go up dir  D:delete  R:rename  s:sort-by  x:special
" ======================================================================
../
./
git-demo/
script.sh*
file.html
file.json
file.txt
lorem.txt
mycopy.txt
sort.txt
~
~
~
~
~
~
~
~
~
~
~
~
~
~
~
~
~/course[-][RO]   CWD: [RO]/home/hacker/course   Line: 8  Column: 1
```

:Explore

It also has a different option. Let's open a file, delete one of the lines, and save it under a new name. Exit and open the two files with vimdiff. Now we can see the differences between them visually. This applies to all sorts of changes and is way better than the plain old diff command output.

Keyboard shortcuts really make a difference and open a whole new world of possibilities when using Vim. It's kind of hard to remember in the beginning, but once you start using them, it will be as simple as clicking a button.

Plugin steroids for Vim

In this section, we will be looking at how we can add external plugins to Vim. Vim has its own programming language for writing plugins, which we saw a glimpse of when writing the `vimrc` file. Luckily, we won't have to learn all of that because most of the stuff we can think of already has a plugin out there. To manage plugins, let's install the plugin manager pathogen. Open: `https://github.com/tpope/vim-pathogen`.

Follow the installation instructions. As you can see, it's a one-line command:

```
mkdir -p ~/.vim/autoload ~/.vim/bundle && \curl -LSso ~/.vim/autoload/
pathogen.vim https://tpo.pe/pathogen.vim
```

And after it finishes, add pathogen to your `.vimrc`:

```
execute pathogen#infect()
```

Most IDEs show a tree layout of the folder structure, in parallel with the open files. Vim can do this also, and the simplest way to achieve this is by installing the plugin called **NERDtree**.

Open: `https://github.com/scrooloose/nerdtree`, and follow the instructions for installing it:

```
cd ~/.vim/bundle git clone https://github.com/scrooloose/nerdtree.git
```

Now we should be all set. Let's open a file and type :NERDtree. We see the tree-like structure of our current folder here, where we can browse and open new files. If we want Vim to replace our IDE, this is certainly a mandatory plugin!

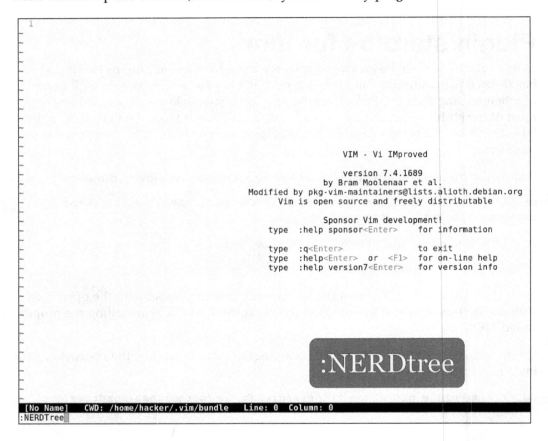

Another awesome plugin that comes in really handy is called **Snipmate** and is used for writing code snippets. To install it, go to this link and follow the instructions: https://github.com/garbas/vim-snipmate.

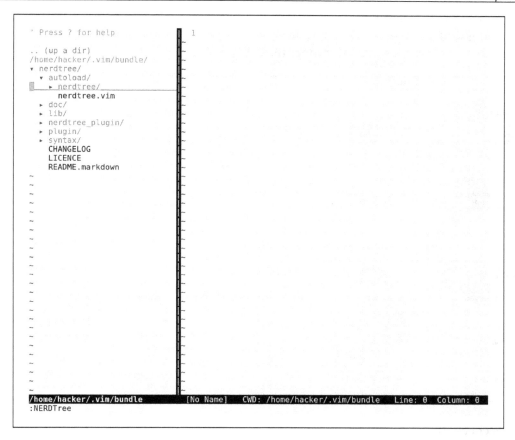

As we can see, before installing `snipmate`, there is another set of plugins that needs to be installed:

- `git clone https://github.com/tomtom/tlib_vim.git`
- `git clone https://github.com/MarcWeber/vim-addon-mw-utils.git`
- `git clone https://github.com/garbas/vim-snipmate.git`
- `git clone https://github.com/honza/vim-snippets.git`

If we take a look at the readme, we can see an example for C files, which has auto completion for the `for` keyword. Let's open a file with a `.c` extension, type `for` and hit *Tab*. We can see the autocomplete working.

We have also installed the `vim-snipmate` package, which comes with lots of snippets for different languages. If we take a look at `~/.vim/bundle/vim-snippets/snippets/`, we can see lots of snippet files:

```
Resolving deltas: 100% (48/48), done.
Checking connectivity... done.
hacker@laptop [08:03:57 AM] [~/.vim/bundle]
-> % git clone https://github.com/garbas/vim-snipmate.git
Cloning into 'vim-snipmate'...
remote: Counting objects: 2644, done.
remote: Total 2644 (delta 0), reused 0 (delta 0), pack-reused 2643
Receiving objects: 100% (2644/2644), 765.30 KiB | 725.00 KiB/s, done.
Resolving deltas: 100% (1158/1158), done.
Checking connectivity... done.
hacker@laptop [08:04:06 AM] [~/.vim/bundle]
-> % git clone https://github.com/honza/vim-snippets.git
Cloning into 'vim-snippets'...
remote: Counting objects: 5884, done.
remote: Total 5884 (delta 0), reused 0 (delta 0), pack-reused 5884
Receiving objects: 100% (5884/5884), 1.21 MiB | 1.22 MiB/s, done.
Resolving deltas: 100% (3753/3753), done.
Checking connectivity... done.
hacker@laptop [08:04:10 AM] [~/.vim/bundle]
-> % vim file.c
hacker@laptop [08:09:15 AM] [~/.vim/bundle]
-> % ls
nerdtree  tlib_vim  vim-addon-mw-utils  vim-snipmate  vim-snippets
hacker@laptop [08:09:23 AM] [~/.vim/bundle]
-> % ls vim-snippets/snippets/
actionscript.snippets   dosini.snippets          java.snippets      po.snippets          snippets.snippets
ada.snippets            d.snippets               jinja.snippets     processing.snippets* sql.snippets
apache.snippets         eelixir.snippets         jsp.snippets       progress.snippets    stylus.snippets
arduino.snippets        elixir.snippets          julia.snippets     puppet.snippets      supercollider.snippets
autoit.snippets         elm.snippets             laravel.snippets   python.snippets      systemverilog.snippets
awk.snippets            erlang.snippets          ledger.snippets    rails.snippets       tcl.snippets
chef.snippets           eruby.snippets           ls.snippets        r.snippets           tex.snippets
clojure.snippets        falcon.snippets          lua.snippets       rst.snippets         textile.snippets
cmake.snippets          fortran.snippets         make.snippets      ruby.snippets        twig.snippets
codeigniter.snippets    go.snippets              mako.snippets      rust.snippets        verilog.snippets
coffee/                 haml.snippets            markdown.snippets  sass.snippets        vhdl.snippets
cpp.snippets            haskell.snippets         mustache.snippets  scala.snippets       vim.snippets
c.snippets              htmldjango.snippets      objc.snippets      scheme.snippets      xml.snippets
cs.snippets             html.snippets            openfoam.snippets  scss.snippets        xslt.snippets
css.snippets            htmltornado.snippets     perl6.snippets     sh.snippets          yii-chtml.snippets
dart.snippets           jade.snippets            perl.snippets      simplemvcf.snippets  yii.snippets
diff.snippets           javascript/              php.snippets       slim.snippets        zsh.snippets
django.snippets         javascript-mocha.snippets plsql.snippets    _.snippets
```

Let's check the `javascript` one:

vim ~/.vim/bundle/vim-snippets/snippets/javascript/javascript.snippets

```
 1 # Functions                                                    1
 2
 3 # prototype
 4 snippet proto
 5     ${1:class_name}.prototype.${2:method_name} = function(${3}) {
 6         ${0}
 7     };
 8 # Function
 9 snippet fun
10     function ${1:function_name}(${2}) {
11         ${0}
12     }
13 # Anonymous Function
14 snippet f "" w
15     function(${1}) {
16         ${0}
17     }
18 # Anonymous Function assigned to variable
19 snippet vaf
20     var ${1:function_name} = function(${2}) {
21         ${0}
22     };
23 # Function assigned to variable
24 snippet vf
25     var ${1:function_name} = function $1(${2}) {
26         ${0}
27     };
28 # Immediate function
29 snippet (f
30     (function(${1}) {
31         ${0}
32     }(${2}));
33 # Minify safe iife
34 snippet ;fe
35     ;(function(${1}) {
36         ${0}
37     }(${2}))
38 # self-defining function
39 snippet sdf
40     var ${1:function_name} = function (${2:argument}) {
41         ${3}
```

```
</snippets/javascript/javascript.snippets   CWD: /home/hacker/.vim/bundl <vim/bundle/file.js   CWD: /home/hacker/.vim/bundle   Line: 0   Column: 0
e   Line: 1  Column: 1                                                   "file.js" [New File]
```

Here we can see all the snippets available. Type `fun` and hit *Tab* for the function autocomplete. The snippets are preconfigured with variables so that you can write a function name and hit *Tab* to go to the next variable to complete. There is a snippet for writing if-else blocks, one for writing `console.log`, and lots of others for common code blocks. The best way to learn them is to go through the file and start using the snippets.

There are lots of plugins out there. People have made all sorts of plugin packs that are guaranteed to put your Vim on steroids. One cool project is `http://vim.spf13.com/`

It's nicknamed the ultimate Vim plugin pack and it basically has plugins and keyboard shortcuts for everything. This is for more advanced users, so be sure to understand the basic concepts before jumping to plugin packs. Remember, the best way to learn is to install plugins manually and play with them one by one.

Vim password manager

Vim can also be used to safely store information, by encrypting text files with different `cryp` methods. To see the `cryp` method that Vim is currently using, type:

```
:set cryptmethod?
```

We can see in our case it is `zip`, which is not actually a `crypto` method and does not offer much in terms of security. To see what different alternatives we have, we can type:

```
:h 'cryptmethod'
```

A page describing the different encryption methods comes up. We can choose from `zip`, `blowfish`, and `blowfish2`.The most secure and recommended one is, of course, `blowfish2`. To change the encryption method, type:

```
:set cryptmethod=blowfish2
```

This can be also added to `vimrc` so that it becomes the default encryption. Now we can safely encrypt files using Vim.

A common scenario would be storing a passwords file.

Let's open up a new file named `passwords.txt`, add some dummy passwords inside, and save it. The next step is to encrypt the file with a password, and for this we type `:X`.

Vim will prompt you for a password twice. If you exit without saving the file, the encryption will not be applied. Now, encrypt it again, save, and exit the file.

When we reopen it, Vim will ask for the same password. If we get this wrong, Vim will show some random characters that come from the failed decryption. Only if we type the correct password will we get the actual file content:

Saving encrypted files with Vim, combined with backing up the file in places like a private `git` repository or a private Dropbox folder, can be an effective way of storing your passwords:

```
Need encryption key for "passwords.txt"
Enter encryption key:
```

It also has the benefit that it's sort of a unique method of storing passwords, compared to using online services that are pretty standard and might get compromised. This can also be referred to as *security through obscurity*.

Instant configuration restoring

The configuration we have seen in this chapter might take some time to set up manually, but, once everything is configured, we can create a script that will restore the Vim configuration instantly.

For this, we paste all the commands issued up to now into a bash script that can be run to bring Vim to the exact same configuration. All that is missing from this script is the vimrc file from the home folder, which we can also restore through a technique called heredocs. Just type cat, redirect the output to vimrc, and use heredoc as input, delimited by eof:

```
 1 #!/bin/bash
 2
 3 mkdir -p ~/.vim/autoload ~/.vim/bundle && \
 4 curl -LSso ~/.vim/autoload/pathogen.vim https://tpo.pe/pathogen.vim
 5
 6 cd ~/.vim/bundle
 7 # nerdtree
 8 git clone https://github.com/scrooloose/nerdtree.git
 9
10 # snipmate
11 git clone https://github.com/tomtom/tlib_vim.git
12 git clone https://github.com/MarcWeber/vim-addon-mw-utils.git
13 git clone https://github.com/garbas/vim-snipmate.git
14 git clone https://github.com/honza/vim-snippets.git
15
16 # xmllint
17 sudo apt install libxml2-utils
18
19 cat > ~/.vimrc << EOF
```

cat > ~/.vimrc << EOF

~/course/configure_vim.sh[+]   CWD: /home/hacker/course   Line: 19 Column: 22
-- INSERT --

```
cat > ~/.vimrc << EOF

...

<vimrc content>

...

EOF
```

Using heredocs is a common technique for manipulating large chunks of text inside bash scripts. Basically it treats a section of code like a separate file (in our case everything after the cat and until the EOF). With this script, we can restore all the Vim configurations we have done and we can also run it on any computer we work on, so that we get our Vim set up in no time!

We hope you have enjoyed this material and see you in the chapter!

CLI – The Hidden Recipe

4

This chapter will start by focusing on sed, one of the tools that can scare a lot of Linux users. We will look at some basic `sed` commands that could make hours of refractor turn into a few minutes. We will see how you can locate any file by using Linux puter. Furthermore, we will see just how remote work will get a whole lot better when Tmux enters our skill set. You can run long lasting commands, split screens, and never lose your work with the help of the best terminal multiplexor. Then, you will learn how to discover and interact with your network with the help of commands like netstat and nmap. Lastly, we will see how Autoenv helps switch environments automatically and how to use rm command to interact with trash from command line using the trash utility.

In this chapter, we will cover the following:

- Understanding the working of sed
- Working with tmux, a terminal multiplexer
- Automatically switching environments using Autoenv
- Using rm command line to remove (delete) files or directories

Sed – one-liner productivity treasure

If a picture is worth 1000 words, then sed one liners are definitely worth a thousand lines of code! One of the most feared commands in the Linux CLI is, you guessed it, sed! It's been feared by programmers and sysadmins everywhere, because of it's cryptic usage, but it can serve as a very powerful tool for quickly editing large amounts of data.

We have created five files to help demonstrate the power of this awesome tool. The first one is a simple file containing the humble line of text: *Orange is the new black.* Let's start by creating a simple `sed` command to replace the word *black* with *white*.

The first argument of sed is the replace command. It's divided into 3 parts by 3 /. The first part is s for substitute, the second part is the word to be replaced, black, in our case, and the third part is the replacement word, white.

The second argument is the input, in our case, a file:

```
sed "s/black/white/" 1.txt
```

```
hacker@laptop [11:17:43 AM] [~/course/sed]
-> % ls
1.txt  2.txt  3.txt  4.xml  5.txt
hacker@laptop [11:17:49 AM] [~/course/sed]
-> % cat 1.txt
Orage is the new black
hacker@laptop [11:17:53 AM] [~/course/sed]
-> % sed "s/black/white/" 1.txt
Orage is the new white
hacker@laptop [11:18:12 AM] [~/course/sed]
-> %
```

Now, the result will be printed on the screen, and you can see the word black has been replaced by white.

Our second example contains yet another line of text, this time with the word black in both upper and lower case. If we run the same command using this new file, we will see that it replaces only the word that matches the case. If we want to do a case insensitive replace, we will add two more characters to the end of our sed command; g and l.

- g: It means global replace, used for replacing all the occurrences in the file. Without this, it will only replace the first argument.

- l: means case insensitive search.

```
sed "s/black/white/gI" 2.txt
```

```
hacker@laptop [11:17:43 AM] [~/course/sed]
-> % ls
1.txt  2.txt  3.txt  4.xml  5.txt
hacker@laptop [11:17:49 AM] [~/course/sed]
-> % cat 1.txt
Orage is the new black
hacker@laptop [11:17:53 AM] [~/course/sed]
-> % sed "s/black/white/" 1.txt
Orage is the new white
hacker@laptop [11:18:12 AM] [~/course/sed]
-> % cat 2.txt
lower case black, upper case Black
hacker@laptop [11:18:17 AM] [~/course/sed]
-> % sed "s/black/white/" 2.txt
lower case white, upper case Black
hacker@laptop [11:18:22 AM] [~/course/sed]
-> % sed "s/black/white/gI" 2.txt
lower case white, upper case white
hacker@laptop [11:18:31 AM] [~/course/sed]
-> %
```

And as you can see, both words have been replaced. If we want to save the results in our file instead of printing to the screen, we use the `-i` argument, which stands for inline replace.

In some scenarios, we might also want to save our initial files, just in case we have an error in the `sed` command. To do this, we specify a suffix after `-i` which will create a backup file. In our case, we use the `.bak` suffix:

```
sed -i.bak "s/black/white/g" 2.txt
```

```
hacker@laptop [11:18:22 AM] [~/course/sed]
-> % sed "s/black/white/gI" 2.txt
lower case white, upper case white
hacker@laptop [11:18:31 AM] [~/course/sed]
-> % sed -i "s/black/white/" 1.txt
hacker@laptop [11:18:55 AM] [~/course/sed]
-> % cat 1.txt
Orage is the new white
hacker@laptop [11:18:58 AM] [~/course/sed]
-> % sed -i.bak "s/black/white/gI" 2.txt
hacker@laptop [11:19:08 AM] [~/course/sed]
-> % ls
1.txt  2.txt  2.txt.bak  3.txt  4.xml  5.txt
hacker@laptop [11:19:09 AM] [~/course/sed]
-> %
```

If we check the content of the files, we can see that the initial file contains the updated text, and the backup file contains the original text.

Now, let's look at a more practical example. Let's say we have a shell script that contains multiple variables and we want to surround our variables with curly brackets:

```
hacker@laptop [11:19:19 AM] [~/course/sed]
-> % cat 3.txt

CWD=$1

echo $CWD
```

In order to do this we will write:

- `s`: It's for substitute.
- `g`: It's for global; meaning replace all occurrences found.
- `\$`: This matches all strings starting with the dollar sign. Here dollar needs to be escaped, so that it's not confused with the *start of the row* anchor.
- We will enclose the string following $ in ( ), so that we can reference it in the replace part of our command.

- `[ ]`: This is for specifying a range of characters
- `A-Z`: It matches all uppercase characters
- `0-9`: It matches all numbers
- `_`: It matches _
- `\+`: Any character in the `[ ]` must appear one or multiple times

In the replace part, we will use:

- `\$`: The dollar sign
- `{ }`: The curly brackets we want to add.
- `\1`: The string that was previously matched in the ()

```
sed 's/\$\([A-Z0-9_]\+\)/\${\1}/g' 3.txt
```

```
hacker@laptop [11:20:24 AM] |~/course/sed|
-> % sed "s/\$\([A-Z0-9_]\+\)/\${\1}/g" 3.txt

CWD=${1}

echo ${CWD}
```

Other common scenarios are replacing content in `xml` or `html` files.

Here we have a basic html file with a `<strong>` text inside. Now, we know that the `<strong>` text has more semantic value for search engine optimizations, so maybe we want to make our strong tags be a simple `<b>` (bold), and manually decide the `<strong>` words in the page. For this we say:

- `s`: This is for substitute.
- `<strong`: The actual text we are searching for.
- `\( \)`: This will be used again for selecting a piece of text, that will be added back.
- `.*`: This means any character, found any number of times. We want to select everything between "`<strong`" and "`strong>`".
- `</`: This is the closing of the tag. This, we want to keep intact.

- `<b\1b>`: Just add `<b b>`, and the text that you previously found in the ( ).

```
sed "s/<strong\(.*</\)strong>/<b\1b>/g" 4.xml
```

```
hacker@laptop [11:20:35 AM] [~/course/sed]
-> % cat 4.xml
<html>
<body>
<p>Some <strong class="red">text</strong></p>
</body>
</html>
```

As you can see, the text was updated correctly, the red class still applies to the new tag, and the old text is still contained between our tags, which is exactly what we wanted:

```
hacker@laptop [11:21:38 AM] [~/course/sed]
-> % sed "s/<strong\(.*<\/\)strong>/<b\1b>/g" 4.xml
<html>
<body>
<p>Some <b class="red">text</b></p>
</body>
</html>
```

Besides replacing, sed can also be used for deleting lines of text. Our `5.txt` file contains all the words from the `lorem ipsum` text. If we wanted to delete the third line of text, we would issue the command:

```
sed -i 3d 5.txt
```

Hit *:e*, to reload the file in vim, and we see the word `dolor` is no longer there. If, for example, we wanted to delete the first 10 lines of the file, we'd simply run:

```
sed -i 1,10d 5.txt
```

Hit *:e*, and you see the lines are no longer there. For our last example, if we scroll down, we can see multiple empty lines of text. These can be deleted with:

```
sed -i "/^$/d" 5.txt
```

```
20 ei.                                        hacker@laptop [11:22:05 AM] [~/course/sed]
21 Ne                                         -> % sed -i 3d 5.txt
22 paulo                                      hacker@laptop [11:22:33 AM] [~/course/sed]
23 intellegebat                              -> % sed -i 1,10d 5.txt
24 eos.                                       hacker@laptop [11:23:01 AM] [~/course/sed]
25 cu                                         -> % sed -i "/^$/d" 5.txt
26 pri                                        hacker@laptop [11:23:31 AM] [~/course/sed]
27 mundi                                      -> % []
28 dicunt
29 nostrum,
30 cu
31 pri
32 idque
33 diceret.
34 Cu
35 magna
36 tation
37 comprehensam
38 nam,
39 ius
40 adipisci
41 vituperata
42 reprehendunt
43 cu.
44 Unum
45 rebum
46 molestiae
47 eam
48 ea.
49 Eros
50 dicam
51 vis
52 te.
53 In
54 est
55 quaeque
56 appareat.
57 ea
58 vim
59 soleat
60 adipiscing
~/course/sed/5.txt    CWD: /home/hacker/course/sed    Line: 40  Column: 1
"5.txt" 221L, 1407C
```

Which stands for:

- ^: Beginning of line anchor
- $: End of line anchor
- d: Delete

Reload the file, and you see that the lines are no longer there.

Now, as you can imagine, these have only been some basic examples. The power of sed is much greater than this, and there are many more possibilities of using it than what we have seen today. We recommend that you gain a good understanding of the features presented here today, as these are the features you will probably use the most. It's not as complicated as it might seem at first, and it really comes in handy in lots of scenarios.

You can run, but you can't hide... from find

Tens of projects, hundreds of folders and thousands of file; does this scenario sound familiar? If the answer is *yes*, then you probably found yourself more than once in a situation where you couldn't find a specific file. The `find` command will help us locate any file in our project and much more. But first, for creating a quick playground, let's download the electron open source project from GitHub:

Git clone `https://github.com/electron/electron`

And `cd` into it:

```
cd electron
```

We see here lots of different files and folders, just like in any normal sized software project. In order to find a particular file, let's say `package.json`, we will use:

```
find . -name package.json
```

```
                    [09:06:31 AM]
-> % git clone https://github.com/electron/electron
Cloning into 'electron'...
remote: Counting objects: 63612, done.
remote: Compressing objects: 100% (74/74), done.
remote: Total 63612 (delta 36), reused 0 (delta 0), pack-reused 63538
Receiving objects: 100% (63612/63612), 17.35 MiB | 3.51 MiB/s, done.
Resolving deltas: 100% (46247/46247), done.
Checking connectivity... done.
                    [09:07:03 AM]
-> % ls
electron
                    [09:07:05 AM]
-> % cd electron
                    [09:07:07 AM]                  |master|
-> % ls
appveyor.yml   CODE_OF_CONDUCT.md   CONTRIBUTING.md   docs-translations   ISSUE_TEMPLATE.md   package.json   script          tools
atom           common.gypi          default_app       electron.gyp        lib                 README-ko.md   spec            vendor
chromium_src   CONTRIBUTING-ko.md   docs              filenames.gypi      LICENSE             README.md      toolchain.gypi
                    [09:07:08 AM]                  |master|
-> % find . -name package.json
./package.json
./spec/package.json
./spec/fixtures/api/relaunch/package.json
./spec/fixtures/api/electron-module-app/node_modules/electron/package.json
./spec/fixtures/api/electron-module-app/node_modules/foo/package.json
./spec/fixtures/api/quit-app/package.json
./default_app/package.json
                    [09:07:20 AM]                  |master|
-> %
```

find . -name package.json

.: This starts the search in the current folder

-name: This helps to search the file name

If we were to look for all readme files in the project, the previous command format is not helpful. We need to issue a case insensitive find. For demonstration purposes, we will also create a readme.md file:

touch lib/readme.md

We will also use the -iname argument for case insensitive search:

find . -iname readme.md

```
./spec/package.json
./spec/fixtures/api/relaunch/package.json
./spec/fixtures/api/electron-module-app/node_modules/electron/package.json
./spec/fixtures/api/electron-module-app/node_modules/foo/package.json
./spec/fixtures/api/quit-app/package.json
./default_app/package.json
hacker@laptop [09:07:20 AM] [~/course/find/electron] [master]
-> % find . -name readme.md
hacker@laptop [09:07:35 AM] [~/course/find/electron] [master]
-> % find . -iname readme.md
./docs-translations/zh-CN/README.md
./docs-translations/th-TH/README.md
./docs-translations/es/README.md
./docs-translations/zh-TW/README.md
./docs-translations/fr-FR/README.md
./docs-translations/pt-BR/README.md
./docs-translations/ru-RU/README.md
./docs-translations/jp/README.md
./docs-translations/ko-KR/README.md
./docs-translations/uk-UA/README.md
./docs-translations/tr-TR/README.md
./docs/README.md
./README.md
hacker@laptop [09:07:39 AM] [~/course/find/electron] [master]
-> % touch lib/readme.md
hacker@laptop [09:07:51 AM] [~/course/find/electron] [master *]
-> % find . -iname readme.md
./lib/readme.md
./docs-translations/zh-CN/README.md
./docs-translations/th-TH/README.md
./docs-translations/es/README.md
./docs-translations/zh-TW/README.md
./docs-translations/fr-FR/README.md
./docs-translations/pt-BR/README.md
./docs-translations/ru-RU/README.md
./docs-translations/jp/README.md
./docs-translations/ko-KR/README.md
./docs-translations/uk-UA/README.md
./docs-translations/tr-TR/README.md
./docs/README.md
./README.md
hacker@laptop [09:07:53 AM] [~/course/find/electron] [master *]
-> %
```

You see here that both `readme.md` and `README.md` have been found. Now, if we were to search for all JavaScript files we would use:

`find . -name "*.js"`

```
./docs/README.md
./README.md
              [09:07:53 AM]                  [master *]
-> % find . -name "*.js"
./lib/common/asar_init.js
./lib/common/reset-search-paths.js
./lib/common/api/crash-reporter.js
./lib/common/api/callbacks-registry.js
./lib/common/api/native-image.js
./lib/common/api/deprecations.js
./lib/common/api/deprecate.js
./lib/common/api/shell.js
./lib/common/api/clipboard.js
./lib/common/api/is-promise.js
./lib/common/api/exports/electron.js
./lib/common/asar.js
./lib/common/init.js
./lib/renderer/web-view/web-view-attributes.js
./lib/renderer/web-view/web-view.js
./lib/renderer/web-view/web-view-constants.js
./lib/renderer/web-view/guest-view-internal.js
./lib/renderer/extensions/web-navigation.js
./lib/renderer/extensions/event.js
./lib/renderer/extensions/storage.js
./lib/renderer/extensions/i18n.js
./lib/renderer/inspector.js
./lib/renderer/api/web-frame.js
./lib/renderer/api/screen.js
./lib/renderer/api/desktop-capturer.js
./lib/renderer/api/ipc-renderer.js
./lib/renderer/api/remote.js
./lib/renderer/api/exports/electron.js
./lib/renderer/override.js
./lib/renderer/content-scripts-injector.js
./lib/renderer/chrome-api.js
./lib/renderer/init.js
./lib/browser/rpc-server.js
./lib/browser/api/menu.js
./lib/browser/api/power-monitor.js
./lib/browser/api/dialog.js
./lib/browser/api/session.js
./lib/browser/api/web-contents.js
./lib/browser/api/system-preferences.js
```

find . -name "*.js"

And as you can see, there are quite a few results. For narrowing down our results, let's limit the find to the `default_app` folder:

`find default_app -name "*.js"`

```
./spec/fixtures/module/preload-webview.js
./spec/fixtures/module/class.js
./spec/fixtures/module/preload-ipc.js
./spec/fixtures/module/fork_ping.js
./spec/fixtures/module/preload-node-off.js
./spec/fixtures/module/create_socket.js
./spec/fixtures/module/process_args.js
./spec/fixtures/module/set-global.js
./spec/fixtures/module/ping.js
./spec/fixtures/module/function.js
./spec/fixtures/module/set-immediate.js
./spec/fixtures/module/no-prototype.js
./spec/fixtures/module/process-stdout.js
./spec/fixtures/module/runas.js
./spec/fixtures/module/print_name.js
./spec/fixtures/module/original-fs.js
./spec/fixtures/module/send-later.js
./spec/fixtures/module/rejected-promise.js
./spec/fixtures/module/answer.js
./spec/fixtures/module/call.js
./spec/fixtures/module/id.js
./spec/fixtures/module/unhandled-rejection.js
./spec/fixtures/module/asar.js
./spec/fixtures/module/property.js
./spec/fixtures/module/locale-compare.js
./spec/fixtures/module/preload.js
./spec/fixtures/module/promise.js
./spec/fixtures/workers/shared_worker.js
./spec/fixtures/workers/worker.js
./spec/fixtures/api/relaunch/main.js
./spec/fixtures/api/electron-module-app/node_modules/electron/index.js
./spec/fixtures/api/electron-module-app/node_modules/foo/index.js
./spec/fixtures/api/quit-app/main.js
./spec/fixtures/pages/service-worker/service-worker.js
./spec/fixtures/pages/save_page/test.js
./default_app/default_app.js
./default_app/main.js
hacker@laptop [09:08:16 AM] [~/course/find/electron] [master *]
-> % find default_app -name "*.js"
default_app/default_app.js
default_app/main.js
hacker@laptop [09:08:28 AM] [~/course/find/electron] [master *]
-> % 
```

As you can see, there are only two `js` files in this folder. And if we were to find all files that are not JavaScript, just add a `!` mark before the name argument:

```
find default_app ! -name "*.js"
```

```
./spec/fixtures/module/create_socket.js
./spec/fixtures/module/process_args.js
./spec/fixtures/module/set-global.js
./spec/fixtures/module/ping.js
./spec/fixtures/module/function.js
./spec/fixtures/module/set-immediate.js
./spec/fixtures/module/no-prototype.js
./spec/fixtures/module/process-stdout.js
./spec/fixtures/module/runas.js
./spec/fixtures/module/print_name.js
./spec/fixtures/module/original-fs.js
./spec/fixtures/module/send-later.js
./spec/fixtures/module/rejected-promise.js
./spec/fixtures/module/answer.js
./spec/fixtures/module/call.js
./spec/fixtures/module/id.js
./spec/fixtures/module/unhandled-rejection.js
./spec/fixtures/module/asar.js
./spec/fixtures/module/property.js
./spec/fixtures/module/locale-compare.js
./spec/fixtures/module/preload.js
./spec/fixtures/module/promise.js
./spec/fixtures/workers/shared_worker.js
./spec/fixtures/workers/worker.js
./spec/fixtures/api/relaunch/main.js
./spec/fixtures/api/electron-module-app/node_modules/electron/index.js
./spec/fixtures/api/electron-module-app/node_modules/foo/index.js
./spec/fixtures/api/quit-app/main.js
./spec/fixtures/pages/service-worker/service-worker.js
./spec/fixtures/pages/save_page/test.js
./default_app/default_app.js
./default_app/main.js
                 [09:08:16 AM]                  [master *]
-> % find default_app -name "*.js"
default_app/default_app.js
default_app/main.js
                 [09:08:28 AM]                  [master *]
-> % find default_app ! -name "*.js"
default_app
default_app/package.json
default_app/index.html
                 [09:08:34 AM]                  [master *]
-> %
```

You can see here all files that don't end their name with `js`. If we were to look for all inodes in the directory, which are of type file, we would use the `-type f` argument:

`find lib -type f`

```
./default_app/default_app.js
./default_app/main.js
hacker@laptop [09:08:16 AM] [~/course/find/electron] [master *]
-> % find default_app -name "*.js"
default_app/default_app.js
default_app/main.js
hacker@laptop [09:08:28 AM] [~/course/find/electron] [master *]
-> % find default_app ! -name "*.js"
default_app
default_app/package.json
default_app/index.html
hacker@laptop [09:08:34 AM] [~/course/find/electron] [master *]
-> % find lib -type f
lib/common/asar_init.js
lib/common/reset-search-paths.js
lib/common/api/crash-reporter.js
lib/common/api/callbacks-registry.js
lib/common/api/native-image.js
lib/common/api/deprecations.js
lib/common/api/deprecate.js
lib/common/api/shell.js
lib/common/api/clipboard.js
lib/common/api/is-promise.js
lib/common/api/exports/electron.js
lib/common/asar.js
lib/common/init.js
lib/renderer/web-view/web-view-attributes.js
lib/renderer/web-view/web-view.js
lib/renderer/web-view/web-view-constants.js
lib/renderer/web-view/guest-view-internal.js
lib/renderer/extensions/web-navigation.js
lib/renderer/extensions/event.js
lib/renderer/extensions/storage.js
lib/renderer/extensions/i18n.js
lib/renderer/inspector.js
lib/renderer/api/web-frame.js
lib/renderer/api/screen.js
lib/renderer/api/desktop-capturer.js
lib/renderer/api/ipc-renderer.js
lib/renderer/api/remote.js
lib/renderer/api/exports/electron.js
lib/renderer/override.js
lib/renderer/content-scripts-injector.js
```

In the same way, we'd use `-type d` to find all directories in a specific location:

`find lib -type d`

```
lib/browser/api/session.js
lib/browser/api/web-contents.js
lib/browser/api/system-preferences.js
lib/browser/api/browser-window.js
lib/browser/api/auto-updater.js
lib/browser/api/menu-item-roles.js
lib/browser/api/content-tracing.js
lib/browser/api/ipc-main.js
lib/browser/api/screen.js
lib/browser/api/navigation-controller.js
lib/browser/api/tray.js
lib/browser/api/menu-item.js
lib/browser/api/protocol.js
lib/browser/api/app.js
lib/browser/api/power-save-blocker.js
lib/browser/api/auto-updater/auto-updater-win.js
lib/browser/api/auto-updater/auto-updater-native.js
lib/browser/api/auto-updater/squirrel-update-win.js
lib/browser/api/exports/electron.js
lib/browser/api/global-shortcut.js
lib/browser/objects-registry.js
lib/browser/desktop-capturer.js
lib/browser/guest-window-manager.js
lib/browser/guest-view-manager.js
lib/browser/init.js
lib/browser/chrome-extension.js
                    [09:08:51 AM]                    [master *]
-> % find lib -type d
lib
lib/common
lib/common/api
lib/common/api/exports
lib/renderer
lib/renderer/web-view
lib/renderer/extensions
lib/renderer/api
lib/renderer/api/exports
lib/browser
lib/browser/api
lib/browser/api/auto-updater
lib/browser/api/exports
                    [09:09:01 AM]                    [master *]
-> %
```

find lib -type **d**

Find can also locate files based on time identifiers. For example, in order to find all files in the /usr/share directory that were modified in the last 24 hours, issue the following command:

```
find /usr/share -mtime -1
```

```
lib/browser/chrome-extension.js
hacker@laptop [09:08:51 AM] [~/course/find/electron] [master *]
-> % find lib -type d
lib
lib/common
lib/common/api
lib/common/api/exports
lib/renderer
lib/renderer/web-view
lib/renderer/extensions
lib/renderer/api
lib/renderer/api/exports
lib/browser
lib/browser/api
lib/browser/api/auto-updater
lib/browser/api/exports
hacker@laptop [09:09:01 AM] [~/course/find/electron] [master *]
-> % find /usr/share -mtime -1
/usr/share/applications
/usr/share/applications/mimeinfo.cache
/usr/share/applications/bamf-2.index
/usr/share/man/man1
/usr/share/man/man8
/usr/share/libnm-gtk
/usr/share/gdb/python/gdb
/usr/share/gdb/python/gdb/function
/usr/share/gdb/python/gdb/command
/usr/share/gdb/python/gdb/printer
/usr/share/gdb/system-gdbinit
/usr/share/gdb/syscalls
/usr/share/bash-completion/completions
/usr/share/GConf
/usr/share/GConf/gsettings
/usr/share/GConf/gsettings.dpkg-cache
/usr/share/dbus-1/services
/usr/share/doc
/usr/share/doc/libnm-gtk-common
/usr/share/doc/gdb
/usr/share/doc/gdb/contrib
/usr/share/doc/gdb/contrib/ari
/usr/share/doc/libnm-gtk0
/usr/share/doc/mysql-client-5.7
/usr/share/doc/linux-firmware
```

I have quite a big list. You can see the -mtime -3 broadens the list even more.

If we were to find, for example, all the files modified in the last hour, we can use -mmin -60:

find ~/.local/share -mmin -60

```
/usr/share/help/hu/file-roller
/usr/share/help/hu/file-roller/figures
/usr/share/help/sl/file-roller
/usr/share/help/sl/file-roller/figures
/usr/share/help/el/file-roller
/usr/share/help/el/file-roller/figures
/usr/share/help/cs/file-roller
/usr/share/help/cs/file-roller/figures
/usr/share/help/fi/file-roller
/usr/share/help/fi/file-roller/figures
/usr/share/help/ja/file-roller
/usr/share/help/ja/file-roller/figures
/usr/share/help/id/file-roller
/usr/share/help/id/file-roller/figures
/usr/share/help/da/file-roller
/usr/share/help/da/file-roller/figures
/usr/share/help/es/file-roller
/usr/share/help/es/file-roller/figures
/usr/share/help/te/file-roller
/usr/share/help/te/file-roller/figures
/usr/share/help/de/file-roller
/usr/share/help/de/file-roller/figures
/usr/share/help/pt_BR/file-roller
/usr/share/help/pt_BR/file-roller/figures
/usr/share/menu
/usr/share/file-roller
                    [09:09:35 AM]                [master *]
-> % find ~/.local/share -mmin -60
/home/hacker/.local/share
/home/hacker/.local/share/clipit/history
/home/hacker/.local/share/zeitgeist/activity.sqlite-shm
/home/hacker/.local/share/zeitgeist/fts.index
/home/hacker/.local/share/zeitgeist/fts.index/position.DB
/home/hacker/.local/share/zeitgeist/fts.index/termlist.baseA
/home/hacker/.local/share/zeitgeist/fts.index/position.baseB
/home/hacker/.local/share/zeitgeist/fts.index/termlist.DB
/home/hacker/.local/share/zeitgeist/fts.index/postlist.DB
/home/hacker/.local/share/zeitgeist/fts.index/record.DB
/home/hacker/.local/share/zeitgeist/fts.index/postlist.baseA
/home/hacker/.local/share/zeitgeist/fts.index/record.baseA
/home/hacker/.local/share/zeitgeist/activity.sqlite-wal
                    [09:10:12 AM]                [master *]
-> %
```

find ~/.local/share -mmin -60

A good folder to search is `~/.local/share`, If we use `-mmin -90`, the list broadens again.

Find can also show us the list of files accessed in the last 24 hours by using the `-atime -1` argument like so:

find ~/.local/share -atime -1

```
/home/hacker/.local/share/Trash/info/a.js.trashinfo
/home/hacker/.local/share/Trash/info/a.html.trashinfo
/home/hacker/.local/share/Trash/info/script.sh.trashinfo
/home/hacker/.local/share/Trash/info/lib.sh.trashinfo
/home/hacker/.local/share/evolution
/home/hacker/.local/share/evolution/memos
/home/hacker/.local/share/evolution/memos/trash
/home/hacker/.local/share/evolution/addressbook
/home/hacker/.local/share/evolution/addressbook/system
/home/hacker/.local/share/evolution/addressbook/system/contacts.db
/home/hacker/.local/share/evolution/addressbook/system/photos
/home/hacker/.local/share/evolution/addressbook/trash
/home/hacker/.local/share/evolution/tasks
/home/hacker/.local/share/evolution/tasks/system
/home/hacker/.local/share/evolution/tasks/system/tasks.ics
/home/hacker/.local/share/evolution/tasks/trash
/home/hacker/.local/share/evolution/mail
/home/hacker/.local/share/evolution/mail/trash
/home/hacker/.local/share/evolution/calendar
/home/hacker/.local/share/evolution/calendar/system
/home/hacker/.local/share/evolution/calendar/system/calendar.ics
/home/hacker/.local/share/evolution/calendar/trash
/home/hacker/.local/share/recently-used.xbel
/home/hacker/.local/share/gsettings-data-convert
/home/hacker/.local/share/gvfs-metadata
/home/hacker/.local/share/gvfs-metadata/home-6863d769.log
/home/hacker/.local/share/gvfs-metadata/home
/home/hacker/.local/share/nautilus
/home/hacker/.local/share/nautilus/scripts
/home/hacker/.local/share/icons
/home/hacker/.local/share/icons/hicolor
/home/hacker/.local/share/icons/hicolor/48x48
/home/hacker/.local/share/icons/hicolor/48x48/apps
/home/hacker/.local/share/icons/hicolor/32x32
/home/hacker/.local/share/icons/hicolor/32x32/apps
/home/hacker/.local/share/icons/hi
/home/hacker/.local/share/icons/hi
/home/hacker/.local/share/icons/hi
/home/hacker/.local/share/icons/hi
/home/hacker/.local/share/icons/hi
/home/hacker/.local/share/unity-settings-daemon
```

find ~/.local/share -atime -1

While working with lots of project files, if sometimes the case in some projects remain empty, and we forget to delete them. In order to locate all empty files just do a:

```
find . -empty
```

```
/home/hacker/.local/share/evolution/calendar/system/calendar.ics
/home/hacker/.local/share/evolution/calendar/trash
/home/hacker/.local/share/recently-used.xbel
/home/hacker/.local/share/gsettings-data-convert
/home/hacker/.local/share/gvfs-metadata
/home/hacker/.local/share/gvfs-metadata/home-6863d769.log
/home/hacker/.local/share/gvfs-metadata/home
/home/hacker/.local/share/nautilus
/home/hacker/.local/share/nautilus/scripts
/home/hacker/.local/share/icons
/home/hacker/.local/share/icons/hicolor
/home/hacker/.local/share/icons/hicolor/48x48
/home/hacker/.local/share/icons/hicolor/48x48/apps
/home/hacker/.local/share/icons/hicolor/32x32
/home/hacker/.local/share/icons/hicolor/32x32/apps
/home/hacker/.local/share/icons/hicolor/16x16
/home/hacker/.local/share/icons/hicolor/16x16/apps
/home/hacker/.local/share/icons/hicolor/128x128
/home/hacker/.local/share/icons/hicolor/128x128/apps
/home/hacker/.local/share/icons/hicolor/128x128/apps/chrome-fhbjgbiflinjbdggehcddcbncdddomop-Default.png
/home/hacker/.local/share/unity-settings-daemon
                [09:10:40 AM]                              [master *]
-> % find . -empty
./lib/readme.md
./.git/refs/tags
./.git/branches
./.git/objects/info
./vendor/boto
./vendor/requests
./vendor/brightray
./vendor/depot_tools
./vendor/crashpad
./vendor/breakpad
./vendor/node
./vendor/native_mate
./chromium_src/chrome/browser/profiles/profile.h
./chromium_src/chrome/browser/profiles/profile_io_d
./chromium_src/chrome/browser/ui/simple_message_box        find . -empty
./chromium_src/grit/generated_resources.h
./script/lib/__init__.py
./spec/fixtures/api/electron-module-app/node_modules/electron/index.js
                [09:11:07 AM]                              [master *]
-> %
```

As we can see, electron has a few empty files. Find will also show us empty directories, or links.

Removing empty files will keep our project clean, but when it comes to reducing size, we sometimes want to know which files are taking up most of the space. Find can also do searches based on file size. For example, let's find all the files larger than 1 mega:

```
find . -size +1M
```

use -1M for smaller.

As we said in the beginning, find can do much more than locating files in your project. Using the -exec argument, it can be combined with almost any other command, which gives it almost infinite capabilities. For example, if we want to find all javascript files that contain the text manager, we can combine find with grep, command as follows:

```
find . -name "*.js" -exec grep -li 'manager' {} \;
```

```
hacker@laptop [09:12:16 AM] [~/course/find/electron] [master *]
-> % find . -iname "*.js" -exec grep -li "manager" {} \;
./lib/renderer/web-view/guest-view-internal.js
./lib/renderer/override.js
./lib/browser/rpc-server.js
./lib/browser/api/browser-window.js
./lib/browser/guest-window-manager.js
./lib/browser/guest-view-manager.js
./lib/browser/init.js
```

This will execute the grep command on all the files returned by find. Let's also search inside the file using vim, so that we verify the result is correct. As you can see, the text "manager" appears in this file. You don't have to worry about {} \;, it's just standard -exec syntax.

Moving on with the practical examples, let's say you have a folder where you want to remove all the files modified in the last 100 days. We can see our default_app folder contains such files. If we combine find with rm like so:

```
find default_app -mtime -100 -exec rm -rf {} \;
```

We can do a quick cleanup. Find can be used for smart backups. For example, if we were to backup all json files in the project we would combine find with the cpio backup utility using a pipe and a standard output redirection:

```
find . -name "*.json" | cpio -o > backup.cpio
```

```
-> % find . -iname "*.json" | cpio -o > backup.cpio
5 blocks
hacker@laptop [09:14:11 AM] [~/course/find/electron] [master *]
-> % ls backup.cpio
backup.cpio
hacker@laptop [09:14:17 AM] [~/course/find/electron] [master *]
-> % file backup.cpio
backup.cpio: cpio archive
```

We can see that this command has created a backup.cpio file, of type cpio archive.

Now this could probably have been written with -exec also, but it's critical you understand that pipes can also be used in this type of scenario, together with redirects.

When doing reports, you may have to count the number of lines written:

- In order to do this, we combine find with wc -l:

  ```
  find . -iname "*.js" -exec wc -l {} \;
  ```

- This will give us all js files and the number of lines. We can pipe this to cut:

  ```
  find . -iname "*.js" -exec wc -l {} \; | cut -f 1 -d ' '
  ```

- To only output the number of lines, and then pipe to the paste command, we do this:

  ```
  find . -iname "*.js" -exec wc -l {} \; | cut -f 1 -d ' ' | paste -sd+
  ```

- The above will merge all our lines with the + sign as a delimiter. This, of course, can translate to an arithmetic operation, which we can calculate using the binary calculator (bc):

  ```
  find . -iname "*.js" -exec wc -l {} \; | cut -f 1 -d ' ' | paste -sd+ | bc
  ```

```
hacker@laptop [09:14:57 AM] [~/course/find/electron] [master *]
-> % find . -iname "*.js" -exec wc -l {} \; | cut -f 1 -d ' ' | paste -sd+
20+37+88+66+1+11+187+1+6+14+53+616+48+294+471+29+107+21+24+59+84+81+13+1+47+37+308+38+250+61+184+133+372+307+6+197+44+248+6+159+5+147+1+3+6+178+6+8
7+23+72+1+67+6+115+116+1+97+77+137+233+183+383+6+12+80+3+22+498+941+1150+45+51+21+101+936+37+163+6+134+839+315+27+248+87+92+313+426+292+456+19+5+29
+4+16+7+4+4+1+4+1+11+4+1+6+7+3+4+5+4+7+1+3+4+1+7+1+5+7+3+25+8+1+12+9+1
hacker@laptop [09:15:09 AM] [~/course/find/electron] [master *]
-> % find . -iname "*.js" -exec wc -l {} \; | cut -f 1 -d ' ' | paste -sd+ | bc
14120
hacker@laptop [09:15:13 AM] [~/course/find/electron] [master *]
-> %
```

This last command will tell us how many lines our javascript files contain. Of course, these are not actual lines of code, as they can be empty lines or comments. For a precise calculation of lines of code, you can use the sloc utility.

In order to mass rename files, like changing the file extension name to node for all js files we can use this command:

```
find . -type f -iname "*.js" -exec rename "s/js$/node/g" {} \;
```

You can see the rename syntax is quite similar to sed. In addition, there are no more .js files left, as all have been renamed to .node:

```
hacker@laptop [09:15:25 AM] [~/course/find/electron] [master *]
-> % find . -iname "*.js" -exec rename "s/js$/node/g" {} \;
hacker@laptop [09:15:59 AM] [~/course/find/electron] [master *]
-> % find . -iname "*.js"
hacker@laptop [09:16:01 AM] [~/course/find/electron] [master *]
```

Some software projects require all source code files to have a copyright header. As this is not required in the beginning, often times we can find ourselves in the situation that we have to add copyright information at the beginning of all our files.

In order to do this, we can combine find with sed like this:

```
find . -name "*.node" -exec sed -i "1s/^/\/** Copyright 2016 all rights reserved *\/\n/" {} \;
```

What this is basically doing is telling the computer to find all .node files, and add the copyright notice in the beginning of each file, followed by a new line.

We can check one random file and, yes, the copyright notice is there:

```
1 /** Copyright all rights reserved */
2 this.onmessage = function (msg) {
3     this.postMessage(msg.data)
4 }
```

Update version numbers in all files:

```
find . -name pom.xml -exec sed -i "s/<version>4.02/<version>4.03/g" {} \;
```

As you can imagine, find has lots of use cases. The examples I've shown you are only the first piece of the pie. Learning find, along with sed and the git cli can set you free from your IDE when it comes to finding, refactoring or working with git, which means you can more easily switch from one IDE to the other, because you don't have to learn all the features. You just use your friendly CLI tools.

tmux – virtual consoles, background jobs and the like

In this section, we will be looking at another great tool called tmux. Tmux comes in particularly handy when working in remote ssh sessions, because it gives you the ability to continue your work from where you left off. It can also replace some of the features in terminator, if you are working, for example, on Mac, and you can't install terminator.

To get started with tmux on Ubuntu, we first need to install it:

```
sudo apt install tmux
```

```
                    [09:32:19 AM]
-> % sudo apt install tmux
```

sudo apt install tmux

Then just run the command:

tmux

```
                    [09:32:19 AM]
-> % sudo apt install tmux
[sudo] password for hacker:
Reading package lists... Done
Building dependency tree
Reading state information... Done
The following NEW packages will be installed:
  tmux
0 upgraded, 1 newly installed, 0 to remove and 6 not upgraded.
Need to get 223 kB of archives.
After this operation, 601 kB of additional disk space will be used.
Get:1 http://ro.archive.ubuntu.com/ubuntu xenial/main amd64 tmux amd64 2.1-3build1 [223 kB]
Fetched 223 kB in 0s (644 kB/s)
Selecting previously unselected package tmux.
(Reading database ... 215883 files and directories currently installed.)
Preparing to unpack .../tmux_2.1-3build1_amd64.deb ...
Unpacking tmux (2.1-3build1) ...
Processing triggers for man-db (2.7.5-1) ...
Setting up tmux (2.1-3build1) ...
                    [09:32:39 AM]
-> % tmux
```

tmux

And you will find yourself inside a brand new virtual console:

For demonstration purposes, we will open up a new tab that you can see the list of open sessions with `tmux ls`:

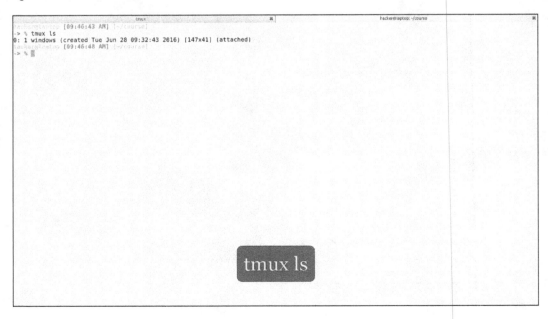

Let's start a new `tmux` named session:

tmux new -s mysession

```
                    [09:46:43 AM]                                    hacker@laptop: ~/course
-> % tmux ls
0: 1 windows (created Tue Jun 28 09:32:43 2016) [147x41] (attached)
                    [09:46:48 AM]
-> % tmux new -s mysession
[detached (from session mysession)]
                    [09:47:30 AM]
-> % tmux ls
0: 1 windows (created Tue Jun 28 09:32:43 2016) [147x41] (attached)
mysession: 1 windows (created Tue Jun 28 09:46:59 2016) [147x41]
                    [09:47:33 AM]
-> %
```

Here we can see that opening a `tmux` session maintains the current directory. To list and switch `tmux` sessions inside `tmux`, hit *Ctrl + B S*.

We can see that we can switch to another tmux session, execute commands inside, and switch back to our initial session if we want to. To detach (leave a session running and go back to the normal terminal) hit *Ctrl + b d*;

Now we can see we have two opened sessions.

To attach to a session:

tmux a -t mysession

```
                    [09:46:43 AM]                                    hacker@laptop: ~/course
-> % tmux ls
0: 1 windows (created Tue Jun 28 09:32:43 2016) [147x41] (attached)
                    [09:46:48 AM]
-> % tmux new -s mysession
[detached (from session mysession)]
                    [09:47:30 AM]
-> % tmux ls
0: 1 windows (created Tue Jun 28 09:32:43 2016) [147x41] (attached)
mysession: 1 windows (created Tue Jun 28 09:46:59 2016) [147x41]
                    [09:47:33 AM]
-> % tmux a mysession
usage: attach-session [-dEr] [-c working-directory] [-t target-session]
                    [09:47:43 AM]
-> % tmux a -t mysession
```

tmux a -t mysession

This scenario comes in handy when you login to a remote server and want to execute a long running task, then leave and come back when it ends. We will replicate this scenario with a quick script called infinity.sh. We will execute it. It's writing to the standard output. Now let's detach from tmux.

If we look at the script, it's just a simple while loop that goes on forever, printing text each second.

Now when we come back to our session, we can see the script was running while we were detached from the session and it's still outputting data to the console. I will manually stop it by hitting *Ctrl + c*.

Alright, let's go to our first tmux session and close it. In order to manually kill a running tmux session, use:

```
tmux kill-session -t mysession
```

tmux kill-session -t mysession

This will kill the running session. If we switch over to our second tab, we can see that we have been logged off tmux. Let's also close this terminator tab, and open a brand new tmux session:

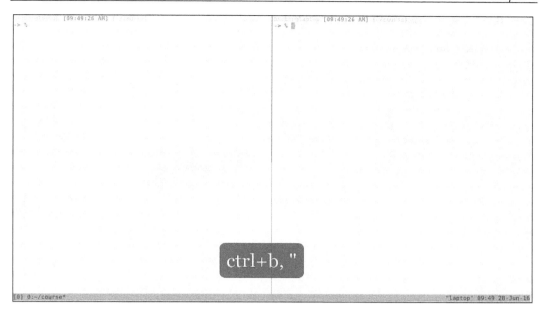

Tmux gives you the possibility to split the screen, just like terminator, horizontally with *Ctrl + b + "*, and vertically with *Ctrl + b + %*. After that, use *Ctrl + b +* arrows to navigate between the panes:

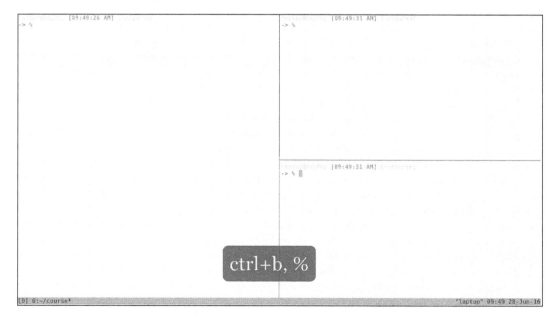

You also have the possibility to create windows (tabs):

- *Ctrl + b c*: create:

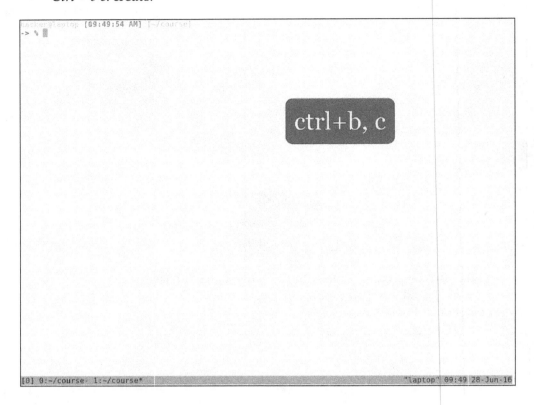

- *Ctrl + b w*: list:

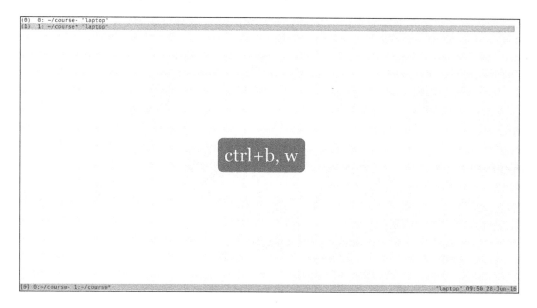

- *Ctrl + b &*: delete

These last functionalities are very similar to what terminator offers.

You can use tmux in situations where you want to have two or more panes or even tabs in your remote ssh connection, but you don't want to open multiple ssh sessions. You could also use it locally, as a terminator replacement, but the keyboard shortcuts are much harder to use. Although they can be changed, you will lose the option to use tmux remotely, because opening a tmux session in another tmux session is discouraged. In addition, configuring new tmux keyboard shortcuts might make tmux a burden when working on lots of servers due to the shortcut differences.

Network – Who's listening?

When working with network applications, it comes in handy to be able to see open ports and connections and to be able to interact with ports on different hosts for testing purposes. In this section, we will be looking at some basic commands for networking and in what situations they might come in handy.

The first command is netstat:

netstat -plnt

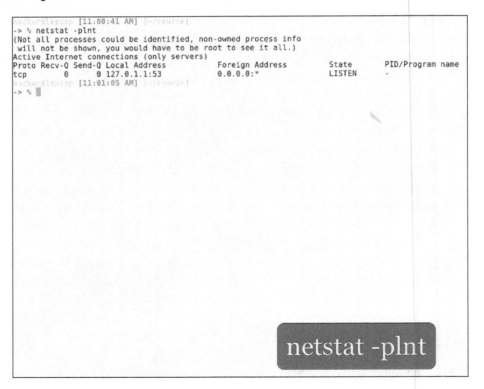

This will show all open ports on our host. You can see here that we only have one open port on a default Ubuntu desktop installation, which is port 53. We can look this up in the special file /etc/services. This file contains all basic port numbers for programs and protocols. We see here port 53 is the DNS server:

```
 1 ░ Network services, Internet style
 2 #
 3 # Note that it is presently the policy of IANA to assign a single well-known
 4 # port number for both TCP and UDP; hence, officially ports have two entries
 5 # even if the protocol doesn't support UDP operations.
 6 #
 7 # Updated from http://www.iana.org/assignments/port-numbers and other
 8 # sources like http://www.freebsd.org/cgi/cvsweb.cgi/src/etc/services .
 9 # New ports will be added on request if they have been officially assigned
10 # by IANA and used in the real-world or are needed by a debian package.
11 # If you need a huge list of used numbers please install the nmap package.
12
13 tcpmux        1/tcp                    # TCP port service multiplexer
14 echo          7/tcp
15 echo          7/udp
16 discard       9/tcp         sink null
17 discard       9/udp         sink null
18 systat       11/tcp         users
19 daytime      13/tcp
20 daytime      13/udp
21 netstat      15/tcp
22 qotd         17/tcp         quote
23 msp     18/tcp                   # message send protocol
24 msp     18/udp
25 chargen      19/tcp         ttytst source
26 chargen      19/udp         ttytst source
27 ftp-data     20/tcp
28 ftp     21/tcp
29 fsp     21/udp         fspd
30 ssh          22/tcp                   # SSH Remote Login Protocol
31 ssh          22/udp
32 telnet       23/tcp
33 smtp         25/tcp         mail
34 time         37/tcp         timserver
35 time         37/udp         timserver
36 rlp     39/udp         resource    # resource location
37 nameserver   42/tcp         name        # IEN 116
38 whois        43/tcp         nicname
39 tacacs       49/tcp                   # Login Host Protocol (TACACS)
40 tacacs       49/udp
41 re-mail-ck   50/tcp                   # Remote Mail Checking Protocol
/etc/services[RO]   CWD: [RO]/home/hacker/course   Line: 1  Column: 1
"/etc/services" [readonly] 612L, 19605C
```

Just by analyzing the output, we cannot determine which program is listening on this port, because this process is not owned by our current user. That's why the *PID/Program Name* column is empty. If we run the same command again with sudo, we see that this process is named dnsmasq and, if we want more information, we can look it up in the man page. It's a lightweight DHCP and caching DNS server:

```
hacker@laptop [11:00:41 AM] [~/course]
-> % netstat -plnt
(Not all processes could be identified, non-owned process info
 will not be shown, you would have to be root to see it all.)
Active Internet connections (only servers)
Proto Recv-Q Send-Q Local Address         Foreign Address       State     PID/Program name
tcp       0      0 127.0.1.1:53           0.0.0.0:*             LISTEN    -
hacker@laptop [11:01:05 AM] [~/course]
-> % vim /etc/services
hacker@laptop [11:01:29 AM] [~/course]
-> % sudo netstat -plnt
Active Internet connections (only servers)
Proto Recv-Q Send-Q Local Address         Foreign Address       State     PID/Program name
tcp       0      0 127.0.1.1:53           0.0.0.0:*             LISTEN    1529/dnsmasq
hacker@laptop [11:01:35 AM] [~/course]
-> %
```

Other useful information we get from this command:

- The program protocol, in this case dhcp.
- Total bytes not copied.
- Total bytes not acknowledged.
- Local and foreign address and port. Getting the port is the main reason we are using this command. This is also important for determining if the port is open just on localhost or if it's listening for incoming connections on the network.
- The state of the port. Usually this is **LISTEN**.
- The PID and program name, which helps us identify which program is listening on what port.

Now, if we run a program that is supposed to be listening on a certain port and we don't know if it's working, we can find out with netstat. Let's open the most basic HTTP server by running the command:

python -m SimpleHTTPServer

```
hacker@laptop [11:00:41 AM] [~/course]
-> % netstat -plnt
(Not all processes could be identified, non-owned process info
 will not be shown, you would have to be root to see it all.)
Active Internet connections (only servers)
Proto Recv-Q Send-Q Local Address          Foreign Address         State       PID/Program name
tcp        0      0 127.0.1.1:53           0.0.0.0:*               LISTEN      -
hacker@laptop [11:01:05 AM] [~/course]
-> % vim /etc/services
hacker@laptop [11:01:29 AM] [~/course]
-> % sudo netstat -plnt
Active Internet connections (only servers)
Proto Recv-Q Send-Q Local Address          Foreign Address         State       PID/Program name
tcp        0      0 127.0.1.1:53           0.0.0.0:*               LISTEN      1529/dnsmasq
hacker@laptop [11:01:35 AM] [~/course]
-> % man dnsmasq
hacker@laptop [11:01:49 AM] [~/course]
-> % python -m SimpleHTTPServer
Serving HTTP on 0.0.0.0 port 8000 ...
```

python -m SimpleHTTPServer

As you can see from the output, it's listening on port 8000 on interface 0.0.0.0. If we open a new pane and run the netstat command, we will see the open the port, and the PID / name.

You probably already know this but, just to be on the safe side, we will look at adding different hostnames as static dns entries on our machine. This is helpful when developing applications that need to connect to servers and the servers change their IP address, or when you want to emulate a remote server on a local machine. For this we type:

```
sudo vim /etc/hosts
```

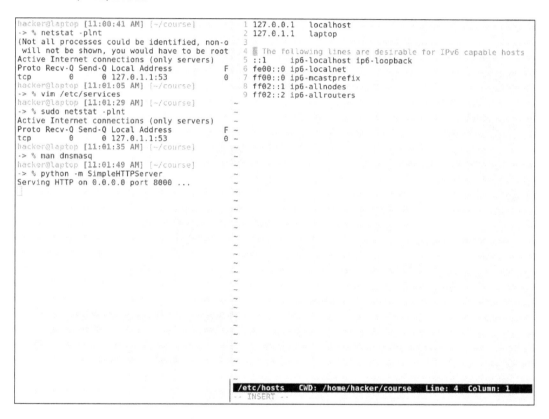

You can quickly understand the format of the file from the existing content. Let's add an alias for our localhost, so that we can access it under a different name. Add the following line:

```
127.0.0.1    myhostname.local
```

We recommend using non existing top level domain names for localhost, such as .local or .dev. This is to avoid overriding any existing address, because /etc/hosts takes precedence in dns resolution. Now, if we open the address in the browser on port 8000, we will see our local Python server running and serving content.

The next command is nmap. As you can see, it is not installed by default on Ubuntu, so let's go ahead and install it by typing:

```
sudo apt install nmap
```

```
Active Internet connections (only servers)
Proto Recv-Q Send-Q Local Address         Foreign Address        State       PID/Program name
tcp        0      0 127.0.1.1:53          0.0.0.0:*              LISTEN      -
hacker@laptop [11:01:05 AM] [~/course]
-> % vim /etc/services
hacker@laptop [11:01:29 AM] [~/course]
-> % sudo netstat -plnt
Active Internet connections (only servers)
Proto Recv-Q Send-Q Local Address         Foreign Address        State       PID/Program name
tcp        0      0 127.0.1.1:53          0.0.0.0:*              LISTEN      1529/dnsmasq
hacker@laptop [11:01:35 AM] [~/course]
-> % man dnsmasq
hacker@laptop [11:01:49 AM] [~/course]
-> % python -m SimpleHTTPServer
Serving HTTP on 0.0.0.0 port 8000 ...
127.0.0.1 - - [05/Jul/2016 11:03:00] "GET / H
TTP/1.1" 200 -
127.0.0.1 - - [05/Jul/2016 11:03:00] code 404
, message File not found
127.0.0.1 - - [05/Jul/2016 11:03:00] "GET /fa
vicon.ico HTTP/1.1" 404 -
127.0.0.1 - - [05/Jul/2016 11:03:00] code 404
, message File not found
127.0.0.1 - - [05/Jul/2016 11:03:00] "GET /fa
vicon.ico HTTP/1.1" 404 -
^CTraceback (most recent call last):
  File "/usr/lib/python2.7/runpy.py", line 174, in _run_module_as_main
    "__main__", fname, loader, pkg_name)
  File "/usr/lib/python2.7/runpy.py", line 72, in _run_code
    exec code in run_globals
  File "/usr/lib/python2.7/SimpleHTTPServer.py", line 235, in <module>
    test()
  File "/usr/lib/python2.7/SimpleHTTPServer.py", line 231, in test
    BaseHTTPServer.test(HandlerClass, ServerClass)
  File "/usr/lib/python2.7/BaseHTTPServer.py", line 599, in test
    httpd.serve_forever()
  File "/usr/lib/python2.7/SocketServer.py", line 231, in serve_forever
    poll_interval)
  File "/usr/lib/python2.7/SocketServer.py", line 150, in _eintr_retry
    return func(*args)
KeyboardInterrupt
hacker@laptop [11:03:11 AM] [~/course]
-> % sudo apt install nmap
```

`sudo apt install nmap`

Nmap is a command used for checking all open ports on a remote host, also known as a port scanner. If we run `nmap` on our network gateway, which, in our case, is `192.68.0.1`, we'll get all of the open ports on the gateway:

Type: **nmap 192.168.0.1**

```
    File "/usr/lib/python2.7/SimpleHTTPServer.py", line 231, in test
      BaseHTTPServer.test(HandlerClass, ServerClass)
    File "/usr/lib/python2.7/BaseHTTPServer.py", line 599, in test
      httpd.serve_forever()
    File "/usr/lib/python2.7/SocketServer.py", line 231, in serve_forever
      poll_interval)
    File "/usr/lib/python2.7/SocketServer.py", line 150, in _eintr_retry
      return func(*args)
KeyboardInterrupt
                [11:03:11 AM]
-> % sudo apt install nmap
Reading package lists... Done
Building dependency tree
Reading state information... Done
The following NEW packages will be installed:
  nmap
0 upgraded, 1 newly installed, 0 to remove and 24 not upgraded.
Need to get 4,638 kB of archives.
After this operation, 21.3 MB of additional disk space will be used.
Get:1 http://ro.archive.ubuntu.com/ubuntu xenial/main amd64 nmap amd64 7.01-2ubuntu2 [4,638 kB]
Fetched 4,638 kB in 7s (635 kB/s)
Selecting previously unselected package nmap.
(Reading database ... 215547 files and directories currently installed.)
Preparing to unpack .../nmap_7.01-2ubuntu2_amd64.deb ...
Unpacking nmap (7.01-2ubuntu2) ...
Processing triggers for man-db (2.7.5-1) ...
Setting up nmap (7.01-2ubuntu2) ...
                [11:03:28 AM]
-> % nmap 192.168.0.1

Starting Nmap 7.01 ( https://nmap.org ) at 2016-07-05 11:03 EEST
Nmap scan report for dlinkrouter (192.168.0.1)
Host is up (0.065s latency).
Not shown: 996 closed ports
PORT      STATE SERVICE
53/tcp    open  domain
80/tcp    open  http
443/tcp   open  https
49152/tcp open  unknown

Nmap done: 1 IP address (1 host up) scanned in 0.77 seconds
                [11:03:36 AM]
-> %
```

As you can see, there is again the `dns` port open, the http and https servers, which are used as a web page for configuring the router, and port `49152`, which, at this time, is not specific to any common protocol-and that's why it is marked as unknown. Nmap does not know for sure that those specific programs are actually running on the host; all it does is verify what ports are open and write the default application that usually runs on that port.

If we are not sure what server we need to, connect to or if we want to know how many servers are in our current network, we can run nmap on the local network address, specifying the network mask as the destination network. We get this information from ifconfig; if our IP address is 192.168.0.159, and our network mask is 255.255.255.0, that means the command will look like this:

nmap -sP 192.168.0.0/24

```
                inet addr:172.17.0.1  Bcast:0.0.0.0  Mask:255.255.0.0
                UP BROADCAST MULTICAST  MTU:1500  Metric:1
                RX packets:0 errors:0 dropped:0 overruns:0 frame:0
                TX packets:0 errors:0 dropped:0 overruns:0 carrier:0
                collisions:0 txqueuelen:0
                RX bytes:0 (0.0 B)  TX bytes:0 (0.0 B)

enp2s0          Link encap:Ethernet  HWaddr 20:89:84:f4:50:97
                UP BROADCAST MULTICAST  MTU:1500  Metric:1
                RX packets:0 errors:0 dropped:0 overruns:0 frame:0
                TX packets:0 errors:0 dropped:0 overruns:0 carrier:0
                collisions:0 txqueuelen:1000
                RX bytes:0 (0.0 B)  TX bytes:0 (0.0 B)

lo              Link encap:Local Loopback
                inet addr:127.0.0.1  Mask:255.0.0.0
                inet6 addr: ::1/128 Scope:Host
                UP LOOPBACK RUNNING  MTU:65536  Metric:1
                RX packets:679 errors:0 dropped:0 overruns:0 frame:0
                TX packets:679 errors:0 dropped:0 overruns:0 carrier:0
                collisions:0 txqueuelen:1
                RX bytes:73014 (73.0 KB)  TX bytes:73014 (73.0 KB)

wlp3s0          Link encap:Ethernet  HWaddr 68:17:29:bf:e2:67
                inet addr:192.168.0.159  Bcast:192.168.0.255  Mask:255.255.255.0
                inet6 addr: fe80::18e9:533a:d12f:82de/64 Scope:Link
                UP BROADCAST RUNNING MULTICAST  MTU:1500  Metric:1
                RX packets:23231 errors:0 dropped:0 overruns:0 frame:0
                TX packets:15862 errors:0 dropped:0 overruns:0 carrier:0
                collisions:0 txqueuelen:1000
                RX bytes:23244583 (23.2 MB)  TX bytes:2348670 (2.3 MB)

hacker@laptop [11:03:46 AM] [~/course]
-> % nmap -sP 192.168.0.0/24

Starting Nmap 7.01 ( https://nmap.org ) at 2016-07-05 11:04 EEST
Nmap scan report for dlinkrouter (192.168.0.1)
Host is up (0.0047s latency).
Nmap scan report for 192-168-0-159.rdsnet.ro (192.168.0.159)
Host is up (0.000057s latency).
Nmap done: 256 IP addresses (2 hosts up) scanned in 3.03 seconds
hacker@laptop [11:04:08 AM] [~/course]
-> %
```

In /24 = 255.255.255.0, basically the network will have ips ranging from 192.168.0.0 to 192.168.0.255. We see here that we have three active hosts, and it even gives us the latency, so we can determine which host is closer.

Nmap is helpful when developing client-server applications, for example, when you want to see what ports are accessible on the server. However, nmap might miss application-specific ports, which are non-standard. To actually connect to a given port, we will be using telnet, which comes preinstalled on Ubuntu desktop. To see if a particular port accepts connections, just type the hostname, followed by the port:

```
telnet 192.168.0.1 80
```

```
          collisions:0 txqueuelen:0
          RX bytes:0 (0.0 B)  TX bytes:0 (0.0 B)

enp2s0    Link encap:Ethernet  HWaddr 20:89:84:f4:50:97
          UP BROADCAST MULTICAST  MTU:1500  Metric:1
          RX packets:0 errors:0 dropped:0 overruns:0 frame:0
          TX packets:0 errors:0 dropped:0 overruns:0 carrier:0
          collisions:0 txqueuelen:1000
          RX bytes:0 (0.0 B)  TX bytes:0 (0.0 B)

lo        Link encap:Local Loopback
          inet addr:127.0.0.1  Mask:255.0.0.0
          inet6 addr: ::1/128 Scope:Host
          UP LOOPBACK RUNNING  MTU:65536  Metric:1
          RX packets:679 errors:0 dropped:0 overruns:0 frame:0
          TX packets:679 errors:0 dropped:0 overruns:0 carrier:0
          collisions:0 txqueuelen:1
          RX bytes:73014 (73.0 KB)  TX bytes:73014 (73.0 KB)

wlp3s0    Link encap:Ethernet  HWaddr 68:17:29:bf:e2:67
          inet addr:192.168.0.159  Bcast:192.168.0.255  Mask:255.255.255.0
          inet6 addr: fe80::18e9:533a:d12f:82de/64 Scope:Link
          UP BROADCAST RUNNING MULTICAST  MTU:1500  Metric:1
          RX packets:23231 errors:0 dropped:0 overruns:0 frame:0
          TX packets:15862 errors:0 dropped:0 overruns:0 carrier:0
          collisions:0 txqueuelen:1000
          RX bytes:23244583 (23.2 MB)  TX bytes:2348670 (2.3 MB)

               [11:03:46 AM]
-> % nmap -sP 192.168.0.0/24

Starting Nmap 7.01 ( https://nmap.org ) at 2016-07-05 11:04 EEST
Nmap scan report for dlinkrouter (192.168.0.1)
Host is up (0.0047s latency).
Nmap scan report for 192-168-0-159.rdsnet.ro (192.168.0.159)
Host is up (0.000057s latency).
Nmap done: 256 IP addresses (2 hosts up) scanned in          seconds
               [11:04:08 AM]
-> % telnet 192.168.0.1 53
Trying 192.168.0.1...
Connected to 192.168.0.1.
Escape character is '^]'.
```

telnet 192.168.0.1 80

If the port is listening and accepts connections, telnet will output a message like this:

- Trying 192.168.0.1...
- Connected to 192.168.0.1
- Escape character is ^]

This means that you can also connect from your application. So if you are having difficulties connecting, it's usually a client problem; the server is working fine.

To get out of telnet, hit: *Ctrl +]*, followed by *Ctrl + d*.

Also, in some cases we need to get the ip address of a particular hostname. The simplest way to do this is to use the host command:

`host ubuntu.com`

```
              RX bytes:0 (0.0 B)  TX bytes:0 (0.0 B)

lo           Link encap:Local Loopback
             inet addr:127.0.0.1  Mask:255.0.0.0
             inet6 addr: ::1/128 Scope:Host
             UP LOOPBACK RUNNING  MTU:65536  Metric:1
             RX packets:679 errors:0 dropped:0 overruns:0 frame:0
             TX packets:679 errors:0 dropped:0 overruns:0 carrier:0
             collisions:0 txqueuelen:1
             RX bytes:73014 (73.0 KB)  TX bytes:73014 (73.0 KB)

wlp3s0       Link encap:Ethernet  HWaddr 68:17:29:bf:e2:67
             inet addr:192.168.0.159  Bcast:192.168.0.255  Mask:255.255.255.0
             inet6 addr: fe80::18e9:533a:d12f:82de/64 Scope:Link
             UP BROADCAST RUNNING MULTICAST  MTU:1500  Metric:1
             RX packets:23231 errors:0 dropped:0 overruns:0 frame:0
             TX packets:15862 errors:0 dropped:0 overruns:0 carrier:0
             collisions:0 txqueuelen:1000
             RX bytes:23244583 (23.2 MB)  TX bytes:2348670 (2.3 MB)
hacker@laptop [11:03:46 AM] [~/course]
-> % nmap -sP 192.168.0.0/24

Starting Nmap 7.01 ( https://nmap.org ) at 2016-07-05 11:04 EEST
Nmap scan report for dlinkrouter (192.168.0.1)
Host is up (0.0047s latency).
Nmap scan report for 192-168-0-159.rdsnet.ro (192.168.0.159)
Host is up (0.000057s latency).
Nmap done: 256 IP addresses (2 hosts up) scanned in 3.03 seconds
hacker@laptop [11:04:08 AM] [~/course]
-> % telnet 192.168.0.1 53
Trying 192.168.0.1...
Connected to 192.168.0.1.
Escape character is '^]'.
^\^]

telnet> Connection closed.
hacker@laptop [11:04:50 AM] [~/course]
-> % host ubuntu.com
ubuntu.com has address 91.189.94.40
ubuntu.com mail is handled by 10 mx.canonical.com.
hacker@laptop [11:05:02 AM] [~/course]
-> % 
```

We've learned only the basics, the minimum elements you need, in order to start working with hostnames and ports. For a deeper understanding of networks and package traffic, we recommend checking out courses on penetration testing or network traffic analyzing tools such as Wireshark. Here's one such course: `https://www.packtpub.com/networking-and-servers/mastering-wireshark`.

Autoenv – Set a lasting, project-based habitat

Projects are different from one another and so are environments. We might be developing an application on our local machine with certain environment variables like debug level, API keys, or memory size. Then we want to deploy the application to a staging or production server, which has other values for the same environment variables. A tool that comes in handy for loading environments on the fly is `autoenv`.

To install it we go to the official GitHub page and follow the instructions:

`https://github.com/kennethreitz/autoenv`

First we will clone the project in our home directory, and then we add the following line to our .zshrc config file, so that every time zsh starts, autoenv is loaded by default:

`source ~/.autoenv/activate.sh`

Now let's create an example workplace with two imaginary projects, project 1 and project 2.

We open an environment file for project 1:

`vim project1/.env`

Let's now imagine that project 1 uses an environment variable called ENV, which we will set to dev:

export ENV=dev

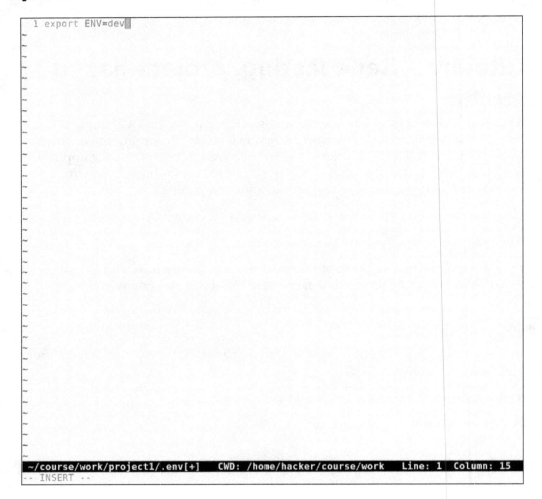

Now let's do the same thing for project 2, but with a different value for ENV; qa:

```
export ENV=qa
```

Save and close both files. Now when we cd in the project 1 folder, we see the following message:

```
autoenv:
autoenv: WARNING:
autoenv: This is the first time you are about to source /home/hacker/
course/work/project1/.env:
autoenv:
autoenv:      --- (begin contents) ----------------------------------
----
autoenv:      export ENV=dev$
autoenv:
autoenv:      --- (end contents) ------------------------------------
----
autoenv:
autoenv: Are you sure you want to allow this? (y/N)
```

Hit *y* to load the file. This happens every time a new environment file is sourced. Now if we grep the environment for the ENV variable, we can see it present and with a value of `dev`:

```
-> % source ~/.zshrc
hacker@laptop [10:03:53 AM] [~/course]
-> % mkdir work
hacker@laptop [10:04:01 AM] [~/course]
-> % cd work
hacker@laptop [10:04:02 AM] [~/course/work]
-> % mkdir project1 project 2
hacker@laptop [10:04:08 AM] [~/course/work]
-> % mkdir project1 project2
mkdir: cannot create directory 'project1': File exists
hacker@laptop [10:04:10 AM] [~/course/work]
-> % ls
2  project  project1  project2
hacker@laptop [10:04:14 AM] [~/course/work]
-> % rmdir 2 project
hacker@laptop [10:04:19 AM] [~/course/work]
-> % ks
zsh: command not found: ks
hacker@laptop [10:04:20 AM] [~/course/work]
-> % ls
project1  project2
hacker@laptop [10:04:21 AM] [~/course/work]
-> % vim project1/.env
hacker@laptop [10:04:45 AM] [~/course/work]
-> % vim project2/.env
hacker@laptop [10:04:58 AM] [~/course/work]
-> % cd project1
autoenv:
autoenv: WARNING:
autoenv: This is the first time you are about to source /home/hacker/course/work/project1/.env:
autoenv:
autoenv:     --- (begin contents) --------------------------------------
autoenv:     export ENV=dev$
autoenv:
autoenv:     --- (end contents) ----------------------------------------
autoenv:
autoenv: Are you sure you want to allow this? (y/N) y
hacker@laptop [10:05:14 AM] [~/course/work/project1]
-> % env | grep -i env
ENV=dev
_=/usr/bin/env
hacker@laptop [10:05:20 AM] [~/course/work/project1]
-> % ..█
```

Now let's change the directory to `project 2`:

```
-> % rmdir 2 project
                 [10:04:19 AM]
-> % ks
zsh: command not found: ks
                 [10:04:20 AM]
-> % ls
project1  project2
                 [10:04:21 AM]
-> % vim project1/.env
                 [10:04:45 AM]
-> % vim project2/.env
                 [10:04:58 AM]
-> % cd project1
autoenv:
autoenv: WARNING:
autoenv: This is the first time you are about to source /home/hacker/course/work/project1/.env:
autoenv:
autoenv:     --- (begin contents) -----------------------------------------
autoenv:     export ENV=dev$
autoenv:
autoenv:     --- (end contents) -------------------------------------------
autoenv:
autoenv: Are you sure you want to allow this? (y/N) y
                 [10:05:14 AM]
-> % env | grep -i env
ENV=dev
_=/usr/bin/env
                 [10:05:20 AM]
-> % ..
                 [10:05:25 AM]
-> % cd project2
autoenv:
autoenv: WARNING:
autoenv: This is the first time you are about to source /home/hacker/course/work/project2/.env:
autoenv:
autoenv:     --- (begin contents) -----------------------------------------
autoenv:     export ENV=qa$
autoenv:
autoenv:     --- (end contents) -------------------------------------------
autoenv:
autoenv: Are you sure you want to allow this? (y/N) y
                 [10:05:33 AM]
-> %
```

We can see that the same warning message is issued. And when we grep for the ENV variable, we now see that its value is qa. If we leave this folder, the environment variable is still defined, and will be defined until some other script overrides it or when the current session is closed. The .env file is sourced, even if we cd to a directory deeper inside project1.

Now let's look at a more complex example for project1.

Let's say we want to get the version from package.json, and we also want to use a variable called COMPOSE_FILE that will specify a different file for docker compose. Docker users know what it's all about, but if you don't.. Google time!

Here is an example:

```
export environment=dev
export version=`cat package.json | grep version | cut -f 4 -d "\""`
export COMPOSE_FILE=docker-compose.yml
```

For this to take effect, we need to first copy a `package.json` file, and test that the `cat` command works:

```
autoenv:       --- (end contents) -----------------------------------------
autoenv:
autoenv: Are you sure you want to allow this? (y/N) y
hacker@laptop [10:05:14 AM] [~/course/work/project1]
-> % env | grep -i env
ENV=dev
_=/usr/bin/env
hacker@laptop [10:05:20 AM] [~/course/work/project1]
-> % ..
hacker@laptop [10:05:25 AM] [~/course/work]
-> % cd project2
autoenv:
autoenv: WARNING:
autoenv: This is the first time you are about to source /home/hacker/course/work/project2/.env:
autoenv:
autoenv:       --- (begin contents) ----------------------------------------
autoenv:       export ENV=qa$
autoenv:
autoenv:       --- (end contents) -----------------------------------------
autoenv:
autoenv: Are you sure you want to allow this? (y/N) y
hacker@laptop [10:05:33 AM] [~/course/work/project2]
-> % env | grep -i env
ENV=qa
_=/usr/bin/env
hacker@laptop [10:05:40 AM] [~/course/work/project2]
-> % cd ..
hacker@laptop [10:05:43 AM] [~/course/work]
-> % env | grep -i env
ENV=qa
_=/usr/bin/env
hacker@laptop [10:05:44 AM] [~/course/work]
-> % vim project1/.env
hacker@laptop [10:06:58 AM] [~/course/work]
-> % cp ../find/electron/package.json project1
hacker@laptop [10:07:17 AM] [~/course/work]
-> % cat project1/package.json | grep version | cut -f 4 -d ""
  "version": "1.2.5",
hacker@laptop [10:07:25 AM] [~/course/work]
-> % cat project1/package.json | grep version | cut -f 4 -d "\""
1.2.5
hacker@laptop [10:07:45 AM] [~/course/work]
-> %
```

Everything seems fine, so let's `cd` into our folder:

```
autoenv:       --- (begin contents) ----------------------------------------
autoenv:       export ENV=qa$
autoenv:
autoenv:       --- (end contents) ------------------------------------------
autoenv:
autoenv: Are you sure you want to allow this? (y/N) y
                 [10:05:33 AM]
-> % env | grep -i env
ENV=qa
_=/usr/bin/env
                 [10:05:40 AM]
-> % cd ..
                 [10:05:43 AM]
-> % env | grep -i env
ENV=qa
_=/usr/bin/env
                 [10:05:44 AM]
-> % vim project1/.env
                 [10:06:58 AM]
-> % cp ../find/electron/package.json project1
                 [10:07:17 AM]
-> % cat project1/package.json | grep version | cut -f 4 -d ""
    "version": "1.2.5",
                 [10:07:25 AM]
-> % cat project1/package.json | grep version | cut -f 4 -d "\""
1.2.5
                 [10:07:45 AM]
-> % vim project1/.env
                 [10:07:57 AM]
-> % cd project1
autoenv:
autoenv: WARNING:
autoenv: This is the first time you are about to source /home/hacker/course/work/project1/.env:
autoenv:
autoenv:       --- (begin contents) ----------------------------------------
autoenv:       export ENV=dev$
autoenv:       export VERSION=`cat package.json | grep version | cut -f 4 -d "'"`$
autoenv:       export COMPOSE_FILE=docker-compose.yml$
autoenv:
autoenv:       --- (end contents) ------------------------------------------
autoenv:
autoenv: Are you sure you want to allow this? (y/N) ▌
```

And as you can see, the environment variables have been set:

```
LC_MONETARY=en_US.UTF-8
UPSTART_INSTANCE=
HOME=/home/hacker
QT_ACCESSIBILITY=1
ORBIT_SOCKETDIR=/tmp/orbit-hacker
XDG_SEAT_PATH=/org/freedesktop/DisplayManager/Seat0
XDG_DATA_DIRS=/usr/share/ubuntu:/usr/share/gnome:/usr/local/share/:/usr/share/:/var/lib/snapd/desktop
LANGUAGE=en_US
COMPIZ_BIN_PATH=/usr/bin/
COMPIZ_CONFIG_PROFILE=ubuntu
XDG_GREETER_DATA_DIR=/var/lib/lightdm-data/hacker
LANG=en_US.UTF-8
LC_NAME=en_US.UTF-8
GTK2_MODULES=overlay-scrollbar
GPG_AGENT_INFO=/home/hacker/.gnupg/S.gpg-agent:0:1
SHLVL=1
WINDOWID=67108868
XDG_VTNR=7
GDM_LANG=en_US
SESSIONTYPE=gnome-session
DBUS_SESSION_BUS_ADDRESS=unix:abstract=/tmp/dbus-hVrqUueOIv
XDG_CURRENT_DESKTOP=Unity
XDG_SESSION_TYPE=x11
GNOME_KEYRING_PID=
LC_TELEPHONE=en_US.UTF-8
QT_LINUX_ACCESSIBILITY_ALWAYS_ON=1
OLDPWD=/home/hacker/course/work/project1
ZSH=/home/hacker/.oh-my-zsh
PAGER=less
LESS=-R
LC_CTYPE=en_US.UTF-8
LSCOLORS=Gxfxcxdxbxegedabagacad
ENV=dev
defIFS=

answer=y                          I
VERSION=1.2.5
COMPOSE_FILE=docker-compose.yml
IFS=

_=/usr/bin/env
                 [10:08:36 AM]
-> % ▌
```

Autoenv can really come in handy, and is not limited to just exporting environment variables. You can do stuff like issuing a reminder when entering a certain project or running a git pull or updating the look and feel of the terminal so that a distinct feel is given for each project.

Don't rm the trash

Commands can be categorized as harmless or harmful. Most commands fall within the first category, but there is one that is very common and that has been known to produce a lot of damage in the world of computers. The dreaded command is rm, which has wiped out numerous hard drives, making precious volumes of data inaccessible. The Linux desktop has borrowed the concept of trash from other desktops and the default action when deleting a file is sending it to the Trash. Sending files there is a good practice, so that no unintentional removing is done. But this trash is no magic location; it's just a hidden folder, usually located in ~/.local.

In this part, we will be looking at a utility tool designed to work with trash. We will install it with:

```
sudo apt install trash-cli
```

This will install multiple commands. Let's look at our current directory that contains quite a few files. Let's assume we don't need the files starting with file.*

In order to remove files we will use:

trash filename

```
-> % sudo apt install trash-cli
Reading package lists... Done
Building dependency tree
Reading state information... Done
The following NEW packages will be installed:
  trash-cli
0 upgraded, 1 newly installed, 0 to remove and 6 not upgraded.
Need to get 22.2 kB of archives.
After this operation, 123 kB of additional disk space will be used.
Get:1 http://ro.archive.ubuntu.com/ubuntu xenial/universe amd64 trash-cli all 0.12.9.14-2 [22.2 kB]
Fetched 22.2 kB in 0s (48.5 kB/s)
Selecting previously unselected package trash-cli.
(Reading database ... 216874 files and directories currently installed.)
Preparing to unpack .../trash-cli 0.12.9.14-2_all.deb ...
Unpacking trash-cli (0.12.9.14-2) ...
Processing triggers for man-db (2.7.5-1) ...
Setting up trash-cli (0.12.9.14-2) ...
                [10:11:33 AM]
-> % ls
file1.html  file.html  file.json  file.txt  find  git         lorem.txt  secret_passwords.txt  sed         words.txt  work
                [10:11:37 AM]
-> % trash file.html file.json file.txt
                [10:11:53 AM]
-> % ls
file1.html  find  git         lorem.txt  secret_passwords.txt  sed         words.txt  work
                [10:11:55 AM]
-> %

                                    trash file.txt
```

(There is a separate command for working with the trash. We will rehash to reload our path.) We list all the trash commands. The command for listing the trash content is:

trash-list

```
-> % sudo apt install trash-cli
Reading package lists... Done
Building dependency tree
Reading state information... Done
The following NEW packages will be installed:
  trash-cli
0 upgraded, 1 newly installed, 0 to remove and 6 not upgraded.
Need to get 22.2 kB of archives.
After this operation, 123 kB of additional disk space will be used.
Get:1 http://ro.archive.ubuntu.com/ubuntu xenial/universe amd64 trash-cli all 0.12.9.14-2 [22.2 kB]
Fetched 22.2 kB in 0s (48.5 kB/s)
Selecting previously unselected package trash-cli.
(Reading database ... 216874 files and directories currently installed.)
Preparing to unpack .../trash-cli_0.12.9.14-2_all.deb ...
Unpacking trash-cli (0.12.9.14-2) ...
Processing triggers for man-db (2.7.5-1) ...
Setting up trash-cli (0.12.9.14-2) ...
hacker@laptop [10:11:33 AM] [~/course]
-> % ls
file1.html  file.html  file.json  file.txt  find  git  infinity.sh  lorem.txt  secret_passwords.txt  sed  test.sh  words.txt  work
hacker@laptop [10:11:37 AM] [~/course]
-> % trash file.html file.json file.txt
hacker@laptop [10:11:53 AM] [~/course]
-> % ls
file1.html  find  git  infinity.sh  lorem.txt  secret_passwords.txt  sed  test.sh  words.txt  work
hacker@laptop [10:11:55 AM] [~/course]
-> % rehash
hacker@laptop [10:12:09 AM] [~/course]
-> % trash-list
2016-06-28 10:11:53 /home/hacker/course/file.txt
2016-06-21 10:46:15 /home/hacker/a.js
2016-06-21 10:46:15 /home/hacker/a.html
2016-06-21 10:46:15 /home/hacker/script.sh
2016-06-21 10:46:16 /home/hacker/lib.sh
2016-06-28 10:11:53 /home/hacker/course/file.json
2016-06-28 10:11:53 /home/hacker/course/file.html
hacker@laptop [10:12:13 AM] [~/course]
-> %
```

Here we see the files that are in our trash. It is only showing the files that were put there with the trash command. We can see the date when they were deleted, the hour, and the exact location. If we'd have had multiple files with the same name and path, they would have been listed here, and we could have identified them by the deletion date.

In order to restore a file from trash we will use the command:

restore-trash

```
-> % sudo apt install trash-cli
Reading package lists... Done
Building dependency tree
Reading state information... Done
The following NEW packages will be installed:
  trash-cli
0 upgraded, 1 newly installed, 0 to remove and 6 not upgraded.
Need to get 22.2 kB of archives.
After this operation, 123 kB of additional disk space will be used.
Get:1 http://ro.archive.ubuntu.com/ubuntu xenial/universe amd64 trash-cli all 0.12.9.14-2 [22.2 kB]
Fetched 22.2 kB in 0s (48.5 kB/s)
Selecting previously unselected package trash-cli.
(Reading database ... 216874 files and directories currently installed.)
Preparing to unpack .../trash-cli_0.12.9.14-2_all.deb ...
Unpacking trash-cli (0.12.9.14-2) ...
Processing triggers for man-db (2.7.5-1) ...
Setting up trash-cli (0.12.9.14-2) ...
               [10:11:33 AM]
-> % ls
file1.html  file.html  file.json  file.txt  find  git            lorem.txt  secret_passwords.txt  sed         words.txt  work
               [10:11:37 AM]
-> % trash file.html file.json file.txt
               [10:11:53 AM]
-> % ls
file1.html  find  git            lorem.txt  secret_passwords.txt  sed         words.txt  work
               [10:11:55 AM]
-> % rehash
               [10:12:09 AM]
-> % trash-list
2016-06-28 10:11:53 /home/hacker/course/file.txt
2016-06-21 10:46:15 /home/hacker/a.js
2016-06-21 10:46:15 /home/hacker/a.html
2016-06-21 10:46:15 /home/hacker/script.sh
2016-06-21 10:46:16 /home/hacker/lib.sh
2016-06-28 10:11:53 /home/hacker/course/file.json
2016-06-28 10:11:53 /home/hacker/course/file.html
               [10:12:13 AM]
-> % restore-trash
   0 2016-06-28 10:11:53 /home/hacker/course/file.txt
   1 2016-06-28 10:11:53 /home/hacker/course/file.json
   2 2016-06-28 10:11:53 /home/hacker/course/file.html
What file to restore [0..2]:
```

It will show us a list of options and ask for a number corresponding to the file we want restored. In this case we will select 1, meaning we want to restore the json file.

We open the file and we can see that the content was not altered in the process.

In order to remove all the files in the trash, we use:

trash-empty

```
Fetched 22.2 kB in 0s (48.5 kB/s)
Selecting previously unselected package trash-cli.
(Reading database ... 216874 files and directories currently installed.)
Preparing to unpack .../trash-cli_0.12.9.14-2_all.deb ...
Unpacking trash-cli (0.12.9.14-2) ...
Processing triggers for man-db (2.7.5-1) ...
Setting up trash-cli (0.12.9.14-2) ...
hacker@laptop [10:11:33 AM] [~/course]
-> % ls
file1.html  file.html  file.json  file.txt  find  git  infinity.sh  lorem.txt  secret_passwords.txt  sed  test.sh  words.txt  work
hacker@laptop [10:11:37 AM] [~/course]
-> % trash file.html file.json file.txt
hacker@laptop [10:11:53 AM] [~/course]
-> % ls
file1.html  find  git  infinity.sh  lorem.txt  secret_passwords.txt  sed  test.sh  words.txt  work
hacker@laptop [10:11:55 AM] [~/course]
-> % rehash
hacker@laptop [10:12:09 AM] [~/course]
-> % trash-list
2016-06-28 10:11:53 /home/hacker/course/file.txt
2016-06-21 10:46:15 /home/hacker/a.js
2016-06-21 10:46:15 /home/hacker/a.html
2016-06-21 10:46:15 /home/hacker/script.sh
2016-06-21 10:46:16 /home/hacker/lib.sh
2016-06-28 10:11:53 /home/hacker/course/file.json
2016-06-28 10:11:53 /home/hacker/course/file.html
hacker@laptop [10:12:13 AM] [~/course]
-> % restore-trash
   0 2016-06-28 10:11:53 /home/hacker/course/file.txt
   1 2016-06-28 10:11:53 /home/hacker/course/file.json
   2 2016-06-28 10:11:53 /home/hacker/course/file.html
What file to restore [0..2]: 1
hacker@laptop [10:12:59 AM] [~/course]
-> % ls
file1.html  file.json  find  git  infinity.sh  lorem.txt  secret_passwords.txt  sed  test.sh  words.txt  work
hacker@laptop [10:13:01 AM] [~/course]
-> % vim fi
hacker@laptop [10:13:12 AM] [~/course]
-> % vim file.json
hacker@laptop [10:13:19 AM] [~/course]
-> % trash-empty
hacker@laptop [10:13:32 AM] [~/course]
-> %
```

This is the equivalent of doing `rm` in the first place. Now if we list the trash again, we see it doesn't have any content.

Although the internet is full of `rm -rf /` jokes, this is actually a serious issue that can cause headaches and wasted time trying to restore the damage caused. If you've been using `rm` for a long time and can't get into the habit of using trash, we suggest adding an alias for `rm` to actually run the trash command instead. In this case, it's a good idea to pile up stacks of files in trash than to risk removing a file that might be needed, before committing, or even removing the whole root partition!

5
Developers' Treasure

In this very chapter, we will kick start by building a web server using Python. We will then see how to process all our images automatically using ImageMagick. Then, we will look at the git flow branching model and how it will help you. Furthermore, we will see how meld command line can help merge our git conflicts. We will then focus on the working of ngrok tool and see how it saves the day by proxying requests coming from the internet to our laptop. We will also explore the versatile query capabilities of jq, the Swiss army knife of JSON! Towards the end, we will explore ways in which one can manage and kill Linux processes.

In this chapter, we will cover the following:

- Shrinking spells and other ImageMagick
- Understanding the work of git flow branching models
- Using ngrok to secure tunnels to localhost
- Getting yourself acquainted with jq

The spot webserver

We have prepared a basic demo `html` file that contains a button, a `div`, a `jquery` function (for helping us do some `ajax` calls), and a script that will try to load static content from our server and put the content inside the `div` tag. The script is trying to load a simple text file on the disk, `/file`:

```
hacker@laptop [10:37:40 AM] [~/course/web]
-> % pwd
/home/hacker/course/web
hacker@laptop [10:38:10 AM] [~/course/web]
-> % ls
file  index.html
hacker@laptop [10:38:15 AM] [~/course/web]
-> % cat index.html
<html>
<body>
    <button onclick="getFile()">Click me!</button>
    <div id="out">

    </div>

    <script src="https://ajax.googleapis.com/ajax/libs/jquery/1.12.4/jquery.min.js"></script>
    <script type="text/javascript" charset="utf-8">
        var getFile = function() {
            $.ajax({
               url: "/file",
               success: function( result ) {
                 $( "#out" ).html( "<strong>" + result + "</strong>" );

               }
            });
        }
    </script>
</body>
</html>
hacker@laptop [10:38:19 AM] [~/course/web]
-> %
```

If we open this file inside our browser, we can see the page content:

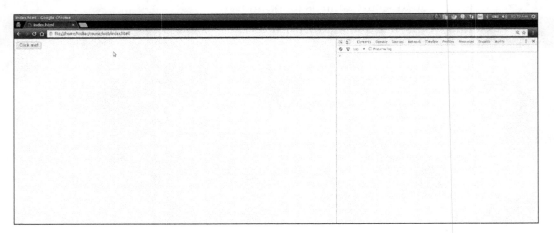

Clicking on the button generates a `javascript` error. It is telling us that we want to do a cross-origin request, which is not allowed by default by the browser. This is to prevent cross-site scripting attacks. What we need to do in order to test our `javascript` code is to serve this file in an HTTP server.

In order to start an HTTP server in the same folder as the file, we type the following command:

```
python -m SimpleHTTPServer
```

```
                [10:37:46 AM]
-> % pwd
/home/hacker/course/web
                [10:38:10 AM]
-> % ls
file  index.html
                [10:38:15 AM]
-> % cat index.html
<html>
<body>
    <button onclick="getFile()">Click me!</button>
    <div id="out">

    </div>

    <script src="https://ajax.googleapis.com/ajax/libs/jquery/1.12.4/jquery.min.js"></script>
    <script type="text/javascript" charset="utf-8">
        var getFile = function() {
            S.ajax({
                url: "/file",
                success: function( result ) {
                    $( "#out" ).html( "<strong>" + result + "</strong>" );

                }
            });
        }
    </script>
</body>
</html>
                [10:38:19 AM]
-> % cat file
Some file content
                [10:38:45 AM]
-> % python -m SimpleHTTPServer
Serving HTTP on 0.0.0.0 port 8000 ...

                        python -m SimpleHTTPServer
```

This is a basic Python module that opens port 8000 on localhost, serving only static content (so, no, you can't use it for php). Let's open the address in the browser:

Click on the **Click me!** button. We see that our file content was loaded in the div beneath the button, which means the browser is no longer blocking us, because we are issuing requests to the same host using the same protocol. Looking at the output from our Python server, we can see all the requests that the browser has made to the server. We can see it's requesting by default a favicon.ico file that doesn't exist and it's giving back a 404 status code:

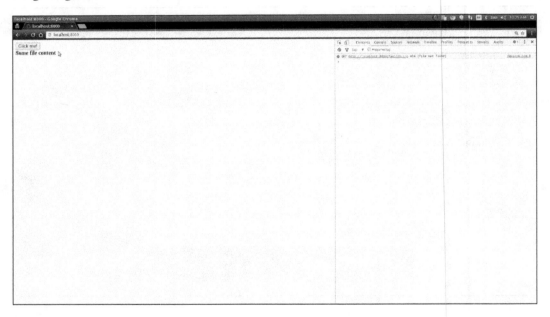

You can find the files used in this project on the GitHub project page.

Also, if we stop the server and go one level up and fire it up again, we can use it as a webdav server, with the possibility of navigating through the files in the current directory. We could, for example, give access to a folder on our local machine to a remote user and allow them to access it through a page in the browser, eliminating the need to install a file server.

Shrinking spells and other ImageMagick

In this chapter, we will learn how to process images from the command line. We will start with the most complex and widely used image command line interface processing toolkit called **ImageMagick**. To install it, run the following:

```
sudo apt install imagemagick
```

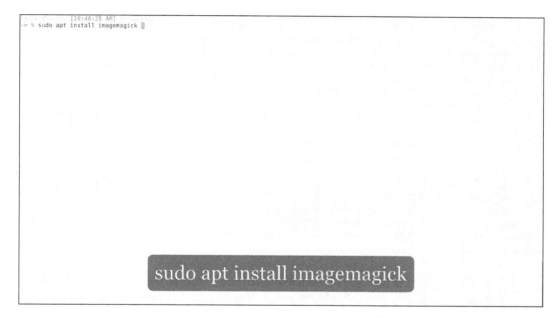

As you can see, we have already installed it.

Now, let's find some images to process. Let's use the default Ubuntu backgrounds that can be found in /usr/share/backgrounds. Let's copy the backgrounds to another location so that we don't alter our default ones.

We'll take a look at the first image in our list: we can see from `ls` that it is a JPEG image of 1.6 MB. To open it and see how it looks, let's use the **eog (eye of gnome)** image viewer:

```
hacker@laptop [10:48:25 AM] [~/course]
-> % sudo apt install imagemagick
[sudo] password for hacker:
Reading package lists... Done
Building dependency tree
Reading state information... Done
imagemagick is already the newest version (8:6.8.9.9-7ubuntu5.1).
imagemagick set to manually installed.
0 upgraded, 0 newly installed, 0 to remove and 6 not upgraded.
hacker@laptop [10:48:41 AM] [~/course]
-> % ls /usr/share/backgrounds
160218-deux-two_by_Pierre_Cante.jpg     Dans_ma_bulle_by_Christophe_Weibel.jpg    Spring_by_Peter_Apas.jpg
Black_hole_by_Marek_Koteluk.jpg         Flora_by_Marek_Koteluk.jpg                TCP118v1_by_Tiziano_Consonni.jpg
Cielo_estrellado_by_Eduardo_Diez_Viñuela.jpg   Icy_Grass_by_Raymond_Lavoie.jpg    The_Land_of_Edonias_by_Γιωργος_Αργυροπουλος.jpg
clock_by_Bernhard_Hanakam.jpg           Night_lights_by_Alberto_Salvia_Novella.jpg   warty-final-ubuntu.png
contest                                 passion_flower_by_Irene_Gr.jpg            Xerus_Wallpaper_Grey_4096x2304.png
hacker@laptop [10:48:57 AM] [~/course]
-> % cp /usr/share/backgrounds .
cp: omitting directory '/usr/share/backgrounds'
hacker@laptop [10:49:03 AM] [~/course]
-> % cp -r /usr/share/backgrounds .
hacker@laptop [10:49:06 AM] [~/course]
-> % cd backgrounds
hacker@laptop [10:49:08 AM] [~/course/backgrounds]
-> % ll
total 20M
-rw-r--r-- 1 hacker hacker 1.6M Jun 28 10:49 160218-deux-two_by_Pierre_Cante.jpg
-rw-r--r-- 1 hacker hacker 1.3M Jun 28 10:49 Black_hole_by_Marek_Koteluk.jpg
-rw-r--r-- 1 hacker hacker 1.3M Jun 28 10:49 Cielo_estrellado_by_Eduardo_Diez_Viñuela.jpg
-rw-r--r-- 1 hacker hacker 1.6M Jun 28 10:49 clock_by_Bernhard_Hanakam.jpg
drwxr-xr-x 2 hacker hacker 4.0K Jun 28 10:49 contest
-rw-r--r-- 1 hacker hacker 1.2M Jun 28 10:49 Dans_ma_bulle_by_Christophe_Weibel.jpg
-rw-r--r-- 1 hacker hacker 1.4M Jun 28 10:49 Flora_by_Marek_Koteluk.jpg
-rw-r--r-- 1 hacker hacker 1.6M Jun 28 10:49 Icy_Grass_by_Raymond_Lavoie.jpg
-rw-r--r-- 1 hacker hacker 1.1M Jun 28 10:49 Night_lights_by_Alberto_Salvia_Novella.jpg
-rw-r--r-- 1 hacker hacker 834K Jun 28 10:49 passion_flower_by_Irene_Gr.jpg
-rw-r--r-- 1 hacker hacker 1.5M Jun 28 10:49 Spring_by_Peter_Apas.jpg
-rw-r--r-- 1 hacker hacker 1.7M Jun 28 10:49 TCP118v1_by_Tiziano_Consonni.jpg
-rw-r--r-- 1 hacker hacker 1.6M Jun 28 10:49 The_Land_of_Edonias_by_Γιωργος_Αργυροπουλος.jpg
-rw-r--r-- 1 hacker hacker 2.6M Jun 28 10:49 warty-final-ubuntu.png
-rw-r--r-- 1 hacker hacker 783K Jun 28 10:49 Xerus_Wallpaper_Grey_4096x2304.png
hacker@laptop [10:49:10 AM] [~/course/backgrounds]
-> % ▓
```

The first and most important part of knowing how to process an image is knowing what that image actually is. To find this out, ImageMagick comes with a tool called **identify**. In its simplest form, you have to feed it an image name and it will output information like the following:

```
identify image_name
```

```
160218-deux-two_by_Pierre_Cante.jpg JPEG 3840x2400 3840x2400+0+0 8-bit
sRGB 1.596MB 0.240u 0:00.230
```

We can see that the file is a JPEG image of 1.6 MB and most importantly, its size is 3,840x2,400 pixels.

If we look at the `warty-final-ubuntu.png` we see that the output format is similar: the size and resolution are higher and the image format is PNG. Let's see what it looks like:

eog warty-final-ubuntu.png

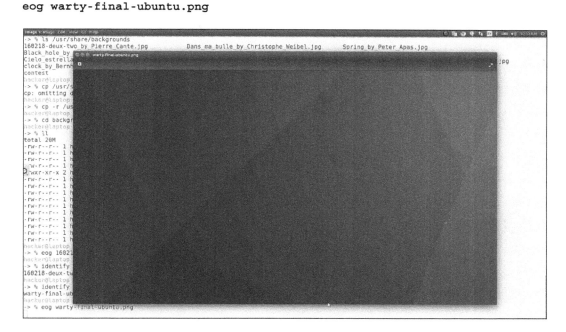

PNG images usually take more space than JPEG images. If you don't have transparency, it is recommended to use `.jpg`. In order to convert from one type to the other, we use the `imagemagick convert` command with two parameters: input filename and output filename:

```
convert file.png file.jpg
```

```
-> % ls /usr/share/backgrounds
160218-deux-two_by_Pierre_Cante.jpg       Dans_ma_bulle_by_Christophe_Weibel.jpg       Spring_by_Peter_Apas.jpg
Black_hole_by_Marek_Koteluk.jpg           Flora_by_Marek_Koteluk.jpg                   TCP118v1_by_Tiziano_Consonni.jpg
Cielo_estrellado_by_Eduardo_Diez_Viñuela.jpg  Icy_Grass_by_Raymond_Lavoie.jpg          The_Land_of_Edonias_by_Γιωργος_Αργυροπουλος.jpg
clock_by_Bernhard_Hanakam.jpg             Night_lights_by_Alberto_Salvia_Novella.jpg   warty-final-ubuntu.png
contest                                   passion_flower_by_Irene_Gr.jpg               Xerus_Wallpaper_Grey_4096x2304.png
hacker@laptop [10:48:57 AM] [~/course]
-> % cp /usr/share/backgrounds .
cp: omitting directory '/usr/share/backgrounds'
hacker@laptop [10:49:03 AM] [~/course]
-> % cp -r /usr/share/backgrounds .
hacker@laptop [10:49:06 AM] [~/course]
-> % cd backgrounds
hacker@laptop [10:49:08 AM] [~/course/backgrounds]
-> % ll
total 20M
-rw-r--r-- 1 hacker hacker 1.6M Jun 28 10:49 160218-deux-two_by_Pierre_Cante.jpg
-rw-r--r-- 1 hacker hacker 1.3M Jun 28 10:49 Black_hole_by_Marek_Koteluk.jpg
-rw-r--r-- 1 hacker hacker 1.3M Jun 28 10:49 Cielo_estrellado_by_Eduardo_Diez_Viñuela.jpg
-rw-r--r-- 1 hacker hacker 1.6M Jun 28 10:49 clock_by_Bernhard_Hanakam.jpg
drwxr-xr-x 2 hacker hacker 4.0K Jun 28 10:49 contest
-rw-r--r-- 1 hacker hacker 1.2M Jun 28 10:49 Dans_ma_bulle_by_Christophe_Weibel.jpg
-rw-r--r-- 1 hacker hacker 1.4M Jun 28 10:49 Flora_by_Marek_Koteluk.jpg
-rw-r--r-- 1 hacker hacker 1.6M Jun 28 10:49 Icy_Grass_by_Raymond_Lavoie.jpg
-rw-r--r-- 1 hacker hacker 1.1M Jun 28 10:49 Night_lights_by_Alberto_Salvia_Novella.jpg
-rw-r--r-- 1 hacker hacker 834K Jun 28 10:49 passion_flower_by_Irene_Gr.jpg
-rw-r--r-- 1 hacker hacker 1.5M Jun 28 10:49 Spring_by_Peter_Apas.jpg
-rw-r--r-- 1 hacker hacker 1.7M Jun 28 10:49 TCP118v1_by_Tiziano_Consonni.jpg
-rw-r--r-- 1 hacker hacker 1.6M Jun 28 10:49 The_Land_of_Edonias_by_Γιωργος_Αργυροπουλος.jpg
-rw-r--r-- 1 hacker hacker 2.6M Jun 28 10:49 warty-final-ubuntu.png
-rw-r--r-- 1 hacker hacker 783K Jun 28 10:49 Xerus_Wallpaper_Grey_4096x2304.png
hacker@laptop [10:49:10 AM] [~/course/backgrounds]
-> % eog 160218-deux-two_by_Pierre_Cante.jpg
hacker@laptop [10:49:39 AM] [~/course/backgrounds]
-> % identify 160218-deux-two_by_Pierre_Cante.jpg
160218-deux-two_by_Pierre_Cante.jpg JPEG 3840x2400 3840x2400+0+0 8-bit sRGB 1.596MB 0.140u 0:00.150
hacker@laptop [10:49:46 AM] [~/course/backgrounds]
-> % identify warty-final-ubuntu.png
warty-final-ubuntu.png PNG 4096x2304 4096x2304 ...
hacker@laptop [10:50:06 AM] [~/course/backgrounds]
-> % eog warty-final-ubuntu.png
hacker@laptop [10:50:27 AM] [~/course/backgrounds]
-> % convert warty-final-ubuntu.png warty-final-ubuntu.jpg
```

convert file.png file.jpg

The format of the output image will be deduced by `convert` from the filename extension. As you can see, the output is a JPEG image with the same resolution, but with a much smaller size than the PNG version: 180 KB compared to 2.6 MB. If we open the image, we can't see any noticeable differences. This is a big thing when it comes to web development, because if we were to use this picture on a web page, it would load as much as 15 times faster than the PNG version.

If we want to crop a region of the image, we can do that with convert. For example, if we want to cut a 500x500 piece of the image, starting at coordinates 100,100, we would use the following:

```
convert -crop "500x500+100+100" warty-final-ubuntu.png warty.jpg
```

As we can see, the output image is at the resolution we requested, but it has a much lower size of only 2.5 KB. Visually analyzing the two images we can see that the cropped one is a section of the big picture. Normally you wouldn't want to guess pixels in the command line, but would use an image processing software, such as GIMP, to do the work for you, so that you can visually select and crop portions of the images. However, when developing software applications, it is often the case that you have to programmatically crop images, in which case this comes in handy.

The `convert` command is also good at creating images. If we want to create an image from a text string, we could use the following:

```
convert -size x80 label:123 nr.jpg
```

```
160218-deux-two_by_Pierre_Cante.jpg JPEG 3840x2400 3840x2400+0+0 8-bit sRGB 1.596MB 0.140u 0:00.150
hackeratoptop [10:49:46 AM] [~/course/backgrounds]
-> % identify warty-final-ubuntu.png
warty-final-ubuntu.png PNG 4096x2304 4096x2304+0+0 8-bit sRGB 2.644MB 0.000u 0:00.000
hackeratoptop [10:50:06 AM] [~/course/backgrounds]
-> % eog warty-final-ubuntu.png
hackeratoptop [10:50:27 AM] [~/course/backgrounds]
-> % convert warty-final-ubuntu.png warty-final-ubuntu.jpg
hackeratoptop [10:50:39 AM] [~/course/backgrounds]
-> % ll
total 20M
-rw-r--r-- 1 hacker hacker 1.6M Jun 28 10:49 160218-deux-two_by_Pierre_Cante.jpg
-rw-r--r-- 1 hacker hacker 1.3M Jun 28 10:49 Black_hole_by_Marek_Koteluk.jpg
-rw-r--r-- 1 hacker hacker 1.3M Jun 28 10:49 Cielo_estrellado_by_Eduardo_Diez_Viñuela.jpg
-rw-r--r-- 1 hacker hacker 1.6M Jun 28 10:49 clock_by_Bernhard_Hanakam.jpg
drwxr-xr-x 2 hacker hacker 4.0K Jun 28 10:49 contest
-rw-r--r-- 1 hacker hacker 1.2M Jun 28 10:49 Dans_ma_bulle_by_Christophe_Weibel.jpg
-rw-r--r-- 1 hacker hacker 1.4M Jun 28 10:49 Flora_by_Marek_Koteluk.jpg
-rw-r--r-- 1 hacker hacker 1.6M Jun 28 10:49 Icy_Grass_by_Raymond_Lavoie.jpg
-rw-r--r-- 1 hacker hacker 1.1M Jun 28 10:49 Night_lights_by_Alberto_Salvia_Novella.jpg
-rw-r--r-- 1 hacker hacker 834K Jun 28 10:49 passion_flower_by_Irene_Gr.jpg
-rw-r--r-- 1 hacker hacker 1.5M Jun 28 10:49 Spring_by_Peter_Apas.jpg
-rw-r--r-- 1 hacker hacker 1.7M Jun 28 10:49 TCP118v1_by_Tiziano_Consonni.jpg
-rw-r--r-- 1 hacker hacker 1.6M Jun 28 10:49 The_Land_of_Edonias_by_Γιωργος_Αργυροπουλος.jpg
-rw-rw-r-- 1 hacker hacker 180K Jun 28 10:50 warty-final-ubuntu.jpg
-rw-r--r-- 1 hacker hacker 2.6M Jun 28 10:49 warty-final-ubuntu.png
-rw-r--r-- 1 hacker hacker 783K Jun 28 10:49 Xerus_Wallpaper_Grey_4096x2304.png
hackeratoptop [10:50:41 AM] [~/course/backgrounds]
-> % identify warty-final-ubuntu.jpg
warty-final-ubuntu.jpg JPEG 4096x2304 4096x2304+0+0 8-bit sRGB 184KB 0.000u 0:00.000
hackeratoptop [10:50:57 AM] [~/course/backgrounds]
-> % eog warty-final-ubuntu.png
hackeratoptop [10:51:21 AM] [~/course/backgrounds]
-> % convert -crop "500x500+100+100" warty-final-ubuntu.jpg warty.jpg
hackeratoptop [10:52:03 AM] [~/course/backgrounds]
-> % identify warty.jpg
warty.jpg JPEG 500x500 500x500+0+0 8-bit sRGB 2.5KB 0.000u 0:00.000
hackeratoptop [10:52:11 AM] [~/course/backgrounds]
-> % eog warty.jpg
hackeratoptop [10:52:32 AM] [~/course/backgrounds]
-> % convert -size x80 label:123 nr.jpg
hackeratoptop [10:52:56 AM] [~/course/backgrounds]
-> % █
```

This will create a JPEG image with a height of 80 pixels, containing the text specified, in this case the string `123`. We can see the output, it is a 3.4 KB image and, if we look at it visually, we see the text `123`:

This can also come in handy in different scenarios where you need to programmatically generate readable images, such as using CAPTCHA software or generating default profile images with the user's initials.

Now let's look at some image shrinking tools outside of `imagemagick`. The first one is a `png` shrinking tool called `pngquant`. We will install it by typing the following:

```
sudo apt install pngquant
```

```
-rw-r--r-- 1 hacker hacker 783K Jun 28 10:49 Xerus_Wallpaper_Grey_4096x2304.png
hacker@laptop [10:50:41 AM] [~/course/backgrounds]
-> % identify warty-final-ubuntu.jpg
warty-final-ubuntu.jpg JPEG 4096x2304 4096x2304+0+0 8-bit sRGB 184KB 0.000u 0:00.009
machine@laptop [10:50:57 AM] [~/course/backgrounds]
-> % eog warty-final-ubuntu.png
hacker@laptop [10:51:21 AM] [~/course/backgrounds]
-> % convert -crop "500x500+100+100" warty-final-ubuntu.jpg warty.jpg
hacker@laptop [10:52:03 AM] [~/course/backgrounds]
-> % identify warty.jpg
warty.jpg JPEG 500x500 500x500+0+0 8-bit sRGB 2.5KB 0.000u 0:00.000
hacker@laptop [10:52:11 AM] [~/course/backgrounds]
-> % eog warty.jpg
hacker@laptop [10:52:32 AM] [~/course/backgrounds]
-> % convert -size x80 label:123 nr.jpg
hacker@laptop [10:52:56 AM] [~/course/backgrounds]
-> % ll
total 20M
-rw-r--r-- 1 hacker hacker 1.6M Jun 28 10:49 160218-deux-two_by_Pierre_Cante.jpg
-rw-r--r-- 1 hacker hacker 1.3M Jun 28 10:49 Black_hole_by_Marek_Koteluk.jpg
-rw-r--r-- 1 hacker hacker 1.3M Jun 28 10:49 Cielo_estrellado_by_Eduardo_Diez_Viñuela.jpg
-rw-r--r-- 1 hacker hacker 1.6M Jun 28 10:49 clock_by_Bernhard_Hanakam.jpg
drwxr-xr-x 2 hacker hacker 4.0K Jun 28 10:49 contest
-rw-r--r-- 1 hacker hacker 1.2M Jun 28 10:49 Dans_ma_bulle_by_Christophe_Weibel.jpg
-rw-r--r-- 1 hacker hacker 1.4M Jun 28 10:49 Flora_by_Marek_Koteluk.jpg
-rw-r--r-- 1 hacker hacker 1.6M Jun 28 10:49 Icy_Grass_by_Raymond_Lavoie.jpg
-rw-r--r-- 1 hacker hacker 1.1M Jun 28 10:49 Night_lights_by_Alberto_Salvia_Novella.jpg
-rw-rw-r-- 1 hacker hacker 3.4K Jun 28 10:52 nr.jpg
-rw-r--r-- 1 hacker hacker 834K Jun 28 10:49 passion_flower_by_Irene_Gr.jpg
-rw-r--r-- 1 hacker hacker 1.5M Jun 28 10:49 Spring_by_Peter_Apas.jpg
-rw-r--r-- 1 hacker hacker 1.7M Jun 28 10:49 TCP118v1_by_Tiziano_Consonni.jpg
-rw-r--r-- 1 hacker hacker 1.6M Jun 28 10:49 The_Land_of_Edonias_by_Γιωργος_Αργυροπουλος.jpg
-rw-rw-r-- 1 hacker hacker 180K Jun 28 10:50 warty-final-ubuntu.jpg
-rw-r--r-- 1 hacker hacker 2.6M Jun 28 10:49 warty-final-ubuntu.png
-rw-rw-r-- 1 hacker hacker 2.5K Jun 28 10:52 warty.jpg
-rw-r--r-- 1 hacker hacker 783K Jun 28 10:49 Xerus_Wallpaper_Grey_4096x2304.png
hacker@laptop [10:52:59 AM] [~/course/ba
-> % identify nr.jpg
nr.jpg JPEG 126x80 126x80+0+0 8-bit Gray
hacker@laptop [10:53:14 AM] [~/course/ba        sudo apt install pngquant
-> % eog nr.jpg
hacker@laptop [10:53:28 AM] [~/course/backgrounds]
-> % sudo apt install pngquant
```

Let's try to shrink the large PNG image that we were looking at earlier. If the image contains transparency and it is necessary to keep it in the PNG format, we would just call `pngquant` with the following image name:

```
pngquant warty-final-ubuntu.png
```

```
-rw-r--r-- 1 hacker hacker 1.6M Jun 28 10:49 clock_by_Bernhard_Hanakam.jpg
drwxr-xr-x 2 hacker hacker 4.0K Jun 28 10:49 contest
-rw-r--r-- 1 hacker hacker 1.2M Jun 28 10:49 Dans_ma_bulle_by_Christophe_Weibel.jpg
-rw-r--r-- 1 hacker hacker 1.4M Jun 28 10:49 Flora_by_Marek_Koteluk.jpg
-rw-r--r-- 1 hacker hacker 1.6M Jun 28 10:49 Icy_Grass_by_Raymond_Lavoie.jpg
-rw-r--r-- 1 hacker hacker 1.1M Jun 28 10:49 Night_lights_by_Alberto_Salvia_Novella.jpg
-rw-rw-r-- 1 hacker hacker 3.4K Jun 28 10:52 nr.jpg
-rw-r--r-- 1 hacker hacker 834K Jun 28 10:49 passion_flower_by_Irene_Gr.jpg
-rw-r--r-- 1 hacker hacker 1.5M Jun 28 10:49 Spring_by_Peter_Apas.jpg
-rw-r--r-- 1 hacker hacker 1.7M Jun 28 10:49 TCP118v1_by_Tiziano_Consonni.jpg
-rw-r--r-- 1 hacker hacker 1.6M Jun 28 10:49 The_Land_of_Edonias_by_Γιωργος_Αργυροπουλος.jpg
-rw-rw-r-- 1 hacker hacker 180K Jun 28 10:50 warty-final-ubuntu.jpg
-rw-r--r-- 1 hacker hacker 2.6M Jun 28 10:49 warty-final-ubuntu.png
-rw-rw-r-- 1 hacker hacker 2.5K Jun 28 10:52 warty.jpg
-rw-r--r-- 1 hacker hacker 783K Jun 28 10:49 Xerus_Wallpaper_Grey_4096x2304.png
              [10:52:59 AM] ~/courses/backgrounds
-> % identify nr.jpg
nr.jpg JPEG 126x80 126x80+0+0 8-bit Gray 256c 3.44KB 0.000u 0:00.000
              [10:53:14 AM] ~/courses/backgrounds
-> % eog nr.jpg
              [10:53:28 AM] ~/courses/backgrounds
-> % sudo apt install pngquant
Reading package lists... Done
Building dependency tree
Reading state information... Done
The following NEW packages will be installed:
  pngquant
0 upgraded, 1 newly installed, 0 to remove and 6 not upgraded.
Need to get 35.4 kB of archives.
After this operation, 113 kB of additional disk space will be used.
Get:1 http://ro.archive.ubuntu.com/ubuntu xenial/universe amd64 pngquant amd64 2.5.0-1 [35.4 kB]
Fetched 35.4 kB in 0s (178 kB/s)
Selecting previously unselected package pngquant.
(Reading database ... 216898 files and directories currently installed.)
Preparing to unpack .../pngquant_2.5.0-1_amd64.deb ...
Unpacking pngquant (2.5.0-1) ...
Processing triggers for man-db (2.7.5-1) ..
Setting up pngquant (2.5.0-1) ...
              [10:53:48 AM] ~/courses/backgrounds
-> % rehash
              [10:53:55 AM] ~/courses/backgrounds
-> % pngquant warty-final-ubuntu.png

                    pngquant image_name
```

By default, it outputs a file with the same name and an added `fs8` extension. We can see that the difference in size is also noticeable (it's smaller by 1 MB, which is almost half the original size). If we visually compare the images, we won't be able to spot any differences:

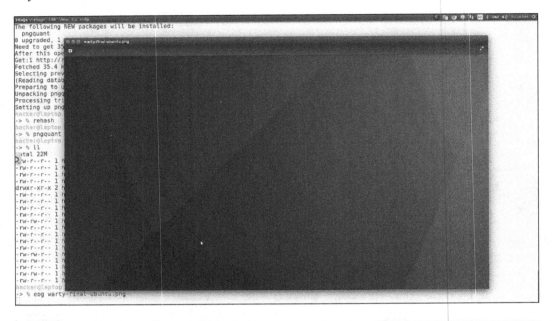

Alright, now let's try and do the same thing for JPEG images.

For this, we'll install the equivalent of `pngquant`, which is `jpegoptim`:

sudo apt install jpegoptim

```
The following NEW packages will be installed:
  pngquant
0 upgraded, 1 newly installed, 0 to remove and 6 not upgraded.
Need to get 35.4 kB of archives.
After this operation, 113 kB of additional disk space will be used.
Get:1 http://ro.archive.ubuntu.com/ubuntu xenial/universe amd64 pngquant amd64 2.5.0-1 [35.4 kB]
Fetched 35.4 kB in 0s (178 kB/s)
Selecting previously unselected package pngquant.
(Reading database ... 216898 files and directories currently installed.)
Preparing to unpack .../pngquant_2.5.0-1_amd64.deb ...
Unpacking pngquant (2.5.0-1) ...
Processing triggers for man-db (2.7.5-1) ...
Setting up pngquant (2.5.0-1) ...
                        [10:53:48 AM]
 > % rehash
                        [10:53:55 AM]
 -> % pngquant warty-final-ubuntu.png
                        [10:54:16 AM]
 -> % ll
total 22M
-rw-r--r-- 1 hacker hacker 1.6M Jun 28 10:49 160218-deux-two by Pierre Cante.jpg
-rw-r--r-- 1 hacker hacker 1.3M Jun 28 10:49 Black hole by Marek Koteluk.jpg
-rw-r--r-- 1 hacker hacker 1.3M Jun 28 10:49 Cielo estrellado by Eduardo Diez Viñuela.jpg
-rw-r--r-- 1 hacker hacker 1.6M Jun 28 10:49 clock by Bernhard Hanakam.jpg
drwxr-xr-x 2 hacker hacker 4.0K Jun 28 10:49 contest
-rw-r--r-- 1 hacker hacker 1.2M Jun 28 10:49 Dans ma bulle by Christophe Weibel.jpg
-rw-r--r-- 1 hacker hacker 1.4M Jun 28 10:49 Flora by Marek Koteluk.jpg
-rw-r--r-- 1 hacker hacker 1.6M Jun 28 10:49 Icy Grass by Raymond Lavoie.jpg
-rw-r--r-- 1 hacker hacker 1.1M Jun 28 10:49 Night lights by Alberto Salvia Novella.jpg
-rw-rw-r-- 1 hacker hacker 3.4K Jun 28 10:52 nr.jpg
-rw-r--r-- 1 hacker hacker 834K Jun 28 10:49 passion flower by Irene Gr.jpg
-rw-r--r-- 1 hacker hacker 1.5M Jun 28 10:49 Spring by Peter Apas.jpg
-rw-r--r-- 1 hacker hacker 1.7M Jun 28 10:49 TCP118v1 by Tiziano Consonni.jpg
-rw-r--r-- 1 hacker hacker 1.6M Jun 28 10:49 The Land of Edonias by Γιωργος Αργυροπουλος.jpg
-rw-rw-r-- 1 hacker hacker 1.6M Jun 28 10:54 warty-final-ubuntu-fs8.png
-rw-rw-r-- 1 hacker hacker 180K Jun 28 10:50 warty-final-ubuntu.png
-rw-r--r-- 1 hacker hacker 2.6M Jun 28 10:49 warty-final-ubuntu.png
-rw-rw-r-- 1 hacker hacker 2.5K Jun 28     sudo apt install jpegoptim
-rw-r--r-- 1 hacker hacker 783K Jun 28 1
                        [10:54:19 AM]
 -> % eog warty-final-ubuntu.png
                        [10:54:51 AM]
 -> % sudo apt install jpegoptim
```

We will call it the same way and we're just going to give it a command-line argument, which is the file to shrink. Let's pick some random images to try and see if we can reduce their size:

```
Get:1 http://ro.archive.ubuntu.com/ubuntu xenial/universe amd64 jpegoptim amd64 1.4.3-1 [18.4 kB]
Fetched 18.4 kB in 0s (88.8 kB/s)
Selecting previously unselected package jpegoptim.
(Reading database ... 216984 files and directories currently installed.)
Preparing to unpack .../jpegoptim_1.4.3-1_amd64.deb ...
Unpacking jpegoptim (1.4.3-1) ...
Processing triggers for man-db (2.7.5-1) ...
Setting up jpegoptim (1.4.3-1) ...
hacker@laptop [10:55:12 AM] [~/course/backgrounds]
-> % rehash
hacker@laptop [10:55:18 AM] [~/course/backgrounds]
-> % jpegoptim TCP118v1_by_Tiziano_Consonni.jpg
TCP118v1_by_Tiziano_Consonni.jpg 3840x2400 24bit N IPTC Exif ICC ICC ICC ICC XMP JFIF  [OK] 1773026 --> 1773026 bytes (0.00%), skipped.
hacker@laptop [10:55:30 AM] [~/course/backgrounds]
-> % ll
total 22M
-rw-r--r-- 1 hacker hacker 1.6M Jun 28 10:49 160218-deux-two_by_Pierre_Cante.jpg
-rw-r--r-- 1 hacker hacker 1.3M Jun 28 10:49 Black_hole_by_Marek_Koteluk.jpg
-rw-r--r-- 1 hacker hacker 1.3M Jun 28 10:49 Cielo_estrellado_by_Eduardo_Diez_Viñuela.jpg
-rw-r--r-- 1 hacker hacker 1.6M Jun 28 10:49 clock_by_Bernhard_Hanakam.jpg
drwxr-xr-x 2 hacker hacker 4.0K Jun 28 10:49 contest
-rw-r--r-- 1 hacker hacker 1.2M Jun 28 10:49 Dans_ma_bulle_by_Christophe_Weibel.jpg
-rw-r--r-- 1 hacker hacker 1.4M Jun 28 10:49 Flora_by_Marek_Koteluk.jpg
-rw-r--r-- 1 hacker hacker 1.6M Jun 28 10:49 Icy_Grass_by_Raymond_Lavoie.jpg
-rw-r--r-- 1 hacker hacker 1.1M Jun 28 10:49 Night_lights_by_Alberto_Salvia_Novella.jpg
-rw-rw-r-- 1 hacker hacker 3.4K Jun 28 10:52 nr.jpg
-rw-r--r-- 1 hacker hacker 834K Jun 28 10:49 passion_flower_by_Irene_Gr.jpg
-rw-r--r-- 1 hacker hacker 1.5M Jun 28 10:49 Spring_by_Peter_Apas.jpg
-rw-r--r-- 1 hacker hacker 1.7M Jun 28 10:49 TCP118v1_by_Tiziano_Consonni.jpg
-rw-r--r-- 1 hacker hacker 1.6M Jun 28 10:49 The_Land_of_Edonias_by_Гιωργος_Αργυροπουλος.jpg
-rw-r--r-- 1 hacker hacker 1.6M Jun 28 10:54 warty-final-ubuntu-fs8.png
-rw-rw-r-- 1 hacker hacker 180K Jun 28 10:50 warty-final-ubuntu.jpg
-rw-r--r-- 1 hacker hacker 2.6M Jun 28 10:50 warty-final-ubuntu.png
-rw-rw-r-- 1 hacker hacker 2.5K Jun 28 10:52 warty.jpg
-rw-r--r-- 1 hacker hacker 783K Jun 28 10:49 Xerus_Wallpaper_Grey_4096x2304.png
hacker@laptop [10:55:33 AM] [~/course/backgrounds]
-> % jpegoptim 160218-deux-two_by_Pierre_Cante.jpg
160218-deux-two_by_Pierre_Cante.jpg 3840x2400 24bit P JFIF  [OK] 1595515 --> 1595515 bytes (0.00%), skipped.
hacker@laptop [10:55:58 AM] [~/course/backgrounds]
-> % jpegoptim nr.jpg
nr.jpg 126x80 8bit N JFIF  [OK] 3442 --> 3442 bytes (0.00%), skipped.
hacker@laptop [10:56:03 AM] [~/course/backgrounds]
-> %
```

As you can see from the output, it is saying **Skipped**. That means the image had already been shrunk (the guys at Ubuntu probably used the same tool before submitting the image). If we try it again on the JPEG produced by imagemagick, you can see that it is also skipped: imagemagick already uses the minimum necessary format.

The image processing tools come in especially handy when it comes to web development, where lots of images need to be used and their size needs to be as small as possible. Command-line tools are really useful because they can be used to automate tasks. Image shrinking is usually added to build tasks, where production versions of websites are prepared. The imagemagick toolkit comes with a lot more tools than the ones we have seen today, so feel free to explore other handy commands from the toolkit. Also, when it comes to graphically processing the images, there are some great open source tools like GIMP and Inkscape that can really help you get your job done, and also save you a lot of money.

Go with the Git flow

Git is by far the most popular version control system out there. In this chapter, we will be looking at a plugin for Git, called **GitFlow**, which proposes a branching model for software projects. This branching model doesn't offer much help when it comes to small projects, but it's a great benefit to medium sized and large projects. We will be looking at a variation of the `git-flow` plugin, called `gitflow-avh`, which adds extra functionality, such as **Git hooks,** https://github.com/petervanderdoes/gitflow-avh.

To install it, we'll follow the instructions on the GitHub page. We are on Ubuntu, so we will follow the installation instructions for Linux.

We can see that it can be directly installed with the `apt` command, but apt doesn't usually contain the latest version of the software, so today we will do a manual installation. We want to pick the stable version, and use the one line command.

Once this is done, let's create a dummy project. We'll create an empty directory and initialize it as a Git repository:

```
git init
```

```
'gitflow/hooks/post-flow-bugfix-start' -> '/usr/local/share/doc/gitflow/hooks/post-flow-bugfix-start'
'gitflow/hooks/post-flow-bugfix-track' -> '/usr/local/share/doc/gitflow/hooks/post-flow-bugfix-track'
'gitflow/hooks/post-flow-feature-delete' -> '/usr/local/share/doc/gitflow/hooks/post-flow-feature-delete'
'gitflow/hooks/post-flow-feature-finish' -> '/usr/local/share/doc/gitflow/hooks/post-flow-feature-finish'
'gitflow/hooks/post-flow-feature-publish' -> '/usr/local/share/doc/gitflow/hooks/post-flow-feature-publish'
'gitflow/hooks/post-flow-feature-pull' -> '/usr/local/share/doc/gitflow/hooks/post-flow-feature-pull'
'gitflow/hooks/post-flow-feature-start' -> '/usr/local/share/doc/gitflow/hooks/post-flow-feature-start'
'gitflow/hooks/post-flow-feature-track' -> '/usr/local/share/doc/gitflow/hooks/post-flow-feature-track'
'gitflow/hooks/post-flow-hotfix-delete' -> '/usr/local/share/doc/gitflow/hooks/post-flow-hotfix-delete'
'gitflow/hooks/post-flow-hotfix-finish' -> '/usr/local/share/doc/gitflow/hooks/post-flow-hotfix-finish'
'gitflow/hooks/post-flow-hotfix-publish' -> '/usr/local/share/doc/gitflow/hooks/post-flow-hotfix-publish'
'gitflow/hooks/post-flow-hotfix-start' -> '/usr/local/share/doc/gitflow/hooks/post-flow-hotfix-start'
'gitflow/hooks/post-flow-release-branch' -> '/usr/local/share/doc/gitflow/hooks/post-flow-release-branch'
'gitflow/hooks/post-flow-release-delete' -> '/usr/local/share/doc/gitflow/hooks/post-flow-release-delete'
'gitflow/hooks/post-flow-release-finish' -> '/usr/local/share/doc/gitflow/hooks/post-flow-release-finish'
'gitflow/hooks/post-flow-release-publish' -> '/usr/local/share/doc/gitflow/hooks/post-flow-release-publish'
'gitflow/hooks/post-flow-release-start' -> '/usr/local/share/doc/gitflow/hooks/post-flow-release-start'
'gitflow/hooks/post-flow-release-track' -> '/usr/local/share/doc/gitflow/hooks/post-flow-release-track'
'gitflow/hooks/pre-flow-feature-delete' -> '/usr/local/share/doc/gitflow/hooks/pre-flow-feature-delete'
'gitflow/hooks/pre-flow-feature-finish' -> '/usr/local/share/doc/gitflow/hooks/pre-flow-feature-finish'
'gitflow/hooks/pre-flow-feature-publish' -> '/usr/local/share/doc/gitflow/hooks/pre-flow-feature-publish'
'gitflow/hooks/pre-flow-feature-pull' -> '/usr/local/share/doc/gitflow/hooks/pre-flow-feature-pull'
'gitflow/hooks/pre-flow-feature-start' -> '/usr/local/share/doc/gitflow/hooks/pre-flow-feature-start'
'gitflow/hooks/pre-flow-feature-track' -> '/usr/local/share/doc/gitflow/hooks/pre-flow-feature-track'
'gitflow/hooks/pre-flow-hotfix-delete' -> '/usr/local/share/doc/gitflow/hooks/pre-flow-hotfix-delete'
'gitflow/hooks/pre-flow-hotfix-finish' -> '/usr/local/share/doc/gitflow/hooks/pre-flow-hotfix-finish'
'gitflow/hooks/pre-flow-hotfix-publish' -> '/usr/local/share/doc/gitflow/hooks/pre-flow-hotfix-publish'
'gitflow/hooks/pre-flow-hotfix-start' -> '/usr/local/share/doc/gitflow/hooks/pre-flow-hotfix-start'
'gitflow/hooks/pre-flow-release-branch' -> '/usr/local/share/doc/gitflow/hooks/pre-flow-release-branch'
'gitflow/hooks/pre-flow-release-delete' -> '/usr/local/share/doc/gitflow/hooks/pre-flow-release-delete'
'gitflow/hooks/pre-flow-release-finish' -> '/usr/local/share/doc/gitflow/hooks/pre-flow-release-finish'
'gitflow/hooks/pre-flow-release-publish' -> '/usr/local/share/doc/gitflow/hooks/pre-flow-release-publish'
'gitflow/hooks/pre-flow-release-start' -> '/usr/local/share/doc/gitflow/hooks/pre-flow-release-start'
'gitflow/hooks/pre-flow-release-track' -> '/usr/local/share/doc/gitflow/hooks/pre-flow-release-track'
                    [11:04:12 AM]
-> % mkdir flow
                    [11:04:37 AM]
-> % cd flow
                    [11:04:39 AM]                    git init
-> % git init
Initialized empty Git repository in /home/hacker/course/flow/.git
                    [11:04:41 AM]                    [master]
-> % 
```

Basic Git usage is not part of this course, and we are assuming that you understand the basics.

All right. A good way to get started with `git-flow` is to read the excellent cheatsheet created by Daniel Kummer:

`http://danielkummer.github.io/git-flow-cheatsheet/`

This provides the basic tips and tricks to get you started quickly with `git-flow`. So the first thing the cheatsheet suggests is to run the following:

git flow init

```
'gitflow/hooks/post-flow-release-finish' -> '/usr/local/share/doc/gitflow/hooks/post-flow-release-finish'
'gitflow/hooks/post-flow-release-publish' -> '/usr/local/share/doc/gitflow/hooks/post-flow-release-publish'
'gitflow/hooks/post-flow-release-start' -> '/usr/local/share/doc/gitflow/hooks/post-flow-release-start'
'gitflow/hooks/post-flow-release-track' -> '/usr/local/share/doc/gitflow/hooks/post-flow-release-track'
'gitflow/hooks/pre-flow-feature-delete' -> '/usr/local/share/doc/gitflow/hooks/pre-flow-feature-delete'
'gitflow/hooks/pre-flow-feature-finish' -> '/usr/local/share/doc/gitflow/hooks/pre-flow-feature-finish'
'gitflow/hooks/pre-flow-feature-publish' -> '/usr/local/share/doc/gitflow/hooks/pre-flow-feature-publish'
'gitflow/hooks/pre-flow-feature-pull' -> '/usr/local/share/doc/gitflow/hooks/pre-flow-feature-pull'
'gitflow/hooks/pre-flow-feature-start' -> '/usr/local/share/doc/gitflow/hooks/pre-flow-feature-start'
'gitflow/hooks/pre-flow-feature-track' -> '/usr/local/share/doc/gitflow/hooks/pre-flow-feature-track'
'gitflow/hooks/pre-flow-hotfix-delete' -> '/usr/local/share/doc/gitflow/hooks/pre-flow-hotfix-delete'
'gitflow/hooks/pre-flow-hotfix-finish' -> '/usr/local/share/doc/gitflow/hooks/pre-flow-hotfix-finish'
'gitflow/hooks/pre-flow-hotfix-publish' -> '/usr/local/share/doc/gitflow/hooks/pre-flow-hotfix-publish'
'gitflow/hooks/pre-flow-hotfix-start' -> '/usr/local/share/doc/gitflow/hooks/pre-flow-hotfix-start'
'gitflow/hooks/pre-flow-release-branch' -> '/usr/local/share/doc/gitflow/hooks/pre-flow-release-branch'
'gitflow/hooks/pre-flow-release-delete' -> '/usr/local/share/doc/gitflow/hooks/pre-flow-release-delete'
'gitflow/hooks/pre-flow-release-finish' -> '/usr/local/share/doc/gitflow/hooks/pre-flow-release-finish'
'gitflow/hooks/pre-flow-release-publish' -> '/usr/local/share/doc/gitflow/hooks/pre-flow-release-publish'
'gitflow/hooks/pre-flow-release-start' -> '/usr/local/share/doc/gitflow/hooks/pre-flow-release-start'
'gitflow/hooks/pre-flow-release-track' -> '/usr/local/share/doc/gitflow/hooks/pre-flow-release-track'
hacker@laptop [11:04:12 AM] [~/course]
-> % mkdir flow
hacker@laptop [11:04:37 AM] [~/course]
-> % cd flow
hacker@laptop [11:04:39 AM] [~/course/flow]
-> % git init
Initialized empty Git repository in /home/hacker/course/flow/.git/
hacker@laptop [11:04:41 AM] [~/course/flow] (master)
-> % git flow init
No branches exist yet. Base branches must be created now.
Branch name for production releases: [master]
Branch name for "next release" development: [develop]

How to name your supporting branch prefixes?
Feature branches? [feature/]
Bugfix branches? [bugfix/]
Release branches? [release/]
Hotfix branches? [hotfix/]
Support branches? [support/]
Version tag prefix? []
Hooks and filters directory? [/home/hacker/course/flow/.git/hooks]
hacker@laptop [11:05:39 AM] [~/course/flow] (develop)
-> % 
```

To configure it, we need to answer a bunch of questions about what names the branches should have in each flow and what the version tag prefix and hooks directory are. Let's just leave the defaults. Now, let's run the following:

git branch

```
'gitflow/hooks/pre-flow-feature-delete' -> '/usr/local/share/doc/gitflow/hooks/pre-flow-feature-delete'
'gitflow/hooks/pre-flow-feature-finish' -> '/usr/local/share/doc/gitflow/hooks/pre-flow-feature-finish'
'gitflow/hooks/pre-flow-feature-publish' -> '/usr/local/share/doc/gitflow/hooks/pre-flow-feature-publish'
'gitflow/hooks/pre-flow-feature-pull' -> '/usr/local/share/doc/gitflow/hooks/pre-flow-feature-pull'
'gitflow/hooks/pre-flow-feature-start' -> '/usr/local/share/doc/gitflow/hooks/pre-flow-feature-start'
'gitflow/hooks/pre-flow-feature-track' -> '/usr/local/share/doc/gitflow/hooks/pre-flow-feature-track'
'gitflow/hooks/pre-flow-hotfix-delete' -> '/usr/local/share/doc/gitflow/hooks/pre-flow-hotfix-delete'
'gitflow/hooks/pre-flow-hotfix-finish' -> '/usr/local/share/doc/gitflow/hooks/pre-flow-hotfix-finish'
'gitflow/hooks/pre-flow-hotfix-publish' -> '/usr/local/share/doc/gitflow/hooks/pre-flow-hotfix-publish'
'gitflow/hooks/pre-flow-hotfix-start' -> '/usr/local/share/doc/gitflow/hooks/pre-flow-hotfix-start'
'gitflow/hooks/pre-flow-release-branch' -> '/usr/local/share/doc/gitflow/hooks/pre-flow-release-branch'
'gitflow/hooks/pre-flow-release-delete' -> '/usr/local/share/doc/gitflow/hooks/pre-flow-release-delete'
'gitflow/hooks/pre-flow-release-finish' -> '/usr/local/share/doc/gitflow/hooks/pre-flow-release-finish'
'gitflow/hooks/pre-flow-release-publish' -> '/usr/local/share/doc/gitflow/hooks/pre-flow-release-publish'
'gitflow/hooks/pre-flow-release-start' -> '/usr/local/share/doc/gitflow/hooks/pre-flow-release-start'
'gitflow/hooks/pre-flow-release-track' -> '/usr/local/share/doc/gitflow/hooks/pre-flow-release-track'
           [11:04:12 AM]
-> % mkdir flow
           [11:04:37 AM]
-> % cd flow
           [11:04:39 AM]
-> % git init
Initialized empty Git repository in /home/hacker/course/flow/.git/
           [11:04:41 AM]                [master]
-> % git flow init
No branches exist yet. Base branches must be created now.
Branch name for production releases: [master]
Branch name for "next release" development: [develop]

How to name your supporting branch prefixes?
Feature branches? [feature/]
Bugfix branches? [bugfix/]
Release branches? [release/]
Hotfix branches? [hotfix/]
Support branches? [support/]
Version tag prefix? []
Hooks and filters directory? [/home/hacker/course/flow/.git/hooks]
           [11:05:39 AM]                [develop]
-> % git branch
* develop
  master
           [11:05:44 AM]                [develop]
-> %
```

We can see that we are now on the develop branch, so no more developing on the master branch. This helps us have a stable master, while not so stable features are kept on the develop branch.

If we go back to the cheatsheet, we can look at the first item, which is a feature branch. Feature branches are useful when developing a specific part of functionality or doing refactoring, but you don't want to break the existing functionality on the develop branch. To create a feature branch, just run the following:

```
git flow feature start feature1
```

```
'gitflow/hooks/pre-flow-release-finish' -> '/usr/local/share/doc/gitflow/hooks/pre-flow-release-finish'
'gitflow/hooks/pre-flow-release-publish' -> '/usr/local/share/doc/gitflow/hooks/pre-flow-release-publish'
'gitflow/hooks/pre-flow-release-start' -> '/usr/local/share/doc/gitflow/hooks/pre-flow-release-start'
'gitflow/hooks/pre-flow-release-track' -> '/usr/local/share/doc/gitflow/hooks/pre-flow-release-track'
hacker@laptop [11:04:12 AM] [~/course]
-> % mkdir flow
hacker@laptop [11:04:37 AM] [~/course]
-> % cd flow
hacker@laptop [11:04:39 AM] [~/course/flow]
-> % git init
Initialized empty Git repository in /home/hacker/course/flow/.git/
hacker@laptop [11:04:41 AM] [~/course/flow] [master]
-> % git flow init
No branches exist yet. Base branches must be created now.
Branch name for production releases: [master]
Branch name for "next release" development: [develop]

How to name your supporting branch prefixes?
Feature branches? [feature/]
Bugfix branches? [bugfix/]
Release branches? [release/]
Hotfix branches? [hotfix/]
Support branches? [support/]
Version tag prefix? []
Hooks and filters directory? [/home/hacker/course/flow/.git/hooks]
hacker@laptop [11:05:39 AM] [~/course/flow] [develop]
-> % git branch
* develop
  master
hacker@laptop [11:05:44 AM] [~/course/flow] [develop]
-> % git flow feature start feature1
Switched to a new branch 'feature/feature1'

Summary of actions:
- A new branch 'feature/feature1' was created, based on 'develop'
- You are now on branch 'feature/feature1'

Now, start committing on your feature. When done, use:

     git flow feature finish feature1

hacker@laptop [11:06:10 AM] [~/course/flow] [feature/feature1]
-> % 
```

This is not the most intuitive description of the feature, but it's good for demonstration purposes. GitFlow will also show us a summary of actions once the feature branch has finished. This has created a new branch called feature/feature1, based on the develop branch and has switched us to that branch. We can also see this from our handy zsh prompt.

Let's open up a file, edit, and save it:

git status

```
How to name your supporting branch prefixes?
Feature branches? [feature/]
Bugfix branches? [bugfix/]
Release branches? [release/]
Hotfix branches? [hotfix/]
Support branches? [support/]
Version tag prefix? []
Hooks and filters directory? [/home/hacker/course/flow/.git/hooks]
                   [11:05:39 AM]                 [develop]
-> % git branch
* develop
  master
                   [11:05:44 AM]                 [develop]
-> % git flow feature start feature1
Switched to a new branch 'feature/feature1'

Summary of actions:
- A new branch 'feature/feature1' was created, based on 'develop'
- You are now on branch 'feature/feature1'

Now, start committing on your feature. When done, use:

     git flow feature finish feature1

                   [11:06:10 AM]                 [feature/feature1]
-> % git branch
  develop
* feature/feature1
  master
                   [11:06:22 AM]                 [feature/feature1]
-> % vim feature1.txt
                   [11:06:42 AM]                 [feature/feature1 *]
-> % git status
On branch feature/feature1
Untracked files:
  (use "git add <file>..." to include in what will be committed)

        feature1.txt                  git status

nothing added to commit but untracked files present (use "git add" to track)
                   [11:06:49 AM]                 [feature/feature1 *]
-> %
```

This command will tell us that we have an uncommitted file. Let's go ahead and commit it.

Now `git commit` is using the `nano` editor for editing the commit message. Since we prefer `vim`, let's go ahead and change the default editor to `vim`. All we need to do is add this line in our `zshrc` and reload it:

export EDITOR=vim

Now when we do a `git commit` Vim opens up, shows us a summary of the commit, and closes.

Now let's assume that we've finished adding a new feature. It's time to merge the feature branch back to develop with the following:

```
git flow feature finish feature1
```

```
  master
         [11:06:22 AM]            [feature/feature1]
-> % vim feature1.txt
         [11:06:42 AM]            [feature/feature1 *]
-> % git status
On branch feature/feature1
Untracked files:
  (use "git add <file>..." to include in what will be committed)

        feature1.txt

nothing added to commit but untracked files present (use "git add" to track)
         [11:06:49 AM]            [feature/feature1 *]
-> % git add feature1.txt
         [11:06:54 AM]            [feature/feature1 *]
-> % git commit
Aborting commit due to empty commit message.
         [11:07:07 AM]            [feature/feature1 *]
-> % vim ~/.zshrc
         [11:07:23 AM]            [feature/feature1 *]
-> % source ~/.zshrc
         [11:07:26 AM]            [feature/feature1 *]
-> % git commit
[feature/feature1 a1b83fe] Added feature 1
 1 file changed, 1 insertion(+)
 create mode 100644 feature1.txt
         [11:07:39 AM]            [feature/feature1]
-> % git flow feature finish feature1
Switched to branch 'develop'
Updating 628ec35..a1b83fe
Fast-forward
 feature1.txt | 1 ~
 1 file changed, 1 insertion(+)
 create mode 100644 feature1.txt
Deleted branch feature/feature1 (was a1b83fe).

Summary of actions:
- The feature branch 'feature/feature1' was merged into 'develop'
- Feature branch 'feature/feature1' has been locally deleted
- You are now on branch 'develop'
         [11:07:54 AM]            [develop]
-> % 
```

Again, to get a summary of actions:

- The feature branch was merged back to develop
- The feature branch has been deleted
- The current branch was switched back to develop

If we do an ls, we see the file from our branch present on the develop branch. Looking at the cheatsheet we see a graphical representation of this process.

Next up is starting a release. Release branches are good for stopping the incoming features and bug fixes from the develop branch, testing the current version, submitting bug fixes on it, and releasing it to the general public.

As we can see, the syntax is similar, the process is similar, the develop is branched to a release branch, but when it comes to finishing the branch, the features are also merged to the master branch, and a tag is cut from this branch. Time to see it in action:

```
git flow release start 1.0.0
```

```
-> % vim ~/.zshrc
                    [11:07:23 AM]                     [feature/feature1 *]
-> % source ~/.zshrc
                    [11:07:26 AM]                     [feature/feature1 *]
-> % git commit
[feature/feature1 a1b83fe] Added feature 1
 1 file changed, 1 insertion(+)
 create mode 100644 feature1.txt
                    [11:07:39 AM]                     [feature/feature1]
-> % git flow feature finish feature1
Switched to branch 'develop'
Updating 628ec35..a1b83fe
Fast-forward
 feature1.txt | 1 +
 1 file changed, 1 insertion(+)
 create mode 100644 feature1.txt
Deleted branch feature/feature1 (was a1b83fe).

Summary of actions:
- The feature branch 'feature/feature1' was merged into 'develop'
- Feature branch 'feature/feature1' has been locally deleted
- You are now on branch 'develop'

                    [11:07:54 AM]                     [develop]
-> % ls
feature1.txt
                    [11:08:09 AM]                     [develop]
-> % git flow release start 1.0.0
Switched to a new branch 'release/1.0.0'

Summary of actions:
- A new branch 'release/1.0.0' was created, based on 'develop'
- You are now on branch 'release/1.0.0'

Follow-up actions:
- Bump the version number now!
- Start committing last-minute fixes in preparing your release
- When done, run:

    git flow release finish '1.0.0'

                    [11:08:57 AM]                     [release/1.0.0]
-> %
```

This switches us over to our `release/1.0.0` branch. Let's add a `releasenotes.txt` file to show what has changed in this release. Added more bugs...Hopefully not!

Let's commit the file.

This is usually the case when you start to run your integration and stress testing, to see if all is well and to check that there are no bugs.

After the testing is finished, we go ahead and finish our release branch:

git flow release finish 1.0.0

```
- You are now on branch 'release/1.0.0'

Follow-up actions:
- Bump the version number now!
- Start committing last-minute fixes in preparing your release
- When done, run:

    git flow release finish '1.0.0'

hacker@laptop [11:08:57 AM] [~/course/flow] [release/1.0.0]
-> % vim releasenotes.txt
hacker@laptop [11:09:27 AM] [~/course/flow] [release/1.0.0 *]
-> % git add releasenotes.txt
hacker@laptop [11:09:33 AM] [~/course/flow] [release/1.0.0 *]
-> % git commit
[release/1.0.0 20389c4] Updated release notes
 1 file changed, 3 insertions(+)
 create mode 100644 releasenotes.txt
hacker@laptop [11:09:42 AM] [~/course/flow] [release/1.0.0]
-> % git flow release finish 1.0.0
Switched to branch 'master'
Merge made by the 'recursive' strategy.
 feature1.txt     | 1 +
 releasenotes.txt | 3 +++
 2 files changed, 4 insertions(+)
 create mode 100644 feature1.txt
 create mode 100644 releasenotes.txt
Switched to branch 'develop'
Merge made by the 'recursive' strategy.
 releasenotes.txt | 3 +++
 1 file changed, 3 insertions(+)
 create mode 100644 releasenotes.txt
Deleted branch release/1.0.0 (was 20389c4).

Summary of actions:
- Release branch 'release/1.0.0' has been merged into 'master'
- The release was tagged '1.0.0'
- Release tag '1.0.0' has been back-merged into 'develop'
- Release branch 'release/1.0.0' has been locally deleted
- You are now on branch 'develop'

hacker@laptop [11:10:06 AM] [~/course/flow] [develop]
-> %
```

It will prompt us for a series of release messages: we will leave all the defaults.

Checking out the summary, we can see that:

- The release branch was merged into master
- A tag was cut from master with the release version
- The tag has also been merged into develop
- The release branch has been deleted
- And we are back on the develop branch

Now, we run the following:

git branch

```
- Start committing last-minute fixes in preparing your release
- When done, run:

    git flow release finish '1.0.0'

                [11:08:57 AM]                  [release/1.0.0]
-> % vim releasenotes.txt
                [11:09:27 AM]                  [release/1.0.0 *]
-> % git add releasenotes.txt
                [11:09:33 AM]                  [release/1.0.0 *]
-> % git commit
[release/1.0.0 20389c4] Updated release notes
 1 file changed, 3 insertions(+)
 create mode 100644 releasenotes.txt
                [11:09:42 AM]                  [release/1.0.0]
-> % git flow release finish 1.0.0
Switched to branch 'master'
Merge made by the 'recursive' strategy.
 feature1.txt     | 1 +
 releasenotes.txt | 3 +++
 2 files changed, 4 insertions(+)
 create mode 100644 feature1.txt
 create mode 100644 releasenotes.txt
Switched to branch 'develop'
Merge made by the 'recursive' strategy.
 releasenotes.txt | 3 +++
 1 file changed, 3 insertions(+)
 create mode 100644 releasenotes.txt
Deleted branch release/1.0.0 (was 20389c4).

Summary of actions:
- Release branch 'release/1.0.0' has been merged into 'master'
- The release was tagged '1.0.0'
- Release tag '1.0.0' has been back-merged into 'develop'
- Release branch 'release/1.0.0' has been locally deleted
- You are now on branch 'develop'

                [11:10:06 AM]                  [develop]
-> % git branch
* develop
  master
                [11:10:35 AM]                  [develop]
-> % █
```

We see that the only two available branches are master and develop:

git tag

```
     git flow release finish '1.0.0'
hacker@laptop [11:08:57 AM] [~/course/flow] [release/1.0.0]
-> % vim releasenotes.txt
hacker@laptop [11:09:27 AM] [~/course/flow] [release/1.0.0 *]
-> % git add releasenotes.txt
hacker@laptop [11:09:33 AM] [~/course/flow] [release/1.0.0 *]
-> % git commit
[release/1.0.0 20389c4] Updated release notes
 1 file changed, 3 insertions(+)
 create mode 100644 releasenotes.txt
hacker@laptop [11:09:42 AM] [~/course/flow] [release/1.0.0]
-> % git flow release finish 1.0.0
Switched to branch 'master'
Merge made by the 'recursive' strategy.
 feature1.txt     | 1 +
 releasenotes.txt | 3 ++-
 2 files changed, 4 insertions(+)
 create mode 100644 feature1.txt
 create mode 100644 releasenotes.txt
Switched to branch 'develop'
Merge made by the 'recursive' strategy.
 releasenotes.txt | 3 ++-
 1 file changed, 3 insertions(+)
 create mode 100644 releasenotes.txt
Deleted branch release/1.0.0 (was 20389c4).

Summary of actions:
- Release branch 'release/1.0.0' has been merged into 'master'
- The release was tagged '1.0.0'
- Release tag '1.0.0' has been back-merged into 'develop'
- Release branch 'release/1.0.0' has been locally deleted
- You are now on branch 'develop'

hacker@laptop [11:10:06 AM] [~/course/flow] [develop]
-> % git branch
* develop
  master
hacker@laptop [11:10:35 AM] [~/course/flow] [develop]
-> % git tag
1.0.0
hacker@laptop [11:10:38 AM] [~/course/flow] [develop]
-> % 
```

This tells us that there is a 1.0.0 tag cut. We can see that the branch now contains two files from the merge of the feature and release branch; and if we also switch to the master branch, we can see that, at this point, master is an exact replica of develop:

```
1 file changed, 3 insertions(+)
 create mode 100644 releasenotes.txt
               [11:09:42 AM]              [release/1.0.0]
-> % git flow release finish 1.0.0
Switched to branch 'master'
Merge made by the 'recursive' strategy.
 feature1.txt     | 1 +
 releasenotes.txt | 3 +++
 2 files changed, 4 insertions(+)
 create mode 100644 feature1.txt
 create mode 100644 releasenotes.txt
Switched to branch 'develop'
Merge made by the 'recursive' strategy.
 releasenotes.txt | 3 +++
 1 file changed, 3 insertions(+)
 create mode 100644 releasenotes.txt
Deleted branch release/1.0.0 (was 20389c4).

Summary of actions:
- Release branch 'release/1.0.0' has been merged into 'master'
- The release was tagged '1.0.0'
- Release tag '1.0.0' has been back-merged into 'develop'
- Release branch 'release/1.0.0' has been locally deleted
- You are now on branch 'develop'

               [11:10:06 AM]              [develop]
-> % git branch
* develop
  master
               [11:10:35 AM]              [develop]
-> % git tag
1.0.0
               [11:10:38 AM]              [develop]
-> % ls
feature1.txt  releasenotes.txt
               [11:10:42 AM]              [develop]
-> % git checkout master
Switched to branch 'master'
               [11:10:47 AM]              [master]
-> % ls
feature1.txt  releasenotes.txt
               [11:10:48 AM]              [master]
-> %
```

GitFlow also comes with an enhanced hooks functionality. If we read the documentation, we can see all the possible hooks in the hooks folder. Let's add a git hook that will be executed before every hotfix branch. For this we just open the template, copy the content, and paste it to a file with the name pre-flow-hotfix-start in our .git/hooks directory.

GitFlow has more workflows than the ones presented. We won't go through all of them, but you can find additional information by visiting the cheatsheet page or by reading the instructions on the GitHub page.

Let's just simply echo a message with the version and origin.

If we look at the hotfix flow, we can see that they are created from the master branch and merged back to master and develop, with a tag on master.

Let's see if it works:

git flow hotfix start 1.0.1

```
Summary of actions:
- Release branch 'release/1.0.0' has been merged into 'master'
- The release was tagged '1.0.0'
- Release tag '1.0.0' has been back-merged into 'develop'
- Release branch 'release/1.0.0' has been locally deleted
- You are now on branch 'develop'

hacker@laptop [11:10:06 AM] [~/course/flow] [develop]
-> % git branch
* develop
  master
hacker@laptop [11:10:35 AM] [~/course/flow] [develop]
-> % git tag
1.0.0
hacker@laptop [11:10:38 AM] [~/course/flow] [develop]
-> % ls
feature1.txt  releasenotes.txt
hacker@laptop [11:10:42 AM] [~/course/flow] [develop]
-> % git checkout master
Switched to branch 'master'
hacker@laptop [11:10:47 AM] [~/course/flow] [master]
-> % ls
feature1.txt  releasenotes.txt
hacker@laptop [11:10:48 AM] [~/course/flow] [master]
-> % vim .git/hooks/pre-flow-hotfix-start
hacker@laptop [11:12:49 AM] [~/course/flow] [master]
-> % git flow hotfix start 1.0.1
Switched to a new branch 'hotfix/1.0.1'

Summary of actions:
- A new branch 'hotfix/1.0.1' was created, based on 'master'
- You are now on branch 'hotfix/1.0.1'

Follow-up actions:
- Start committing your hot fixes
- Bump the version number now!
- When done, run:

    git flow hotfix finish '1.0.1'

hacker@laptop [11:13:17 AM] [~/course/flow] [hotfix/1.0.1]
-> %
```

Apparently not. Something went wrong, our script was not executed and we need to delete our branch:

`git flow hotfix delete 1.0.1`

```
-> % git branch
* develop
  master
                [11:10:35 AM]               |develop|
-> % git tag
1.0.0
                [11:10:38 AM]               |develop|
-> % ls
feature1.txt  releasenotes.txt
                [11:10:42 AM]               |develop|
-> % git checkout master
Switched to branch 'master'
                [11:10:47 AM]               |master|
-> % ls
feature1.txt  releasenotes.txt
                [11:10:48 AM]               |master|
-> % vim .git/hooks/pre-flow-hotfix-start
                [11:12:49 AM]               |master|
-> % git flow hotfix start 1.0.1
Switched to a new branch 'hotfix/1.0.1'

Summary of actions:
- A new branch 'hotfix/1.0.1' was created, based on 'master'
- You are now on branch 'hotfix/1.0.1'

Follow-up actions:
- Start committing your hot fixes
- Bump the version number now!
- When done, run:

     git flow hotfix finish '1.0.1'

                [11:13:17 AM]               [hotfix/1.0.1]
-> % git flow hotfix delete 1.0.1
Switched to branch 'master'
Deleted branch hotfix/1.0.1 (was e4d8d51).

Summary of actions:
- Hotfix branch 'hotfix/1.0.1' has been deleted.
- You are now on branch 'master'

                [11:13:52 AM]               [master]
-> %
```

Analyzing the `git hooks` directory, we see that our hook does not have execution permissions. After adding execution permissions, and running the `git hook` command again, we can see our message on the top of the hotfix output. Let's finish this hotfix with the following:

`git flow hotfix finish 1.0.1`

```
-> % ll .git/hooks
total 44K
-rwxrwxr-x 1 hacker hacker  478 Jun 28 11:04 applymsg-msg.sample
-rwxrwxr-x 1 hacker hacker  896 Jun 28 11:04 commit-msg.sample
-rwxrwxr-x 1 hacker hacker  189 Jun 28 11:04 post-update.sample
-rwxrwxr-x 1 hacker hacker  424 Jun 28 11:04 pre-applypatch.sample
-rwxrwxr-x 1 hacker hacker 1.7K Jun 28 11:04 pre-commit.sample
-rw-rw-r-- 1 hacker hacker  632 Jun 28 11:12 pre-flow-hotfix-start
-rwxrwxr-x 1 hacker hacker 1.3K Jun 28 11:04 prepare-commit-msg.sample
-rwxrwxr-x 1 hacker hacker 1.4K Jun 28 11:04 pre-push.sample
-rwxrwxr-x 1 hacker hacker 4.8K Jun 28 11:04 pre-rebase.sample
-rwxrwxr-x 1 hacker hacker 3.6K Jun 28 11:04 update.sample
hacker@laptop [11:14:04 AM] ~/course/flow [master]
-> % chmod +x .git/hooks/pre-flow-hotfix-start
hacker@laptop [11:14:20 AM] ~/course/flow [master]
-> % git flow hotfix start 1.0.1
This is a hotfix for 1.0.1 from origin
Switched to a new branch 'hotfix/1.0.1'

Summary of actions:
- A new branch 'hotfix/1.0.1' was created, based on 'master'
- You are now on branch 'hotfix/1.0.1'

Follow-up actions:
- Start committing your hot fixes
- Bump the version number now!
- When done, run:

     git flow hotfix finish '1.0.1'

hacker@laptop [11:14:28 AM] ~/course/flow [hotfix/1.0.1]
-> % git flow hotfix finish 1.0.1
Switched to branch 'develop'
Deleted branch hotfix/1.0.1 (was e4d8d51).

Summary of actions:
- Hotfix branch 'hotfix/1.0.1' has been merged into 'master'
- The hotfix was tagged '1.0.1'
- Hotfix branch 'hotfix/1.0.1' has been locally deleted
- You are now on branch 'develop'

hacker@laptop [11:14:53 AM] ~/course/flow [develop]
-> %
```

As you can see, the commands are quite straightforward. There is also an `oh-my-zsh` plugin that you can activate to have command line completion.

As we said earlier, this is a plugin suitable for teams of developers working on multiple features, fixing bugs, and releasing hotfixes all at the same time. GitFlow is simple to learn, and helps teams have a correct workflow where they can easily prepare patches for production code, without worrying about the extra functionalities developed on the master branch.

You can tweak the `config` as you like: some people prefer to place the `hooks` folder in a different place so that it is committed on the `git repo` and they don't have to worry about copying the files over; others continue to develop on the master branch and use a separate branch such as customer for the production code.

Merging Git conflicts with ease

Now let's look at another improvement that we can bring to `git`. Most tasks are easy to execute from the command line, but some tasks, such as merging, require a specialist's eye for understanding the different format.

Let's open the `feature` file from our previous chapter, edit it, add a new line, and save it:

git diff

git diff

The `git diff` command will show us colored text explaining the differences between the `git` file and the modified file, but some people find this format hard to understand:

```
diff --git a/feature1.txt b/feature1.txt
index 814c83c..b9d3702 100644
--- a/feature1.txt
+++ b/feature1.txt
@@ -1 +1,2 @@
-File created in feature 1
+File created in feature 2
+And new line
(END)
```

git diff

Luckily, we can tell `git` to use external tools when it comes to merge and one external tool that we can use is called **Meld**. Let's install it using the following:

```
sudo apt install meld
```

```
                    [11:17:15 AM]                    [develop]
-> % ls
feature1.txt  releasenotes.txt
                    [11:17:30 AM]                    [develop]
-> % vim feature1.txt
                    [11:17:43 AM]                    [develop *]
-> % git diff
                    [11:17:55 AM]                    [develop *]
-> % sudo apt install meld
```

After this, we can run the following command:

`git difftool`

```
Reading package lists... Done
Building dependency tree
Reading state information... Done
The following additional packages will be installed:
  python-gi-cairo
The following NEW packages will be installed:
  meld python-gi-cairo
0 upgraded, 2 newly installed, 0 to remove and 6 not upgraded.
Need to get 463 kB of archives.
After this operation, 3,007 kB of additional disk space will be used.
Do you want to continue? [Y/n]
Get:1 http://ro.archive.ubuntu.com/ubuntu xenial/universe amd64 python-gi-cairo amd64 3.20.0-0ubuntu1 [6,246 B]
Get:2 http://ro.archive.ubuntu.com/ubuntu xenial/universe amd64 meld all 3.14.2-1 [457 kB]
Fetched 463 kB in 0s (917 kB/s)
Selecting previously unselected package python-gi-cairo.
(Reading database ... 216911 files and directories currently installed.)
Preparing to unpack .../python-gi-cairo 3.20.0-0ubuntu1 amd64.deb ...
Unpacking python-gi-cairo (3.20.0-0ubuntu1) ...
Selecting previously unselected package meld.
Preparing to unpack .../archives/meld_3.14.2-1_all.deb ...
Unpacking meld (3.14.2-1) ...
Processing triggers for hicolor-icon-theme (0.15-0ubuntu1) ...
Processing triggers for shared-mime-info (1.5-2ubuntu0.1) ...
Processing triggers for man-db (2.7.5-1) ...
Processing triggers for libglib2.0-0:amd64 (2.48.1-1-ubuntu16.04.1) ...
Processing triggers for bamfdaemon (0.5.3~bzr0+16.04.20160523-0ubuntu1) ...
Rebuilding /usr/share/applications/bamf-2.index...
Processing triggers for gnome-menus (3.13.3-6ubuntu3) ...
Processing triggers for desktop-file-utils (0.22-1ubuntu5) ...
Processing triggers for mime-support (3.59ubuntu1) ...
Setting up python-gi-cairo (3.20.0-0ubuntu1) ...
Setting up meld (3.14.2-1) ...
hacker@laptop [11:18:08 AM] [~/course/flow] [develop *]
-> % git difftool

This message is displayed because 'diff.tool' is not configured.
See 'git difftool --tool-help' or 'git help config' for more details.
'git difftool' will now attempt to use one of the following tools:
meld opendiff kdiff3 tkdiff xxdiff kompare gvimdiff diffuse diffmerge ecmerge p4merge araxis bc codecompare vimdiff emerge

Viewing (1/1): 'feature1.txt'
Launch 'meld' [Y/n]:
```

It will ask us if we want to launch Meld as an external program for viewing the file. It's also giving us a list of tools that it can use for displaying the difference. Hit y to open Meld:

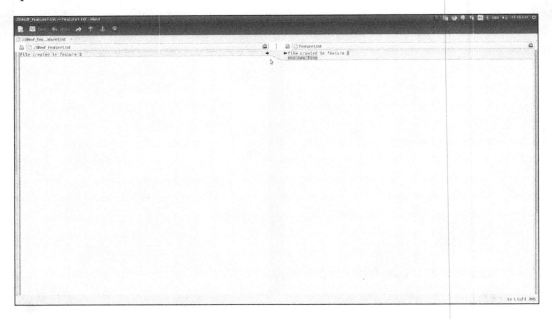

Now we can easily see the two files side by side and the differences between them. We can see that 1 has been changed to 2 and a new line has been added. Based on this output we can easily decide if we want to add it or not. Let's commit the file as it is.

Next, we will look at merge conflicts. Let's manually create a branch called **test** and **edit** the same file, commit it, and then switch back to the develop branch. Let's update the same file, commit it, and then try to merge the test branch: and, of course, there is a merge conflict.

For resolving the conflict, we will be using the following command:

`git mergetool`

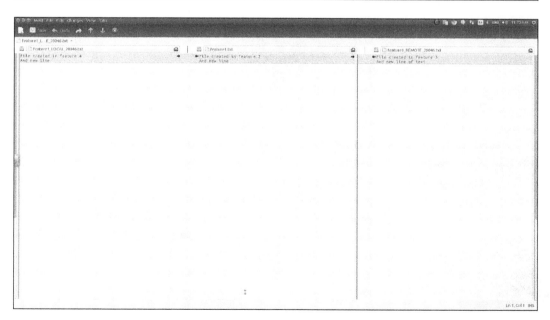

Again, it offers to open Meld. In Meld we can see the three files:

- On the left is the file from our current branch
- On the right is the file from the remote branch
- In the middle is the resulting file that will be created

Let's say that we decide the correct version for the feature is 4 and that we also want to add of text:

git commit -a

```
hackers@laptop [11:20:17 AM] [~/course/flow] [develop *]
-> % git commit feature1.txt
[develop 8bb82c9] Updated feature
 1 file changed, 1 insertion(+), 1 deletion(-)
hackers@laptop [11:20:27 AM] [~/course/flow] [develop]
-> % git merge test
Auto-merging feature1.txt
CONFLICT (content): Merge conflict in feature1.txt
Automatic merge failed; fix conflicts and then commit the result.
hackers@laptop [11:20:34 AM] [~/course/flow] [develop *]
-> % git mergetool

This message is displayed because 'merge.tool' is not configured.
See 'git mergetool --tool-help' or 'git help config' for more details.
'git mergetool' will now attempt to use one of the following tools:
meld opendiff kdiff3 tkdiff xxdiff tortoisemerge gvimdiff diffuse diffmerge ecmerge p4merge araxis bc codecompare vimdiff emerge
Merging:
feature1.txt

Normal merge conflict for 'feature1.txt':
  {local}: modified file
  {remote}: modified file
Hit return to start merge resolution tool (meld):

(meld:20118): Gtk-CRITICAL **: gtk_container_foreach: assertion 'GTK_IS_CONTAINER (container)' failed

(meld:20118): Gtk-CRITICAL **: gtk_container_foreach: assertion 'GTK_IS_CONTAINER (container)' failed

(meld:20118): Gtk-CRITICAL **: gtk_container_foreach: assertion 'GTK_IS_CONTAINER (container)' failed

(meld:20118): Gtk-CRITICAL **: gtk_container_foreach: assertion 'GTK_IS_CONTAINER (container)' failed

(meld:20118): Gtk-CRITICAL **: gtk_container_foreach: assertion 'GTK_IS_CONTAINER (container)' failed

(meld:20118): Gtk-CRITICAL **: gtk_container_foreach: assertion 'GTK_IS_CONTAINER (container)' failed

(meld:20118): Gtk-CRITICAL **: gtk_container_foreach: assertion 'GTK_IS_CONTAINER (container)' failed

(meld:20118): Gtk-CRITICAL **: gtk_container_foreach: assertion 'GTK_IS_CONTAINER (container)' failed
hackers@laptop [11:21:17 AM] [~/course/flow] [develop *]
-> % vim feature1.txt
hackers@laptop [11:21:25 AM] [~/course/flow] [develop *]
-> % git commit -a
```

You can see the predefined commit message. Don't forget to remove the temporary file that was created at the merge:

```
 1 Merge branch 'test' into develop
 2
 3 # Conflicts:
 4 #   feature1.txt
 5 #
 6 # It looks like you may be committing a merge.
 7 # If this is not correct, please remove the file
 8 #   .git/MERGE_HEAD
 9 # and try again.
10
11
12 # Please enter the commit message for your changes. Lines starting
13 # with '#' will be ignored, and an empty message aborts the commit.
14 # On branch develop
15 # All conflicts fixed but you are still merging.
16 #
17 # Changes to be committed:
18 #   modified:   feature1.txt
19 #
20 # Untracked files:
21 #   feature1.txt.orig
22 #
```

git commit -a

```
~/course/flow/.git/COMMIT_EDITMSG   CWD: /home/hacker/course/flow   Line: 1   Column: 1
"~/course/flow/.git/COMMIT_EDITMSG" 22L, 500C
```

In general, most modern IDEs offer plugins for working with `git`, including merging and `diffs`. We recommend that you get more acquainted with the command-line tools, because then you don't need to learn a new `git` plugin when switching from one IDE to another.

The `git` command works the same way across Linux, Mac, and Windows. It is a tool that developers use a lot and being fluent in it will boost your productivity.

From localhost to instant DNS

Often, especially when working with other people or when developing integrations with online services, we have to make our computer accessible from the Internet. This information could be obtained from our trusty router, but wouldn't it be easier if we just had a tool that makes our computer port publicly accessible?

Luckily for us there is such a tool!

Meet `ngrok`, the versatile one line command that makes you forget about router configuration and continuous redeploys. `Ngrok` is a simple tool that exposes a port from our computer to a unique domain name publicly available on the Internet.

How does it do it?

Well, let's see it in action!

Go to the website, click on the **Download** button, and choose your destiny. In our case, our destiny is the Linux package in 64-bit. Next, go to the terminal, unzip the file, and copy its contents to the bin folder:

- `cd` downloads
- `unzip ngrok.zip`
- `mv ngrok ~/bin`

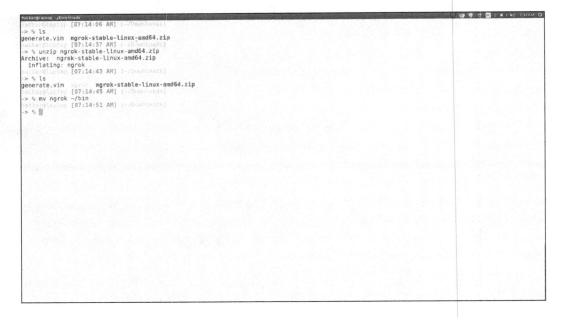

Now do a rehash and type the following:

```
ngrok http 80
```

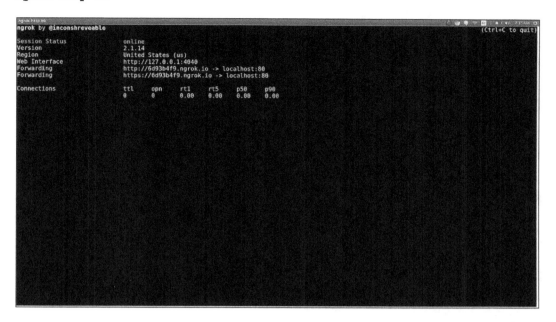

We can see that port forwarding for ports 80 and 443 is running on our local 80 port, at a custom `ngrok` subdomain name. We can also see the region of the server, which by default is located in the US. If we are in a different region we can set this with the following:

```
ngrok http 80 --region eu
```

The ngrok server is located in Europe. In order to test our ngrok server, let's use our trusty Python server to show a simple HTML page:

```
python -m SimpleHTTPServer
```

Then restart ngrok with the HTTP traffic forwarded from port 8000, the default Python web server port:

```
ngrok http 8000 --region eu
```

Click on the link provided by ngrok, and we will see our web page accessible to the Internet.

That's it. No configuration, no account, no headaches. Just a simple one line command that we can run from anywhere. The subdomain provided by ngrok is a generated one and will change every time we restart ngrok. We have the option of using our custom domain name like Linux https://ngrok.com/, but only after acquiring a paid account.

The ngrok also has a web interface at http://127.0.0.1:4040 where we can see statistics and logs.

Power comes from ease of use and `ngrok` provides us with that power:

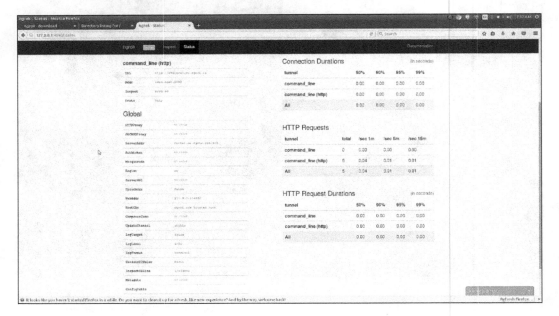

Here are some specific scenarios for using this powerful tool:

- When testing integrations with online services that require a callback `url`, such as oAuth login and online payments
- When developing mobile applications that connect to a local service
- When we want to expose an `ssh` port
- When we want to give our clients access to a webpage on our laptop, to show them some code, maybe

JSON jamming in the new age

Nowadays, JSON is everywhere, in web `apis`, in configuration files, even in logs. JSON is the default format used to structure data. Because it is used so much, there will be times when we will need to process JSON from the command line. Could you imagine doing this with `grep`, `sed`, or other conventional tools? That would be quite a challenge.

Luckily for us, there is a simple Command-line tool called `jq` that we can use to query JSON files. It comes with its own language syntax, as we will see in just a few minutes.

First let's install `jq` with the following command:

```
sudo apt install jq
```

Now let's use an example file, a dummy access log in JSON format: `access.log`, which we can also find in the course GitHub repository.

Let's start with some simple queries:

`jq . access.log`

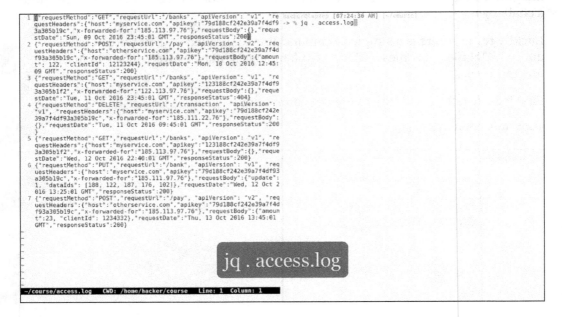

We will print the JSON objects back to the screen, in a pretty format:

```
1  {"requestMethod":"GET","requestUrl":"/banks", "apiVersion": "v1","re
   questHeaders":{"host":"myservice.com","apikey":"79d188cf242e39a7f4df9
   3a305b19c","x-forwarded-for":"185.113.97.76"},"requestBody":{},"reque
   stDate":"Sun, 09 Oct 2016 23:45:01 GMT","responseStatus":200}
2  {"requestMethod":"POST","requestUrl":"/pay", "apiVersion": "v2", "req
   uestHeaders":{"host":"otherservice.com","apikey":"79d188cf242e39a7f4d
   f93a305b19c","x-forwarded-for":"185.113.97.76"},"requestBody":{"amoun
   t": 122, "clientId": 12123244},"requestDate":"Mon, 10 Oct 2016 12:45:
   09 GMT","responseStatus":200}
3  {"requestMethod":"GET","requestUrl":"/banks", "apiVersion": "v1", "re
   questHeaders":{"host":"myservice.com","apikey":"123188cf242e39a7f4df9
   3a305b1f2","x-forwarded-for":"122.113.97.76"},"requestBody":{},"reque
   stDate":"Tue, 11 Oct 2016 23:45:01 GMT","responseStatus":404}
4  {"requestMethod":"DELETE","requestUrl":"/transaction", "apiVersion":
   "v1", "requestHeaders":{"host":"myservice.com","apikey":"79d188cf242e
   39a7f4df93a305b19c","x-forwarded-for":"185.111.22.76"},"requestBody":
   {},"requestDate":"Tue, 11 Oct 2016 09:45:01 GMT","responseStatus":200
   }
5  {"requestMethod":"GET","requestUrl":"/banks", "apiVersion": "v1", "re
   questHeaders":{"host":"myservice.com","apikey":"123188cf242e39a7f4df9
   3a305b1f2","x-forwarded-for":"185.113.97.76"},"requestBody":{},"reque
   stDate":"Wed, 12 Oct 2016 22:40:01 GMT","responseStatus":200}
6  {"requestMethod":"PUT","requestUrl":"/bank", "apiVersion": "v1", "req
   uestHeaders":{"host":"myservice.com","apikey":"79d188cf242e39a7f4df93
   a305b19c","x-forwarded-for":"185.111.97.76"},"requestBody":{"update":
   1, "dataIds": [188, 122, 187, 176, 102]},"requestDate":"Wed, 12 Oct 2
   016 13:25:01 GMT","responseStatus":200}
7  {"requestMethod":"POST","requestUrl":"/pay", "apiVersion": "v2", "req
   uestHeaders":{"host":"otherservice.com","apikey":"79d188cf242e39a7f4d
   f93a305b19c","x-forwarded-for":"185.113.97.76"},"requestBody":{"amoun
   t":23, "clientId": 1234332},"requestDate":"Thu, 13 Oct 2016 13:45:01
   GMT","responseStatus":200}
```

```
   "requestDate": "Wed, 12 Oct 2016 22:40:01 GMT",
   "responseStatus": 200
 {
   "requestMethod": "PUT",
   "requestUrl": "/bank",
   "apiVersion": "v1",
   "requestHeaders": {
     "host": "myservice.com",
     "apikey": "79d188cf242e39a7f4df93a305b19c",
     "x-forwarded-for": "185.111.97.76"
   },
   "requestBody": {
     "update": 1,
     "dataIds": [
       188,
       122,
       187,
       176,
       102
     ]
   },
   "requestDate": "Wed, 12 Oct 2016 13:25:01 GMT",
   "responseStatus": 200
 {
   "requestMethod": "POST",
   "requestUrl": "/pay",
   "apiVersion": "v2",
   "requestHeaders": {
     "host": "otherservice.com",
     "apikey": "79d188cf242e39a7f4df93a305b19c",
     "x-forwarded-for": "185.113.97.76"
   },
   "requestBody": {
     "amount": 23,
     "clientId": 1234332
   },
   "requestDate": "Thu, 13 Oct 2016 13:45:01 GMT",
   "responseStatus": 200
 }
```

```
~/course/access.log    CWD: /home/hacker/course    Line: 1  Column: 1
hacker@laptop [07:24:46 AM] [~/course]
-> %
```

If we want to grab the `request` method from each request, run the following:

```
jq '.requestMethod' access.log
```

```
1  {"requestMethod":"GET","requestUrl":"/banks", "apiVersion": "v1","re
   questHeaders":{"host":"myservice.com","apikey":"79d188cf242e39a7f4df9
   3a305b19c","x-forwarded-for":"185.113.97.76"},"requestBody":{},"reque
   stDate":"Sun, 09 Oct 2016 23:45:01 GMT","responseStatus":200}
2  {"requestMethod":"POST","requestUrl":"/pay", "apiVersion": "v2", "req
   uestHeaders":{"host":"otherservice.com","apikey":"79d188cf242e39a7f4d
   f93a305b19c","x-forwarded-for":"185.113.97.76"},"requestBody":{"amoun
   t": 122, "clientId": 12123244},"requestDate":"Mon, 10 Oct 2016 12:45:
   09 GMT","responseStatus":200}
3  {"requestMethod":"GET","requestUrl":"/banks", "apiVersion": "v1", "re
   questHeaders":{"host":"myservice.com","apikey":"123188cf242e39a7f4df9
   3a305b1f2","x-forwarded-for":"122.113.97.76"},"requestBody":{},"reque
   stDate":"Tue, 11 Oct 2016 23:45:01 GMT","responseStatus":404}
4  {"requestMethod":"DELETE","requestUrl":"/transaction", "apiVersion":
   "v1", "requestHeaders":{"host":"myservice.com","apikey":"79d188cf242e
   39a7f4df93a305b19c","x-forwarded-for":"185.111.22.76"},"requestBody":
   {},"requestDate":"Tue, 11 Oct 2016 09:45:01 GMT","responseStatus":200
5  {"requestMethod":"GET","requestUrl":"/banks", "apiVersion": "v1", "re
   questHeaders":{"host":"myservice.com","apikey":"123188cf242e39a7f4df9
   3a305b1f2","x-forwarded-for":"185.113.97.76"},"requestBody":{},"reque
   stDate":"Wed, 12 Oct 2016 22:40:01 GMT","responseStatus":200}
6  {"requestMethod":"PUT","requestUrl":"/bank", "apiVersion": "v1", "req
   uestHeaders":{"host":"myservice.com","apikey":"79d188cf242e39a7f4df93
   a305b19c","x-forwarded-for":"185.111.97.76"},"requestBody":{"update":
   1, "dataIds": [188, 122, 187, 176, 102]},"requestDate":"Wed, 12 Oct 2
   016 13:25:01 GMT","responseStatus":200}
7  {"requestMethod":"POST","requestUrl":"/pay", "apiVersion": "v2", "req
   uestHeaders":{"host":"otherservice.com","apikey":"79d188cf242e39a7f4d
   f93a305b19c","x-forwarded-for":"185.113.97.76"},"requestBody":{"amoun
   t":23, "clientId": 1234332},"requestDate":"Thu, 13 Oct 2016 13:45:01
   GMT","responseStatus":200}
```

```
   "apikey": "79d188cf242e39a7f4df93a305b19c",
   "x-forwarded-for": "185.111.97.76"
 },
 "requestBody": {
   "update": 1,
   "dataIds": [
     188,
     122,
     187,
     176,
     102
   ]
   "requestDate": "Wed, 12 Oct 2016 13:25:01 GMT",
   "responseStatus": 200
 {
   "requestMethod": "POST",
   "requestUrl": "/pay",
   "apiVersion": "v2",
   "requestHeaders": {
     "host": "otherservice.com",
     "apikey": "79d188cf242e39a7f4df93a305b19c",
     "x-forwarded-for": "185.113.97.76"
   },
   "requestBody": {
     "amount": 23,
     "clientId": 1234332
   },
   "requestDate": "Thu, 13 Oct 2016 13:45:01 GMT",
   "responseStatus": 200
 }
```

```
hacker@laptop [07:24:46 AM] [~/course]
-> % jq '.requestMethod' access.log
"GET"
"POST"
"GET"
"DELETE"
"GET"
"PUT"
"POST"
hacker@laptop [07:25:06 AM] [~/course]
-> %
```

```
~/course/access.log    CWD: /home/hacker/course    Line: 1  Column: 1
```

This will print the request method from each json object. Notice the double quotes around each method:

If we want to use the output as input to other scripts we probably don't want the double quotes and that is where the `-r` (raw output) comes in handy:

```
jq '.requestMethod' -r access.log
```

```
1 {"requestMethod":"GET","requestUrl":"/banks","apiVersion":"v1","re         "apikey":"79d188cf242c39a7f4df93a305b19c",
  questHeaders":{"host":"myservice.com","apikey":"79d188cf242e39a7f4df9         "x-forwarded-for": "185.111.97.76"},
  3a305b19c","x-forwarded-for":"185.113.97.76"},"requestBody":{},"reque       "requestBody": {
  stDate":"Sun, 09 Oct 2016 23:45:01 GMT","responseStatus":200}               "update": 1,
2 {"requestMethod":"POST","requestUrl":"/pay","apiVersion":"v2","req           "dataIds": [
  uestHeaders":{"host":"otherservice.com","apikey":"79d188cf242e39a7f4d            188,
  f93a305b19c","x-forwarded-for":"185.113.97.76"},"requestBody":{"amoun            122,
  t": 122, "clientId": 12123244},"requestDate":"Mon, 10 Oct 2016 12:45:            187,
  09 GMT","responseStatus":200}                                                    176,
3 {"requestMethod":"GET","requestUrl":"/banks","apiVersion":"v1","re              162
  questHeaders":{"host":"myservice.com","apikey":"123188cf242e39a7f4df9          ]
  3a305b1f2","x-forwarded-for":"122.113.97.76"},"requestBody":{},"reque        },
  stDate":"Tue, 11 Oct 2016 23:45:01 GMT","responseStatus":404}              "requestDate": "Wed, 12 Oct 2016 13:25:01 GMT",
4 {"requestMethod":"DELETE","requestUrl":"/transaction","apiVersion":         "responseStatus": 200
  "v1","requestHeaders":{"host":"myservice.com","apikey":"79d188cf242e      }
  39a7f4df93a305b19c","x-forwarded-for":"185.111.22.76"},"requestBody":      {
  {},"requestDate":"Tue, 11 Oct 2016 09:45:01 GMT","responseStatus":200        "requestMethod": "POST",
  }                                                                            "requestUrl": "/pay",
5 {"requestMethod":"GET","requestUrl":"/banks","apiVersion":"v1","re           "apiVersion": "v2",
  questHeaders":{"host":"myservice.com","apikey":"123188cf242e39a7f4df9        "requestHeaders": {
  3a305b1f2","x-forwarded-for":"185.113.97.76"},"requestBody":{},"reque          "host": "otherservice.com",
  stDate":"Wed, 12 Oct 2016 22:40:01 GMT","responseStatus":200}                  "apikey": "79d188cf242e39a7f4df93a305b19c",
6 {"requestMethod":"PUT","requestUrl":"/bank","apiVersion":"v1","req             "x-forwarded-for": "185.113.97.76"
  uestHeaders":{"host":"myservice.com","apikey":"79d188cf242e39a7f4df93        },
  a305b19c","x-forwarded-for":"185.111.97.76"},"requestBody":{"update":        "requestBody": {
  1, "dataIds": [188, 122, 187, 176, 102]},"requestDate":"Wed, 12 Oct 2          "amount": 23,
  016 13:25:01 GMT","responseStatus":200}                                        "clientId": 1234332
7 {"requestMethod":"POST","requestUrl":"/pay","apiVersion":"v2","req           },
  uestHeaders":{"host":"otherservice.com","apikey":"79d188cf242e39a7f4d        "requestDate": "Thu, 13 Oct 2016 13:45:01 GMT",
  f93a305b19c","x-forwarded-for":"185.113.97.76"},"requestBody":{"amoun        "responseStatus": 200
  t":23, "clientId": 1234332},"requestDate":"Thu, 13 Oct 2016 13:45:01      }
  GMT","responseStatus":200}
                                        [07:24:46 AM]
                                -> % jq '.requestMethod' access.log
```

jq '.requestMethod' -r access.log

```
                                                "POST"
                                        [07:25:06 AM]
                                -> % jq '.requestMethod' -r access.log
~/course/access.log   CWD: /home/hacker/course   Line: 1   Column: 1
```

The `jq` is often used for big data queries at a much smaller scale:

```
1 {"requestMethod":"GET","requestUrl":"/banks","apiVersion":"v1","re            176,
  questHeaders":{"host":"myservice.com","apikey":"79d188cf242e39a7f4df9           162
  3a305b19c","x-forwarded-for":"185.113.97.76"},"requestBody":{},"reque        ]
  stDate":"Sun, 09 Oct 2016 23:45:01 GMT","responseStatus":200}              },
2 {"requestMethod":"POST","requestUrl":"/pay","apiVersion":"v2","req          "requestDate": "Wed, 12 Oct 2016 13:25:01 GMT",
  uestHeaders":{"host":"otherservice.com","apikey":"79d188cf242e39a7f4d        "responseStatus": 200
  f93a305b19c","x-forwarded-for":"185.113.97.76"},"requestBody":{"amoun      {
  t": 122, "clientId": 12123244},"requestDate":"Mon, 10 Oct 2016 12:45:        "requestMethod": "POST",
  09 GMT","responseStatus":200}                                                "requestUrl": "/pay",
3 {"requestMethod":"GET","requestUrl":"/banks","apiVersion":"v1","re           "apiVersion": "v2",
  questHeaders":{"host":"myservice.com","apikey":"123188cf242e39a7f4df9        "requestHeaders": {
  3a305b1f2","x-forwarded-for":"122.113.97.76"},"requestBody":{},"reque          "host": "otherservice.com",
  stDate":"Tue, 11 Oct 2016 23:45:01 GMT","responseStatus":404}                  "apikey": "79d188cf242e39a7f4df93a305b19c",
4 {"requestMethod":"DELETE","requestUrl":"/transaction","apiVersion":            "x-forwarded-for": "185.113.97.76"
  "v1","requestHeaders":{"host":"myservice.com","apikey":"79d188cf242e        },
  39a7f4df93a305b19c","x-forwarded-for":"185.111.22.76"},"requestBody":        "requestBody": {
  {},"requestDate":"Tue, 11 Oct 2016 09:45:01 GMT","responseStatus":200          "amount": 23,
  }                                                                              "clientId": 1234332
5 {"requestMethod":"GET","requestUrl":"/banks","apiVersion":"v1","re           },
  questHeaders":{"host":"myservice.com","apikey":"123188cf242e39a7f4df9        "requestDate": "Thu, 13 Oct 2016 13:45:01 GMT",
  3a305b1f2","x-forwarded-for":"185.113.97.76"},"requestBody":{},"reque        "responseStatus": 200
  stDate":"Wed, 12 Oct 2016 22:40:01 GMT","responseStatus":200}
6 {"requestMethod":"PUT","requestUrl":"/bank","apiVersion":"v1","req                                          [07:24:46 AM]
  uestHeaders":{"host":"myservice.com","apikey":"79d188cf242e39a7f4df93   -> % jq '.requestMethod' access.log
  a305b19c","x-forwarded-for":"185.111.97.76"},"requestBody":{"update":    "GET"
  1, "dataIds": [188, 122, 187, 176, 102]},"requestDate":"Wed, 12 Oct 2    "GET"
  016 13:25:01 GMT","responseStatus":200}                                  "DELETE"
7 {"requestMethod":"POST","requestUrl":"/pay","apiVersion":"v2","req       "GET"
  uestHeaders":{"host":"otherservice.com","apikey":"79d188cf242e39a7f4d    "PUT"
  f93a305b19c","x-forwarded-for":"185.113.97.76"},"requestBody":{"amoun    "POST"
  t":23, "clientId": 1234332},"requestDate":"Thu, 13 Oct 2016 13:45:01                         [07:25:06 AM]
  GMT","responseStatus":200}                                           -> % jq '.requestMethod' -r access.log
                                                                         GET
                                                                         POST
                                                                         GET
                                                                         DELETE
                                                                         GET
                                                                         PUT
                                                                         POST
                                                                                          [07:25:26 AM]
~/course/access.log   CWD: /home/hacker/course   Line: 1   Column: 1   -> %
```

Say, for example, if we want to calculate a statistic of request methods on the log file, we could run the following:

```
jq '.requestMethod' -r access.log | sort | uniq -c
```

Now we can see a count of get, put, post, and delete requests. If we want the same type of calculation for another field, say apikey, we can run the following:

```
jq '.requestHeaders.apikey' -r access.log | sort | uniq -c
```

```
 1 {"requestMethod":"GET","requestUrl":"/banks", "apiVersion": "v1", "re        "apiVersion": "v2",
   questHeaders":{"host":"myservice.com","apikey":"79d188cf242e39a7f4df9        "requestHeaders": {
   3a305b19c","x-forwarded-for":"185.113.97.76"},"requestBody":{},"reque          "host": "otherservice.com",
   stDate":"Sun, 09 Oct 2016 23:45:01 GMT","responseStatus":200}                  "apikey": "79d188cf242e39a7f4df93a305b19c",
 2 {"requestMethod":"POST","requestUrl":"/pay", "apiVersion": "v2", "req           "x-forwarded-for": "185.113.97.76"
   uestHeaders":{"host":"otherservice.com","apikey":"79d188cf242e39a7f4d        },
```

```
 3                                                                               }
   stDate":"Tue, 11 Oct 2016 23:45:01 GMT","responseStatus":404}
 4 {"requestMethod":"DELETE","requestUrl":"/transaction", "apiVersion":      -> % jq '.requestMethod' access.log
   "v1", "requestHeaders":{"host":"myservice.com","apikey":"79d188cf242e      "GET"
   39a7f4df93a305b19c","x-forwarded-for":"185.111.22.76"},"requestBody":      "POST"
   {},"requestDate":"Tue, 11 Oct 2016 09:45:01 GMT","responseStatus":200      "GET"
 5 {"requestMethod":"GET","requestUrl":"/banks", "apiVersion": "v1", "re      "DELETE"
   questHeaders":{"host":"myservice.com","apikey":"123188cf242e39a7f4df9      "GET"
   3a305b1f2","x-forwarded-for":"185.113.97.76"},"requestBody":{},"reque      "PUT"
   stDate":"Wed, 12 Oct 2016 22:40:01 GMT","responseStatus":200}              "POST"
 6 {"requestMethod":"PUT","requestUrl":"/bank", "apiVersion": "v1", "req      accesslog~ > % jq '.requestMethod' -r access.log
   uestHeaders":{"host":"myservice.com","apikey":"79d188cf242e39a7f4df9
   a305b19c","x-forwarded-for":"185.111.97.76"},"requestBody":{"update":      GET
   1, "dataIds": [188, 122, 187, 176, 102]},"requestDate":"Wed, 12 Oct 2      GET
   016 13:25:01 GMT","responseStatus":200}                                    DELETE
 7 {"requestMethod":"POST","requestUrl":"/pay", "apiVersion": "v2", "req      GET
   uestHeaders":{"host":"otherservice.com","apikey":"79d188cf242e39a7f4d      PUT
   f93a305b19c","x-forwarded-for":"185.113.97.76"},"requestBody":{"amoun      POST
   t":23, "clientId": 1234332},"requestDate":"Thu, 13 Oct 2016 13:45:01
   GMT","responseStatus":200}                                           [07:25:26 AM]
                                                                        -> % jq '.requestMethod' -r access.log | sort | uniq -c
                                                                           1 DELETE
                                                                           3 GET
                                                                           2 POST
                                                                           1 PUT
                                                                                            [07:25:54 AM]
                                                                        -> % jq '.requestHeaders.apikey' -r access.log | sort | uniq -c
                                                                           2 123188cf242e39a7f4df93a305b1f2
                                                                           5 79d188cf242e39a7f4df93a305b19c
 ~/course/access.log   CWD: /home/hacker/course   Line: 1  Column: 1                         [07:26:24 AM]
                                                                        -> %
```

Since that the syntax for accessing nested fields is to just use the dot as a delimiter between them. Also notice that we are using single quotes instead of double quotes to mark our query as a string. As you probably know, the difference between single and double quotes in shell scripting is that double-quoted strings will try to expand variables, while single quoted strings will be treated as a fixed string.

To query for the request bodies, we will be using the following command:

```
jq '.requestBody' access.log
```

jq '.requestBody' access.log

As we can see from the output, even empty request bodies are logged and will be printed by `jq`:

To skip printing empty bodies, we can use jq's query language to select all documents without an empty body:

```
jq 'select(.requestBody != {}) | .requestBody' access.log
```

If we want to refine our search even more and only print the first element in the `dataIds` object of the request body, use the following:

```
jq 'select(.requestBody.dataIds[0] != null) | .requestBody.dataIds[0]'
access.log
```

We can even perform arithmetic operations with the returned value, such as incrementing it:

```
jq 'select(.requestBody.dataIds[0] != null) | .requestBody.dataIds[0] +
1' access.log
```

There are many more examples and use cases for jq: just go to the official jq page and visit the tutorial there:

https://stedolan.github.io/jq/tutorial/

There we can see an example of consuming a rest API that returns `json` and pipes it to `jq`. To print a `json` with the commit messages from a `github` repository, run the following:

```
curl 'https://api.github.com/repos/stedolan/jq/commits?per_page=5' | jq
-r '[.[] | {message: .commit.message}]'
```

As we said, there are many more examples in the documentation, and many more use cases. `jq` is a pretty powerful tool, and a must when interacting with `json` from the command line.

No more mister nice guy

The kernel and command line in Linux are stable and powerful. Their reliability has been proven throughout the years, with modern legends about Linux servers running for multiple years in a row without restarting. However, graphical interfaces are not the same, and they sometimes fail or become unresponsive. This can become annoying and it's always good to have a quick way of killing unresponsive windows. Prepare to meet `xkill`.

First, let's replicate an unresponsive window. Go to the terminal and start `gedit:` and then hit *Ctrl + z*. This will send `gedit` to the background, while the window is still visible. Trying to click inside the window a couple of times will tell Ubuntu that there is no process handling this window anymore and Ubuntu will make it gray:

Hit *Ctrl* + *z*:

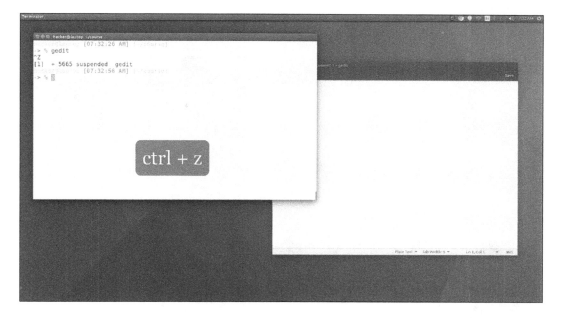

This will send `gedit` to the background, while the window is still visible. Trying to click inside the window a couple of times will tell Ubuntu that there is no process handling this window anymore and Ubuntu will make it grey:

To avoid the process of grepping for the `pid` of the window and then killing that process we use a little trick. Go to the terminal and run the following:

xkill

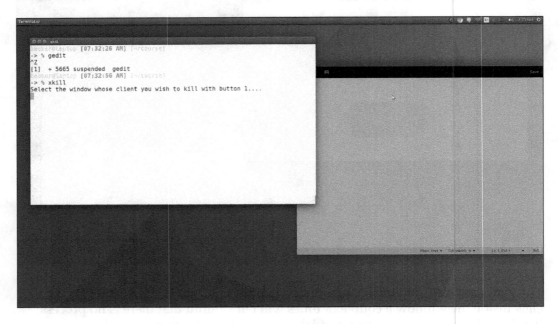

Now we see that the mouse pointer has changed to an x.

Be careful not to click on anything. Hit *Alt + Tab* to bring back the `gedit` window, and then click it. The `xkill` command will find and kill the process of the window we just clicked on.

This trick can be used on any type of window; it's like shooting your windows!

OK, but what happens if the whole system becomes unresponsive and you can't type anything in the command line? That might happen, especially on older systems. You can hit the **on/off** button on your laptop or server, but in some circumstances, this is not possible.

What we are going to show you now is an old trick kept secret by Linux gurus for a very long time; nobody really talks about it because it's so powerful that it can do damage in the hands of the wrong people. Please make sure you save all your work and close all programs before trying the fatal keyboard shortcut that will force a restart of your Linux system. Hold down *Alt + PrtScrn* and at the same time type the following:

reisub

If you've tried it, it means that your computer restarted and you had to come back to this course and continue where you left off.

Practice this command with great caution and please don't use it to restart your computer on a regular basis. Use it only when the **graphical user interface (GUI)** is not responding.

Another trick: if the GUI is not responding and you have unsaved work, you can recover some of it from the command line, by accessing one of Linux's virtual terminals. Ubuntu starts, by default, seven virtual terminals and the graphical user interface starts on terminal 7. To access any of the seven terminals use *Ctrl + Alt + F1* to *F7*. A prompt will appear asking you to log in and, after logging in, you can run some commands to close processes and save work before exiting. To get back to the user interface, hit *Ctrl + Alt + F1*.

6
Terminal Art

All work and no play makes Jack a dull boy. Even though the command line seems boring to a lot of people, it can become great fun. It all comes down to your imagination. Terminals can be stylish and can give a good impression, especially the ones we see in the movies. Colors, ASCII art, and animations can make our terminal come alive. So, here comes some terminal art!

In this chapter, we will cover the following:

- Working with some Linux commands to have fun with

Ever heard of fortune cookies? Do you want to have them without getting fat? Just run the following `apt` command to install the utilities that we will be using in this chapter:

```
sudo apt install fortune cowsay cmatrix
```

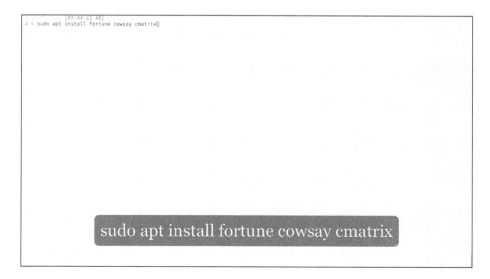

Then run this command:

fortune

```
                    [08:04:22 AM] [~/course]
-> % sudo apt install fortune cowsay cmatrix
[sudo] password for hacker:
Reading package lists... Done
Building dependency tree
Reading state information... Done
Note, selecting 'fortune-mod' instead of 'fortune'
fortune-mod is already the newest version (1:1.99.1-7).
Suggested packages:
  cmatrix-xfont filters
The following NEW packages will be installed:
  cmatrix cowsay cowsay-off
0 upgraded, 3 newly installed, 0 to remove and 0 not upgraded.
Need to get 37.5 kB of archives.
After this operation, 162 kB of additional disk space will be used.
Get:1 http://ro.archive.ubuntu.com/ubuntu xenial/universe amd64 cmatrix amd64 1.2a-5build2 [15.8 kB]
Get:2 http://ro.archive.ubuntu.com/ubuntu xenial/universe amd64 cowsay all 3.03+dfsg1-15 [18.0 kB]
Get:3 http://ro.archive.ubuntu.com/ubuntu xenial/universe amd64 cowsay-off all 3.03+dfsg1-15 [3,640 B]
Fetched 37.5 kB in 1s (28.8 kB/s)
Selecting previously unselected package cmatrix.
(Reading database ... 236548 files and directories currently installed.)
Preparing to unpack .../cmatrix_1.2a-5build2_amd64.deb ...
Unpacking cmatrix (1.2a-5build2) ...
Selecting previously unselected package cowsay.
Preparing to unpack .../cowsay_3.03+dfsg1-15_all.deb ...
Unpacking cowsay (3.03+dfsg1-15) ...
Selecting previously unselected package cowsay-off.
Preparing to unpack .../cowsay-off_3.03+dfsg1-15_all.deb ...
Unpacking cowsay-off (3.03+dfsg1-15) ...
Processing triggers for man-db (2.7.5-1) ...
Setting up cmatrix (1.2a-5build2) ...
Setting up cowsay (3.03+dfsg1-15) ...
Setting up cowsay-off (3.03+dfsg1-15) ...
                    [08:04:42 AM] [~/course]
-> % fortune
He was part of my dream, of course -- but then I was part of his dream too.
                -- Lewis Carroll
                    [08:04:48 AM] [~/course]
-> % fortune
No violence, gentlemen -- no violence, I beg of you!  Consider the furniture!
                -- Sherlock Holmes
                    [08:04:52 AM] [~/course]
-> % 
```

When running this command, you get fortunes, quotes, and jokes, in a random order. If we combine the command with cowsay, we will get the same fortunes, delivered with an image of a cow:

fortune | cowsay

```
Get:3 http://ro.archive.ubuntu.com/ubuntu xenial/universe amd64 cowsay-off all 3.03+dfsg1-15 [3,640 B]
Fetched 37.5 kB in 1s (28.8 kB/s)
Selecting previously unselected package cmatrix.
(Reading database ... 236548 files and directories currently installed.)
Preparing to unpack .../cmatrix_1.2a-5build2_amd64.deb ...
Unpacking cmatrix (1.2a-5build2) ...
Selecting previously unselected package cowsay.
Preparing to unpack .../cowsay_3.03+dfsg1-15_all.deb ...
Unpacking cowsay (3.03+dfsg1-15) ...
Selecting previously unselected package cowsay-off.
Preparing to unpack .../cowsay-off_3.03+dfsg1-15_all.deb ...
Unpacking cowsay-off (3.03+dfsg1-15) ...
Processing triggers for man-db (2.7.5-1) ...
Setting up cmatrix (1.2a-5build2) ...
Setting up cowsay (3.03+dfsg1-15) ...
Setting up cowsay-off (3.03+dfsg1-15) ...
                    [08:04:42 AM]
-> % fortune
He was part of my dream, of course -- but then I was part of his dream too.
                    -- Lewis Carroll
                    [08:04:48 AM]
-> % fortune
No violence, gentlemen -- no violence, I beg of you!  Consider the furniture!
                    -- Sherlock Holmes
                    [08:04:52 AM]
-> % fortune
You'll never be the man your mother was!
                    [08:04:56 AM]
-> % fortune | cowsay

/ It is a wise father that knows his own \
| child.                                  |
|                                         |
| -- William Shakespeare, "The Merchant   |
\ of Venice"                              /
 -----------------------------------------
        \   ^__^
         \  (oo)_____
            (__)\       )\/\
                ||----w |
                ||     ||
                    [08:05:06 AM]
-> %
```

fortune | cowsay

To make this recurrent, we can include it as the last line in our `zshrc` file. Then, every time we open a new terminal window, a cow will deliver a fortune to us.

Now this may not be useful (even though it's kinda fun) so, let's do some productive wizardry.

Let's predict the weather!

All you need is a `curl` command:

curl -4 http://wttr.in/London

```
Selecting previously unselected package cmatrix.
(Reading database ... 236548 files and directories currently installed.)
Preparing to unpack .../cmatrix_1.2a-5build2_amd64.deb ...
Unpacking cmatrix (1.2a-5build2) ...
Selecting previously unselected package cowsay.
Preparing to unpack .../cowsay_3.03+dfsg1-15_all.deb ...
Unpacking cowsay (3.03+dfsg1-15) ...
Selecting previously unselected package cowsay-off.
Preparing to unpack .../cowsay-off_3.03+dfsg1-15_all.deb ...
Unpacking cowsay-off (3.03+dfsg1-15) ...
Processing triggers for man-db (2.7.5-1) ...
Setting up cmatrix (1.2a-5build2) ...
Setting up cowsay (3.03+dfsg1-15) ...
Setting up cowsay-off (3.03+dfsg1-15) ...
hacker@laptop [08:04:42 AM] [~/course]
-> % fortune
He was part of my dream, of course -- but then I was part of his dream too.
                -- Lewis Carroll
hacker@laptop [08:04:48 AM] [~/course]
-> % fortune
No violence, gentlemen -- no violence, I beg of you!  Consider the furniture!
                -- Sherlock Holmes
hacker@laptop [08:04:52 AM] [~/course]
-> % fortune
You'll never be the man your mother was!
hacker@laptop [08:04:56 AM] [~/course]
-> % fortune | cowsay
 _____
/ It is a wise father that knows his own \
| child.                              |
|                                     |
| -- William Shakespeare, "The Merchant |
\ of Venice"                          /
 -----------------------------------
        \   ^__^
         \  (oo)_____
            (__)\       )\/\
                ||----w |
                ||     ||
hacker@laptop [08:05:06 AM] [~/course]
-> % vim ~/.zshrc
hacker@laptop [08:05:48 AM] [~/course]
-> % curl -4 http://wttr.in/London
```

curl -4 http://wttr.in/London

This will show, in a nice format, a three-day weather forecast for the specified city, in this case, London:

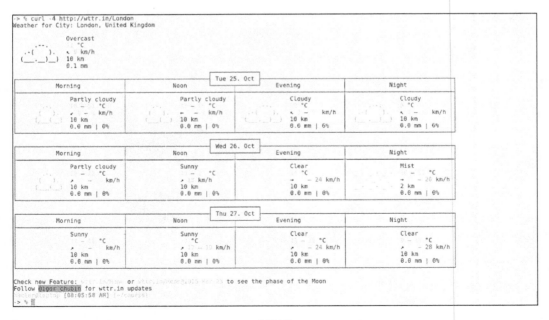

Now, with our newly learned skills, let's put together a shell script that gives us the weather forecast:

Open ~/bin/wttr and type the following:

```
#!/bin/bash
CITY=${1:-London}
curl -4 http://wttr.in/${CITY}
```

Give it execution rights and assign a default city, let's say London. Now, run this:

```
wttr
```

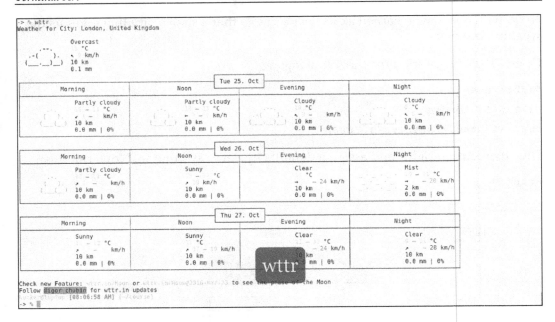

We get the weather forecast for London. Now, run this:

wttr paris

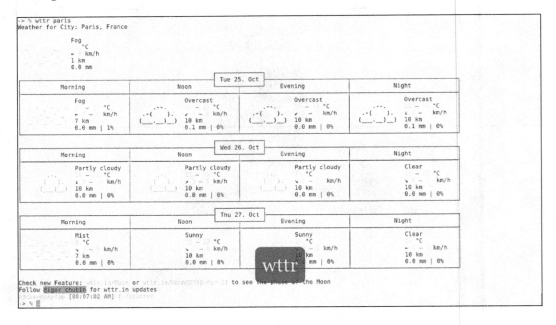

We get the weather forecast for Paris. Working in the command line for the first time may seem like entering the Matrix and, if that's the case, why not create that environment?

Run this command:

```
cmatrix
```

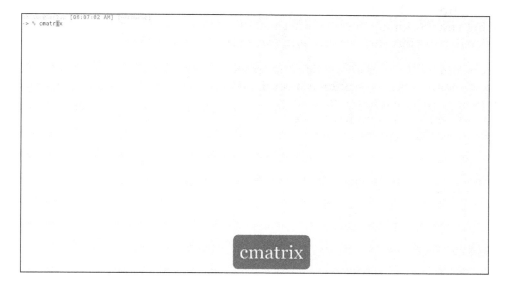

Let your friends be amazed by the complicated stuff you are doing in that cryptic terminal. Terminals are not boring!

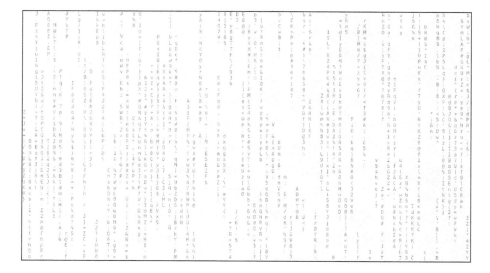

They have beautiful colors, easy-to-read output, and they display compact information that puts users in control of their own system.

Terminals can be customized and interacted with and they increase your productivity while leaving your mouse to sleep the endless sleep of inefficiency.

Of course, all these skills don't come to you overnight, and they require careful tweaking from each user in order to be tailored to their own taste and way of thinking and working. However, after that, they'll fit like a tailored suit, and become an extension of your way of work and sometimes even your job.

We hope you've enjoyed all the tips and tricks we've provided, and had fun learning them. Remember that education is a continuous process, so don't stop here! Stay hungry and surf the Internet to keep track of the latest tools and techniques that will transform you into a productivity beast!

Index